MORAL THINKING

MORAL THINKING

Its Levels, Method, and Point

BY

R. M. HARE

CLARENDON PRESS . OXFORD

Oxford University Press, Walton Street, Oxford OX2 6DP

Oxford New York
Athens Auckland Bangkok Bombay
Calcutta Cape Town Dar es Salaam Delhi
Florence Hong Kong Istanbul Karachi
Kuala Lumpur Madras Madrid Melbourne
Mexico City Nairobi Paris Singapore
Taipei Tokyo Toronto

and associated companies in
Berlin Ibadan

Oxford is a trade mark of Oxford University Press

Published in the United States by
Oxford University Press Inc., New York

British Library Cataloguing in Publication Data
Hare, R. M.
Moral thinking.
1. Ethics
I. Title
170   BJ604.H/
ISBN 0-19-824660-9 Pbk

10

Printed in Hong Kong
on acid-free paper

PREFACE

I offer this book to the public now rather than later, not because I think it needs no improvement, but because of a sense of urgency—a feeling that if these ideas were understood, philosophers might do more to help resolve important practical issues. These are issues over which people are prepared to fight and kill one another; and it may be that unless some way is found of talking about them rationally and with hope of agreement, violence will finally engulf the world. Philosophers have in recent years become increasingly aware of the role that they might have in preventing this; but they have lacked any clear idea of what constitutes a good argument on practical questions. Often they are content with appeals to their own and others' intuitions or prejudices; and since it is these prejudices which fuelled the violence in the first place, this is not going to help.

I have had to leave many questions unresolved, including even some that I mentioned in my earlier book *Freedom and Reason* as requiring solution. But nobody can hope to write the last word on a philosophical subject; the most he can do is to advance the discussion of it by making at least some things clearer. In particular, I wish that I could have given a fuller and more satisfactory account of prudential thinking. David Richards, David Haslett and Richard Brandt have done much to clarify it in their books, and Derek Parfit, from whom I have learnt a lot, will, I am sure, do more in his when it appears.

The relation between this and my first two books is similar to the relation between those two: I have tried not to presume knowledge of their contents; but those who want a fuller account of what is here summarized will turn to them. The same applies to the numerous recent papers of mine in which some of the ideas here presented were first sketched. But one of these papers seems crucial enough to

the argument to be incorporated in this book; I have
therefore to thank the Tanner Trustees for allowing me to
use, in a revised form in chh. 2 and 3, my Tanner Lecture
given at Utah State University in 1978—a small part of
their great generosity to me.

On the few points on which I have disagreed with what I
said in my first two books, I have tried to make this clear. I
have left in the text, for the reader's convenience, the cross-
references to my other books and papers which I put in
earlier drafts for my own guidance; the system of abbrevi-
ations is explained at the beginning of the bibliography,
whither I have consigned all publication details in order to
cut down the number of footnotes.

The suggestions I make in this book are not new; they
are adaptations and, I hope, clarifications of ideas which
are to be found in many of the great thinkers of the past.
But I have tried, by examining the logic of moral argument,
to make a coherent whole out of these pieces, and by
distinguishing the levels of moral thinking, to provide
answers to objections which have prevented the ideas of
those thinkers from being accepted. This may also help us
to see how philosophers like Kant and the utilitarians,
often thought to be at loggerheads, in fact each had hold of
a part of the truth.

I am not, however, attempting the exegesis of any of
these writers, much as I have learnt from them. In
particular, I am, when I speak of intuition, neither
attacking nor defending Sidgwick; my intended targets are
more recent, and will be recognized. Nor do I claim to
know just what Kant meant; I have been inspired by him to
say certain things, but when I look to see where *he* said
them, I always get lost. Thomas Nagel must not be insulted
if I say the same of him.

Too many people have helped me for all to be
mentioned; their names alone would fill most of a page. But
I must especially thank some who have been kind enough
to look at part or all of earlier typescripts and give me their
useful comments, or with whom I have most profitably

discussed these questions. They may well not agree with what I have done in response, but I owe a lot to them. They include, besides those already mentioned, Kenneth Arrow, Jonathan Bennett, Simon Blackburn, Daniel Dennett, Raymond Frey, Jonathan Glover, James Griffin, John Harsanyi, John Howes, Joel Kupperman, Richard Lee, John McDowell, John Mackie, Alan Montefiore, Lynda Paine, Joseph Raz, Amartya Sen, Peter Singer, Aaron Sloman, James Urmson and Zeno Vendler. I also owe much to other people's writings, too many to list. I have not been able to discuss in the text Włodzimierz Rabinowicz's recent highly technical but useful book *Universalizability*; I found much in it with which one can still agree, even if one thinks that the thesis of universalizability has a conceptual foundation.

Oxford University generously gave me a whole year's sabbatical leave, which I was privileged to spend at the Center for Advanced Study in the Behavioral Sciences at Stanford. I returned having written this and another book, and yet feeling as if my wife and I had had a wonderful holiday. This shows what a very happy environment has been created there for study and writing. I owe thanks to my colleagues there for much stimulating talk, and to them and still more to the Director and his staff for constant and unfailing kindnesses. Dorothy Brothers especially, who put the final draft on the Center's word processor, showed great forbearance in dealing with my many afterthoughts.

Above all, I must express my gratitude to my wife, for making clear to me by her example the truth of some things which I rather feebly and aridly say in ch. 11: that the quality of mutual love and affection between people, without which our life would have few joys, cannot be had without the right dispositions; and that these dispositions, therefore, are the condition of both happiness and morality. She has shown this to me throughout our life together, but most recently, not only by patient copyreading and checking of my text, but by keeping me sane during the writing of it.

What convinces me more than anything of the importance and substantial correctness of the account of moral thinking here given is the fact that in many studies of practical moral issues, only some of which have been written up and published, it has clarified those issues for me more than any other method which I have seen suggested. Since my main aim in doing moral philosophy has always been to obtain this practical help, I dedicate this book to all who feel the need for such clarification. These include some but not all moral philosophers, but nearly all ordinary people at one time or another. Among these, my grandchildren may come to be reckoned; I should like to think that, through greater understanding of these problems, they may be spared some of the moral muddles which now afflict us.

Corpus Christi College,   R.M.H.
Oxford,
1981

CONTENTS

PART I. LEVELS

PART II. METHOD

PART III. POINT

PART I

LEVELS

And truly I too speak as one who knows not—only guesses. But that there is a difference in kind between right opinion and knowledge, this, it seems to me, I do *not* guess; but of the few things, if any, that I would claim to know, this is one.

PLATO, *Meno* 98b

I

INTRODUCTION

1.1 The enterprise on which we are embarking will certainly be misunderstood unless I start by explaining its nature. This is a work of moral philosophy. To the adjective 'moral' we shall be recurring (3.4 ff.). It suffices now to say that we are all often faced with moral questions, some more tormenting than others; and that most of us, when we have to answer these questions, do some thinking about them. It will be generally agreed that this kind of thinking, like any other, can be done well or badly. It is the task of moral philosophy to help us do it better. To say this, however, is not to define the subject; for there may be other ways of improving our thinking besides doing philosophy. We need to know *in what respects* our moral thinking might be better done if we studied moral philosophy, and how the philosophy would bring this about.

Clearly the improvement will be in rationality (a concept which we shall be discussing more fully later, 12.4). We want the moral philosopher to help us do our moral thinking more rationally. If we say this, we presuppose that there is a rational way or method of going about answering moral questions; and this means that there are some canons or rules of moral thinking, to follow which is to think rationally. The moral philosopher asks what these canons are. He finds this out by, first of all, studying the questions which we call 'moral', in order to understand better what we are asking. Some questions which we ask *seem* not to need this preliminary inquiry into their nature. For example, it might be claimed that those who asked whether there existed a North West Passage to China knew perfectly well what they were asking, and what empirical discoveries would justify an affirmative answer. The answer would be 'Yes' if, and only if, somebody could navigate around the north of Canada and get to China that way. The same applies to those who ask whether there is a reliable way of preventing the common cold. It applies also to the very different question, whether there is a prime number between seven and thirteen, though in this case the method used is not empirical.

I said, '*seem* not to need this preliminary inquiry into their nature'. But the existence of the philosophies of science and of mathematics indicates that in the opinion of many philosophers, who may well be right, even the questions about the common cold and the prime numbers can have the same sort of inquiry made into them as we shall be making into moral questions. As for the North West Passage, there is not yet, so far as I know, a philosophy of geography; but the theory of knowledge, or epistemology, could certainly handle the difficulties about this question which can be made to arise if we are good enough sceptics.

In all these cases the first step towards answering a question rationally is to understand it (cf. Moore, 1903:vii), which entails understanding the words in which it is posed (H 1979a). The reward for learning about their meanings or uses is that we are at the same time learning something of the canons for thinking logically about questions containing them (*LM* 2.4). For they, like all other words, owe their meanings partly or wholly to their logical properties.[1] In the case of some words, for example

[1] For a recent expression of a similar view see Sellars (1980:81): 'It is obviously true that the meaning of a logical word is a function of its contribution to the implications of sentences in which it occurs. That this is true, at least in

'all', their logical properties exhaust their meaning. We know everything we could know about the meaning of 'all' if we know what inferences we can validly make from and to propositions containing it; and to learn its meaning is to take at least the first step towards knowing what inferences we can validly make. We do not have, indeed, to know the whole of quantification theory, which systematizes the logic of 'all' and 'some', before we can be said to know the meaning of 'all'; but knowing its meaning at least puts us in a position to develop quantification theory.

In the case of other words, the logical properties determine only part of the meaning. The words 'blue' and 'red' are both predicate-words (or adjectives); that means that they can occupy only predicate-places in sentences. [2] The logic appropriate to them is therefore predicate-logic, and is the same for them both. But though these words get part of their meanings from their logical properties as predicate-words, and in this part of their meanings are identical, they get the rest of their meanings (that in which 'blue' differs from 'red') from something other than their logical properties. No amount of logic will show us the difference between blue and red.

It will be my contention that the more general words used in moral discourse[3] (though not only there), such as 'ought' and 'must', which we shall be mainly studying, are in this respect like 'all' rather than like 'red' and 'blue'. This, if true, may be to some people surprising, and would be of fundamental importance; for if it were true that 'ought' and 'must' owed their meanings entirely to their logical properties, we ought to be able in principle to learn

---

part, of the meaning of *every* word may be less obvious, but is certainly of equal importance.'

[2] These include places which represent predicate-places in deep structure. Where such a word occupies a subject-place, for example (as when we say 'Blue is a primary colour'), the noun 'blue', which is not strictly speaking even the same word as the adjective, gets its meaning via a nominalization of the sentence-form '*x* is blue'.

[3] For brevity I shall in what follows say 'the moral words' (H 1979e:115).

all about the canons for thinking about questions posed in these terms by studying the meanings of the words and developing the appropriate logic. We shall see later to what extent this is true.

At any rate, the first step that the moral philosopher has to take, in order to help us think better (i.e. more rationally) about moral questions, is to get to understand the meanings of the words used in asking them; and the second step, which follows directly from the first, is to give an account of the logical properties of the words, and thus of the canons of rational thinking about moral questions. Thus in its formal aspect moral philosophy is a branch of what is now often called philosophical logic; but this is different only in name from the most securely based of the things that used to be called metaphysics. And this word may remind us that Kant called his book on these questions *Groundwork of the Metaphysic of Morals*.

It would, however, be wrong to say that all we have to do, in order to think well and rationally about moral questions, is logic or metaphysics. We shall be saved from this mistake if we pay attention to the work of those writers who, along with Kant, have in modern times contributed most to our understanding of these issues, namely the utilitarians. Many people think, even now, and in spite of some illuminating things that John Stuart Mill (1861:chh.1 *s.f.*, 5) said about the relation between his theory and Kant's, that Kant and the utilitarians stand at opposite poles of moral philosophy. But, as we shall see, the formal, logical properties of the moral words, the understanding of which we owe above all to Kant, yield a system of moral reasoning whose conclusions have a content identical with that of a certain kind of utilitarianism (2.6, 3.3, 6.1 f.). Utilitarianism itself is compounded of two ingredients, a formal and a substantial; and the formal element needs only to be rephrased in order to come extremely close to Kant; there is a very close relation between Bentham's 'Everybody to count for one, nobody for more than one' (*ap*. Mill, 1861:ch. 5 *s.f.*) and Kant's 'Act only on that maxim through which you can at the same time will that it should become a universal law' (1785:52).

But utilitarianism also has a substantial element. In order to decide what we ought to do, we have, according to the utilitarians, to study not only the logical properties of the moral words, but the preferences of the people whom our actions will affect; and it is an empirical question what these are. It is commonly thought that Kant would have dissented; I doubt this, but shall not be able to go into this historical question. At any rate the kind of utilitarianism which I shall be advocating has both a formal element (a reformulation of the requirement that moral principles be properly universal) and the substantial element just mentioned, which brings our moral thinking into contact with the world of reality. The normative consequences of our utilitarian theory are consequences of these two elements in combination: that is to say, it is not just a theory in normative ethics, nor just a theory in metaethics, but both in double harness (though the elements are not to be confused with one another).

1.2 One of the crucial questions we shall be facing is, 'How far can we get by the logical study of the moral words?' At what stage do we have to take into account, in our moral thinking, facts about the way things and people are, in the world as it is? Does a moral system for practical use have to be adequate to all logically possible worlds, as some arguments used by moral philosophers assume (e.g. Rescher, 1975:78; cf. H 1979b:144)? Or will it do if it is adequate to conditions in *this* world? The answer which I shall be suggesting is that we can get a long way by logic alone—further than many people have thought; but that, in the selection of principles for use in this world of ours, facts about the world and the people in it are relevant (3.2, 5.1, 9.9). So a complete moral system will depend both on logical and on empirical theses—which makes it all the more important to be clear which are which.

When we have sorted out the logical from the empirical theses, we have to ask whether there will then remain a

further element in our moral thought, consisting in pieces
of thinking which are neither about how the world is, nor
about the logical properties of words. It is important not to
mistake what I have in mind here. Some philosophers
speak as if there were what they call *ontological* questions
which are neither about the logical properties of words nor
about matters of empirical fact. We shall not be concerning
ourselves with this possibility—certainly, if moral philosophy can be done without ontology, as I think it can, that
makes it a lot easier. What I have in mind is a different
problem: are there, besides questions about the logical
properties of words, and questions about how the world is,
irreducibly *evaluative* or *prescriptive* questions which are
not to be decided either by determining how the world is or
by determining what words mean? When we have done all
we can by way of discovering the facts about the world in
which we do our moral thinking, and elucidating the
logical properties of the moral words and thus establishing
the canons of moral thought, will there remain something
to be done which is neither logic nor fact-finding, but
pure evaluation or prescription—an exercise of Kant's
'rational will' or Aristotle's 'choice'[4]—and how large, if so,
is the field of operation of this element in our moral
thinking?

In my earlier writings (e.g. *LM* ch. 4) I have insisted that
there is this further element; and I shall not in this book be
retracting that view. But I shall be doing what will seem, to
those who do not understand quite what is going on, to be
very like retracting it. For I shall be maintaining that, if we
assumed a perfect command of logic and of the facts, they
would constrain so severely the moral evaluations that we
can make, that in practice we would be bound all to agree to
the same ones. In terms of the title of a previous book of
mine, the freedom which we have as moral thinkers is a

---

[4] The difference between Aristotle's *prāktikē dianoia* (closely related to, if not
identical with, *proairesis* or choice) and Kant's *praktische Vernunft* (which he
equated with the will) is not so great as some have supposed. See Aristotle,
1139[b]17 and Kant, 1785:36.

freedom to reason, i.e. to make rational moral evaluations; and the rules of this reasoning, which are determined by the concepts occurring in the questions we are answering, bring it about that, over the most important part of morality, we shall, if we are rational, exercise our freedom in only one way (12.6 ff.).

I shall endeavour to show this without introducing any considerations which are not founded on philosophical logic and established by its ordinary procedures. This distinguishes the method used here totally from that of most other modern moral philosophers, who appeal at every turn to their own and (they hope) their readers' moral intuitions. That is to say, in establishing the rules of moral reasoning I shall not allow myself to make moves other than those which philosophical logic can validate. If I am successful in this, my position will be much securer than theirs.

What do I mean by 'the ordinary procedures' of 'philosophical logic'? To illustrate what I mean, I will take an example from another part of logic than that which concerns the moral philosopher. Suppose that we were investigating, not any moral word, but the word 'must' in its other sense in which it corresponds to the necessity-operator of ordinary modal logic. I mean the sense occurring in the sentence 'He must be in the garden' (said by someone because he has quite adequate reasons for being sure that he is in the garden), which is to be contrasted with the deontic (e.g. moral) sense of 'must' as in 'One must always keep one's promises', or 'I must not let him down'. We might be interested in one particular logical property of this word—one which is, indeed, closely analogous to the property of universalizability which I wish to ascribe to 'must' in its deontic sense and to its near neighbour 'ought'. It is a logical feature of 'must' that one cannot consistently say: 'He must be in the garden, but I can conceive of another situation, identical in all its universal properties to this one, except that the corresponding person is not in the garden'. ('All its universal

properties' must, of course, be understood as including all
the properties of the person in question himself, and
excluding only his purely numerical identity as that
individual.)

In this respect 'must be' differs from 'is'. It is not
inconsistent to say 'He *is* in the garden, but I can conceive
of another situation, identical in all its universal properties
to this one, except that the corresponding person is not in
the garden'. The reason why this statement becomes
inconsistent (or, not to put too fine a point on it, at least
logically at fault), if 'must be' is substituted for 'is', is that
there cannot be any necessity about his being there unless
there is some law-like, universal proposition which holds,
such that his not being there would be, in this situation, a
breach of it. If there is no such law-like proposition which
holds, there is no necessity, though he might be there all
the same.

It must be noticed that it is not only logical necessity, but
also causal and other kinds of necessity, which have this
feature. We shall be seeing in a moment that it holds also of
the kind of deontic necessity which is expressed by 'must'
in its other, deontic sense, and by 'ought'.

But how could we establish that the 'must' of ordinary
modal logic has this feature? How, for that matter, do we
establish that *any* word has *any* logical property? How do
we establish that the word 'all' has the property which
makes self-contradictory the statement 'All the books on
that shelf are by Wittgenstein, and there is one of them
which is not by Wittgenstein'? Or how do we establish that
the word 'if' has the property which forbids us on pain of
inconsistency to say things of the form 'If p then q; and p;
and not q'? Or how do we establish that the word 'not' has
the property which makes self-contradictory the claim to
have discovered something which both has and does not
have the same quality? How, even, do we establish that we
cannot without contradiction say 'There is a dog in the
garden, and there is no animal in the garden'? These are big

questions, to which I have to some extent addressed myself elsewhere (*LM* 2.4; H 1960); but for now let us say simply this, that we can tell when people are contradicting themselves because we know the language they are speaking. If we want to use that dreadful and very dangerous word, there *are* linguistic 'intuitions', and the disciplines of logic and linguistics rely on them. (There are moral intuitions too, but they need keeping in their place or they will make havoc of moral philosophy, as we shall see: 1.3, 2.5, 4.1 ff., 8.1 ff.) We are able in simple cases[5] to recognize deviant use, or misuse, of the logical connectives such as 'and', for example, because we have learnt how to use them, which is the same thing as learning what they mean. And self-contradiction is one kind of misuse.

We do not need to claim, although it *could* be claimed, that in order to set up a logic it suffices to give meanings, in terms of inference-rules for statements containing them, to all the words or signs to be used in it. The late Mr. Prior (1960) thought that he had a conclusive argument against this claim. He pointed out that it would be possible to have a logical connective 'tonk', which was defined in terms of the following two inference-rules:

From P infer P-tonk-Q
From P-tonk-Q infer Q
    for any P, Q.

The first of these rules is analogous to one which holds for the sign of disjunction ('or') in ordinary logic, and the second to one which holds for the sign of conjunction ('and'). The inclusion in our language of a sign governed by both these rules would, as Prior rightly says, enable any proposition to be derived from any other. But it is not clear what we are to conclude from this. Prior thinks that we have to conclude that any attempt to base a logic on what Sir Karl Popper (1947a:286; 1947b:220) has called

[5] Complex cases are to be handled analogously to the treatment of indirect entailments in *LM* 2.4.

'inferential definitions' of the logical signs is a washout from the start. But it may be that a more modest conclusion is all that we can draw, namely that if we want to have such a logic that is going to be of use, or to have a language in which we can say things without simultaneously implying every other statement that can be expressed in the language, we shall have to be careful *what* rules we define our signs in terms of. This would be analogous to the requirement that when setting up logics in the old way by means of axioms, etc., we should be careful *what* axioms we include, if we are not going to get into similar trouble.

But be that as it may, I shall not be deterred by Prior's argument from holding that a study of the meanings of the words in our language is the first step towards obtaining an account of the logical properties of those words, and thus of the canons of reasoning on questions containing the words. The situation is no different when we come to the moral words. The deontic 'must' and 'ought' are in many ways like the 'must' of ordinary modal logic. We have to be able to recognize, as we *can* recognize if we have learnt how to use these words, or learnt what they mean, that certain uses of them are logically deviant. The thesis of universalizability, which is one of the main elements in a true account of the structure of moral thinking (*FR* 2.5), has the consequence that it is a misuse of the word 'ought' to say 'You ought, but I can conceive of another situation, identical in all its properties to this one, except that the corresponding person ought not'. The same would be true if for 'ought' we substituted the deontic 'must'. And if it is asked how we know that this is a misuse, the answer, whatever it is, is going to be of the same sort as with the 'must' of modal logic. So I am not going to say any more in general about how we establish logical theses of this sort; it is a problem for the whole of logic, not just for that part of logic which concerns the moral concepts.

1.3 However, one very severe warning must now be uttered before I go on. It is only too tempting, when we have said what I have just said about knowing misuses of words when we see them, to go on to take a seemingly small but actually fatal step, and say that in the same way, for example, if we have learnt to use a word like 'ought', we just know that one ought not to tell lies. This is the step (made easy by the existence of some seductive 'borderline cases', 1.5, 4.3) from speaking, justifiably and usefully, of linguistic intuitions as the basis of logic, to speaking, and thereby introducing a pernicious error, of moral intuitions as the basis of moral thinking. Moral intuitions there certainly are, and I shall later be giving an account of them; but if we regard them as the *basis* of moral thinking in the same way as linguistic intuitions are the basis of logic, we shall wreck the entire enterprise, for a reason which I will now explain.

The crucial difference between linguistic and moral intuitions is that the latter, unlike the former, claim to establish matters of moral substance. Linguistic intuitions can support theses in empirical linguistics and, in a subtler way, in philosophical logic. In the first case, the native speakers of a language are the authorities on how it is spoken. In the second, the intention of a speaker on how his words are to be taken (what they imply) is authoritative. If, when he said "The smoke comes from the forward or the after hold', he meant to exclude its coming from both, he can tell us. And since language is mainly for communication between people, the speakers of a language will usually agree on how the words in it are to be taken. This agreement can be formalized after mutual discussion. But there is nothing to stop a particular speaker using a word in a different way from others in his community; provided that he makes this clear, no confusion will result.

The important point is that the kinds of intuitions that are appealed to by empirical linguists and by philosophical logicians can *never* yield either statements or precepts of substance about morals. They are in this respect quite different from moral intuitions, although these certainly exist and have a place in our moral thought. We do feel certain that it is wrong to torture people for fun. But our

authority as native speakers of our language, and our
authority on what we intend to imply by our words, do not
suffice, as they might if we were doing logic or linguistics,
to establish the correctness of what we thus affirm or
prescribe. Nor does the collective authority of our
community. That way lies relativism or subjectivism,
which all the writers who appeal to intuitions are seeking to
avoid. If anybody says that it is all right to torture people
for fun, he is differing from the rest of us, but is making no
logical or linguistic error. His error, if it can be called that,
is an error of moral substance. If we can get the better of
him in argument, it will not be by appealing to linguistic
intuitions alone (though they can be used to reveal the logic
of the argument), nor by appeal to moral intuitions (for
they have no probative force, and the two sides in the most
important moral arguments will have different intuitions).

The appeal to moral intuitions will never do as a basis for
a moral system. It is certainly possible, as some thinkers
even of our times have done, to collect all the moral
opinions of which they and their contemporaries feel most
sure, find some relatively simple method or apparatus
which can be represented, with a bit of give and take, and
making plausible assumptions about the circumstances of
life, as generating all these opinions; and then pronounce
that that is the moral system which, having reflected, we
must acknowledge to be the correct one. But they have
absolutely no authority for this claim beyond the original
convictions, for which no ground or argument was given.
The 'equilibrium' they have reached is one between forces
which might have been generated by prejudice, and no
amount of reflection can make that a solid basis for
morality. It would be possible for two mutually inconsistent systems to be defended in this way; all that this
would show is that their advocates had grown up in
different moral environments.

Having said this, however, it is important to notice that
there do exist legitimate uses, in moral philosophy, of the
appeal to received opinion, some of which I have described

elsewhere (H 1971c:117). The procedure which I have just been criticizing can be represented as hypothetico-deductive, like that of much scientific inquiry. We are to frame hypotheses in the form of moral principles, and check them against the data of received opinions (having first subjected these to a certain amount of reflection). There is, however, another kind of hypothetico-deductive pro-cedure which is quite acceptable, and must be distin-guished from this unsatisfactory one. The hypotheses in this more acceptable procedure are not moral principles but linguistic hypotheses about what people do *mean* when they use the moral words. This procedure can take two forms, one of which is implicit in what I have already said. In this first procedure the hypotheses are linguistic and the data against which we check them are also linguistic, i.e. the recognition by native speakers that certain locutions are deviant or non-deviant. Among the kinds of deviance that especially interest the moral philosopher in his capacity of logician are self-contradictions. Thus, if it is alleged that some moral word has a certain meaning, and we find ordinary people perfectly ready to accept as not self-contradictory what would, according to the proposed meaning, be self-contradictory statements, that will be a reason for abandoning the proposal as a proposal about what people *do* mean by their words (though of course it could still be proposed that we should take to using the words in a different way).

The second form of the procedure is more complex. In it, the hypotheses are still linguistic, but the data against which they are checked are not. Suppose that we know enough about human beings to be sure that they have, for the most part, certain desires, aversions, and the like. And suppose that, given these desires, and given a certain hypothesis about what the moral words mean, and thus about what forms of moral reasoning are valid, and given, further, the assumption that human beings do, on the whole, with some exceptions, reason validly, we can derive from the hypothesis about meanings the prediction that human beings will reach certain moral conclusions in their reasoning, and thus come to have certain moral opinions. If we find that they do in fact, generally speaking, have those opinions, the hypothesis about the meanings of their words has at least escaped refutation. In short, we are allowed to retain, provisionally, those hypotheses about the meanings of words which, if true, and if we are right about what human beings are like, would account for them having the moral opinions which they do have.

Note that, in order to follow this second procedure, we do not have, any more than in the first, to assume, as the philosophers I have been criticizing do, that the moral opinions of ordinary people are correct; we have to assume only that they are the natural outcomes of the fact that people are as they are, on the hypothesis that the words have certain meanings. It might even be that there were various fallacies in reasoning into which it was easy to fall. In that case we might explain people's moral opinions by saying that they had fallen into one of these fallacies, in spite of using the words in the way stated in the hypothesis. The hypothesis has only to stand up against the facts of people's linguistic behaviour; *any* explanation of the behaviour that squares with the hypothesis and is in other ways acceptable will leave the hypothesis unscathed, even if we do not presuppose the correctness of people's moral opinions or of their logic.

In 4.1 we shall be making an extended use of a method which is a development of this. It is possible to test similar linguistic hypotheses, not against what people say about morals (given assumptions about their motivations) but against what philosophical theories get advanced. If there are certain mistakes which philosophers would very naturally make about the meanings and uses of moral words, if the truth about them were what it is, and we find these mistakes being frequently made, then the hypothesis that that is the truth about them has survived an important test.

It must be added that there is yet another kind of hypothetico-deductive procedure which is quite legitimate. This seeks to check, not linguistic hypotheses, but hypotheses in moral anthropology, against people's moral opinions. This procedure is in principle quite straightforward: we hypothesize that certain moral opinions are current in a given society, and then observe the linguistic and other behaviour of the society to see whether in fact they are. I mention this further procedure merely in order to point out the limits of what we can achieve by this and the other acceptable procedures just described, by way of observing people's opinions and how they express them. Nowhere here can we find a way of checking the *correctness* of any moral opinions. To suppose that we can is to confuse moral philosophy with various kinds of empirical science such as anthropology and linguistics, as some moral philosophers appear to be doing (H 1973a: ad init.).

It has been my aim, without any appeal to moral intuitions as certificates of the correctness of moral judgements, to find out what people do mean by the moral words. Having done this, we should be at liberty to recommend the adoption of a different use; but I shall not be doing this, because all the work I have done in moral philosophy, including that set out in this book, has convinced me that our ordinary moral concepts, once their use is clarified, are serviceable. Having established this use and thus a logic for moral thinking, I shall have put us in a position to use this logic, supplemented with other ingredients, in moral reasoning about practical issues. In this book I shall be only explaining in a general way how this can be done; I have in other places applied the method recommended to many practical issues in order to satisfy myself that it works (see bibliography), and shall no doubt be doing more of the same. I am optimistic enough to hope that any reader who understands the method will find it easy to apply.

1.4 But at this point we must consider an objection to such a procedure which is often made. How, it is said, can moral conclusions of substance be founded on premisses

about our uses of words? This would seem to offend
against two canons which have had a great deal of support.
First of all, it is usually held that conclusions of substance
cannot be derived from premisses about the uses of words;
and I have in effect been maintaining just this. Secondly,
supporters of Hume's Law[6] ('No "ought" from an "is"'),
of whom, with qualifications (H 1977b:468 ff.), I am one,
will protest that one cannot get evaluative conclusions out
of factual premisses about word-usage.

The first of these objections is answered by saying that I
am not suggesting a derivation of substantial conclusions
from linguistic premisses *alone*. We shall see later how the
substance gets in. The second objection is harder to deal
with lucidly; I will make a preliminary attempt now, and
hope that the answer will become clearer when the main
argument of the book has been set out (12.6 ff.). The first
point to get clear is that there is no question of a logical
deduction of moral conclusions from factual premisses of
any kind (4.2). What is being proposed is that certain
canons of reasoning, of an entirely formal sort, are to be
established by appeal to linguistic intuitions, and then, by
reasoning in accordance with these, using, as I have just
said, some substantial premisses, we arrive at answers to
our moral questions—but not by deduction nor by any
other kind of 'linear inference' (*FR* 6.1 f.).

The nature of the substantial premisses is of course
crucial. It might be said that if they were non-moral, non-
evaluative, non-prescriptive statements of fact, Hume's
Law would still have been breached, whatever the logic;
but that if they were prescriptive, nothing would have been
achieved, because the problem would remain of how these
substantial prescriptive premisses themselves are to be
established. This problem I shall not be able to deal with
now; its solution lies in seeing, as we shall see later, that the
requirement to universalize our prescriptions, which is
itself a logical requirement if we are reasoning morally,

---

[6] What Hume himself meant in 1739:III, 1, i is disputed (Hudson, 1969).

demands that we treat *other people's* prescriptions (i.e. their desires, likings, and, in general, preferences) as if they were our own (5.3, 6.1 ff.). So it is not that we are going by logic from facts to prescriptions; it is rather that logic compels us, having ascertained facts about what others are prescribing or will prescribe, to treat these prescriptions on a par with our own original prescriptions in our moral reasoning. The reader will rightly be suspicious of this suggestion (so was I when it first occurred to me); but I ask him to be patient and sympathetic, and see whether it does not, after all, work.

1.5 Aside from this major problem, there are subsidiary ones which can conveniently be dealt with here. First of all, would not the 'linguistic method', as we may call it, make us the slaves of our existing conceptual scheme? It must be admitted that in the hands of some recent writers it has done just that (4.3 *s.f.*). Our moral language contains some words, which I have elsewhere called 'secondarily evaluative words', whose very use, in their full evaluative sense, commits us to substantial moral evaluations. An example is 'lazy'; people who do not admire hard work simply do not use this term or its opposite 'industrious', or if they do, use them purely descriptively (*FR* 2.7, 10.1 ff.; *LM* 7.5). It is possible, by concentrating on such words, to create the impression that our conceptual scheme, and the very meanings of our words, from which we cannot escape, commit us to the adoption of certain norms of conduct. The view is thus easily propagated that *all* linguistic intuitions concerning *any* moral words incorporate moral intuitions, or that no distinction can be sustained between the two kinds of intuition.

This, however, is a mere conjuring trick. We do not have to use these words at all; or, if we do, we can use them in a purely descriptive sense without evaluative commitments so that, even here, the adoption of the moral commitment is in principle separable from the adoption of the word (4.3). There exist in language, besides these secondarily evaluative words, words like 'ought' and 'wrong' which do not incapsulate particular moral commitments; and we shall be wise, if we wish to avoid being the slaves of our language, to pay attention to these more general words of commendation and disapproval. The attempt by naturalists to play the same trick with these more general words has been unsuccessful. If '*F*' is any secondarily evaluative condemnatory adjective, we can always ask 'Granted that it would be *F*, would it be *wrong*?' There may, for example, be a secondarily evaluative use of 'unjust', corresponding to our intuitive principles of justice (9.6); but what we need in the end to decide is, not merely whether an act would be unjust, but whether it would be wrong.

But even in the case of the more non-committal moral words, it might be objected that, if I am going to found an entire system of moral reasoning on their meanings, I shall be tying our moral thinking to concepts which we *happen*, contingently, to have in our language. Other peoples might have different conceptual schemes, and these might generate different canons of moral reasoning, and thus lead them to different answers to their moral questions.

It is of great importance to see why this objection misses the target. I am not suggesting that we are tied to using words in the way that we do, or to having the conceptual scheme that we have. But if we were to alter the meanings of our words, we should be altering the questions we were asking, and perhaps answering, in terms of them. We come into moral philosophy asking certain moral questions, and the questions are posed in terms of certain concepts. If we go on trying to answer *those* questions, we are stuck with *those* concepts. We may, indeed, try to clarify them, and they probably need it; but unless we are to give up the questions, any new form of words that we use to express our questions must satisfy us as a reformulation of *those* questions (*LM* 5.8).

I cannot forbid any philosopher, or anybody else, to start asking questions different from those which are expressed in terms of the moral words as we now use them. The new questions may be important and fruitful ones. But if it were being suggested that we should not just ask the new questions as well as the old ones, but give up asking the old ones, I should require to be satisfied, not merely that the new ones are important, but that the old ones are unimportant. And it would be hard to satisfy me of this without at least as full an investigation of the old ones as has been undertaken in this book and in my other writings, but leading to different conclusions from my own.

It is very possible that this investigation will reveal unclarities and especially ambiguities in our moral questions. Think, for example, of the different things that 'Haven't I a right to do what I want with my own property?' could mean (9.2 f.), or 'Ought I to be doing what I am doing?' (*LM* 11.2, *FR* 5.6). Many times in this book I shall be suggesting clarifications and disambiguations which will help us to pinpoint more exactly the questions we are asking. But, as I said, as speakers we remain the authorities on what we intend by our words and thus on what questions we are asking.

The crucial point is that, although we can ask what questions we wish, *whatever* questions we ask will be posed in terms of certain concepts; and that means that, *whatever* questions we ask, we shall have, if we are going to think rationally about the answers to them, to understand the concepts. I have tried to do this in the case of the concepts which I find occurring in questions which do trouble me, and, I am sure, many other people (*FR* 6.5; Moore, 1903:6). I do not for a moment deny the value of proposing new, and perhaps clearer, conceptual schemes, which can be used to generate logics that provide models of practical reasoning procedures. I have tried my hand at this myself (*LM* 12.1 ff.). But anybody who does this, if he is going to shed light on the moral problems which vex us here and now, will have to show that the new models and concepts can be used in order to pose the same problems as were giving us difficulty; otherwise the difficulties will simply not have been faced. And this cannot be done without a study of the difficulties presented by our existing conceptual scheme.

If anybody were to find himself unable to accept the methodological proposals I have been making, it would be open to him to achieve the same ends as I am seeking in this book by a different method. My own strategy has been to expose the logic of the moral concepts as we have them, and show that they generate certain canons of moral reasoning which will lead to our adopting a certain method of substantial normative moral thinking. I then (11.1 ff.) say what is the point of having such concepts, or such words in our language, and why we should, in our own interest, adopt this manner of speaking and thinking. If anybody either does not believe that I have given a true account of the moral concepts as we have them, or thinks that investigations of the logic of words in ordinary language are unhelpful, either because they yield no determinate results, or because, even if they did, these would have no force in moral arguments, it would be open to him to proceed in a different way. He could set out the logic of an artificial language, identical in its properties with the logic which I claim our ordinary words have; then he could show that anybody reasoning in such a language would have to think in the way in which *I* say our existing concepts constrain us to think; and then he could, using the same arguments as I shall use, show that there would be an advantage in our adopting such a language. Though I should not like such a method as much as my own (for it requires us to persuade people to adopt an entirely new language, whereas mine only requires that they articulate the understanding they already have of their existing concepts), I do not think that the difference between the results of the two methods would be very substantial.

1.6   My hope then is that by investigating the meanings of the moral words we shall manage to generate logical canons which will govern our moral thinking. But what *are* the logical properties of the moral words that will generate these canons? For two of them I can refer to previous writings of mine; and these are the two which will do the work in the rest of this book. They are the so-called universalizability and prescriptivity of moral judgements. Both properties are shared with other, non-moral, evaluative judgements; and the second, prescriptivity, is not possessed by all moral judgements, but only by a central class of them, which, however, will be the class we shall be concerned with in our theory of moral reasoning (*LM* 8.2, 10.2 ff.; *FR* 2.2, 2.8, 3.3).Universalizability can be explained in various equivalent ways; it comes to this, that if we make different moral judgements about situations which we admit to be identical in their universal descriptive properties, we contradict ourselves. By 'different', I mean 'such that, if they were made about the same situation, they would be inconsistent with one another'.

The prescriptivity of moral judgements can be explained formally as the property of entailing at least one imperative (*LM* 11.2; *FR* 2.8). But since this presupposes an understanding of 'imperative', which perhaps cannot be achieved without first explaining 'prescriptive', a fuller but more informal explanation may be more helpful. We say something prescriptive if and only if, for some act A, some situation S and some person P, if P were to assent (orally) to what we say, and not, in S, do A, he logically must be assenting insincerely (*LM* 1.7, 2.2).

The mere fact that what we say could be given as a reason for acting in some way does not make it prescriptive. That the hotel faces the sea could be given as a reason for taking a room there, but to say that it does is not to say something prescriptive; for somebody who did not like looking at the sea could sincerely assent, and yet not take a room there. On the other hand, if we say that it is a better hotel than the one on the other side of the road, there is a sense of 'better than' (the prescriptive sense) in which a person who assented orally to our judgement, yet, when faced with a choice between the two hotels (other things such as price being equal), chose the other hotel, must have been saying something that he did not really think. For if, in assenting, he assented sincerely to something prescriptive, he must think it is better, and thus prefer it, and thus, in the appropriate situation and other things being equal, choose it (H 1963b, sec. vi). The example could easily be adapted to make a similar point about the prescriptivity, in certain uses, of 'right', 'ought', and (*a fortiori*) 'must'.

I must also explain that I shall be following my usual practice (*FR* 2.8) of using the words 'evaluative' and 'value-judgement' to apply to utterances which are both prescriptive and universalizable (or actually universal). I shall also use the terms 'evaluative meaning' and 'prescriptive meaning' for the element in the meaning of value-judgements which gives them their prescriptivity. The presence of this element does not prevent their also having a descriptive element in their meaning, so that it can be said to be in some sense right to apply them to certain kinds of things and not others (*FR* 2.1 ff.). But I use the term 'descriptive judgement (or statement)' only for judgements lacking any such prescriptive or evaluative meaning, i.e. those whose meaning is purely descriptive. It must also be noted that not all moral judgements are evaluative or prescriptive (there are some which merely apply accepted standards without endorsing them); and that not all evaluative or universally prescriptive judgements are moral (aesthetic judgements for example are universalizable). All this is more fully explained elsewhere (*LM* 11.2; *FR* 2.8, 8.2; 3.5).

It is not necessary to my argument to insist that 'ought', for example, is *never* used non-prescriptively (it sometimes is) or non-universalizably. Many words have various senses (for example 'all' and 'if'). All that is necessary is for there to be a recognizable sense in which it has the properties which I have claimed. People who then ask moral questions *in this sense*—as, I think, we do much of the time—are bound by the logical rules which these properties dictate. If they want to switch to *different* questions, that is up to them.

The moral word which exhibits these properties most

clearly and consistently is one which has not featured very much in my past writings, because it is not in fact much used in ordinary moral discourse, for reasons which are interesting. This word is the deontic 'must', already referred to. It is much plainer that 'must' is prescriptive and universalizable than that 'ought' is. Reverting to our analogy with the other sense of 'must' (that of ordinary modal logic), we can find a way to display this very clearly. We have already seen (1.2) that 'must' in both its senses has the property of universalizability. The ordinary modal 'must' does not have, like the deontic 'must', the property of prescriptivity; but it has an analogue to it. Most systems of modal logic contain either axioms or theorems to the effect that if something *must be* so, it *is* so. Now if, in deontic logic, we were to introduce a similar axiom, with the simple change of the proposition governed by the operator into the imperative mood, we should have an axiom or theorem to the effect 'If you must do something, then do it', where the 'must' is deontic. The deontic 'must' is then treated in the same way as the 'must' of ordinary necessity, except that it governs an imperative; and, accordingly, the statement that the imperative is necessary entails the imperative itself, just as the statement that a statement is necessary entails that statement itself (Fisher, 1962).

I merely suggest this device without further justifying it, since I am not an expert in modal logic. What is much more interesting is to ask whether the deontic 'must' of ordinary language has the property of prescriptivity thus displayed. It looks as if it does; for it would be self-contradictory to say, using the deontic 'must', 'You must do it, but don't'. Even more interesting is to ask why, if this is so, we cannot extend this thesis to cover the deontic 'ought' as well, in its typical senses as used by human beings. The reasons are essentially those given in *FR* 5.4 and amplified in 3.7 of this book. The word 'must', even in ordinary language, does approximate, in its deontic use, to the 'holy' or 'angelic' character which, adapting Kant's terminology to a new

use, I ascribed in *FR* 5.5 to the idealized artificial 'ought' of
LM 12.4, which, it may be remembered, did not provide
the escape-routes for backsliders charted, in respect of the
ordinary 'ought', in both books; and that is why it is so little
used. It is much odder to say 'I must' at the moment at
which one is backsliding (i.e. doing what one says one must
not do) than it is to do this with 'ought'. One could not
without raising logical as well as moral eyebrows say 'I
must not let him down', and at the same moment deliberately do just that. If anybody said this, the 'inverted
commas' would be palpable. Since, for reasons which I
have given and shall give, we need the flexibility provided
by 'ought' (*FR* 5.5; 3.7), that is the word we mostly use.
But 'ought' aspires to the status of 'must', and, as we shall
see, in rigorous, critical, moral reasoning has to be used like
it. I shall therefore in what follows continue to use the word
'ought', with the proviso that it is to be used in our
reasoning *as if* it were always fully prescriptive, and *as if* its
prescriptions were not to be overridden, though we
humans do not always so use it. Thus, our moral reasoning
will be of the same form as that which angels would use,
even though our human limitations may make us backslide
from the results of it.

There remains a further logical property of moral
language, besides universalizability and prescriptivity,
namely that which distinguishes *moral* from other evaluative judgements. The name I shall give to this property
is 'overridingness' (a notion I have just used in anticipation). But the account we have to give of this
differentia is rather complex, and will have to wait until I
have said something about the different levels of moral
thinking, as I shall be doing in the next chapter. We shall
return to it in ch. 3.

MORAL CONFLICTS

2.1 In this chapter I shall be introducing a distinction between two levels of moral thinking. The distinction is not original; it occurs already in Plato and Aristotle. The seeds of it are to be found in Plato's distinction between knowledge and right opinion, as in the passage cited at the head of ch. 1. This is the basis of his division between the classes in his Republic, and the educations proper to them (3.1; H 1982). It reappears in Aristotle's distinction between right motivation and practical wisdom, virtues of character and of intellect, the 'that' and the 'why'. It was made use of by the classical utilitarians in answering their critics (Mill, 1861: ch. 5; cf. Rawls, 1955). But it may be doubted whether its immense importance has yet been realized. It will be made to do a great deal of work in this book; and it is hardly an exaggeration to say that more confusion is caused, both in theoretical ethics and in practical moral issues, by the neglect of this distinction than by any other factor.

I shall be using the distinction, first in order to shed light on some disputes in metaethics which have recently troubled us, and secondly in order to defend a version of utilitarianism against an extremely common type of objection which would not be made by anybody who understood the distinction. But the uses made of the distinction in this book by no means exhaust its usefulness; in particular, the philosophy of education, as I shall be briefly hinting, can gain a great deal of illumination from it.

I shall be calling the two levels the intuitive and the critical, following my practice in recent papers (e.g. H 1979b:146). Earlier I called them level 1 and level 2 (e.g. H 1976a:122); but it is clearer to have more self-explanatory names for them. To these two levels of moral thinking has to be added a third level, the metaethical, at which we are operating when we discuss the meanings of the moral words and the logic of moral reasoning. The intuitive and critical levels of thinking are both, unlike the metaethical, concerned with moral questions of substance; but they handle them in different ways, each appropriate to the different circumstances in which, and purposes for which, the thinking is done.

The way in which I shall seek to explain the two levels is by discussing the problem of moral conflicts. By this I mean situations in which we seem to have conflicting duties. The views held by moral philosophers about conflicts of duties are an extremely good diagnostic of the comprehensiveness and penetration of their thought about morality; superficiality is perhaps more quickly revealed by what is said about this problem than in any other way. Those who say, roundly, that there can just be irresoluble conflicts of duties are always those who have confined their thinking about morality to the intuitive level. At this level the conflicts are indeed irresoluble; but at the critical level there is a requirement that we resolve the conflict, unless we are to confess that our thinking has been incomplete. We are not thinking critically if we just say 'There is a conflict of duties; I ought to do A, and I ought to do B, and I can't do both'. But at the intuitive level it is perfectly permissible to say this. The critical level is that at which the minister was operating who put a placard on the 'wayside pulpit' outside his church in Yorkshire (as reported to me by Mr. Anthony Kenny) saying 'If you have conflicting duties, one of them isn't your duty'.

It can readily be agreed, however, that it is sometimes the case that a person thinks that he ought to do A, and also thinks that he ought to do B, but cannot do both. For example, he may have made a promise, and circumstances may have intervened, by no fault of his, such that he has an urgent duty to perform which precludes his fulfilling the promise. To start with the kind of trivial example which used to be favoured by intuitionist philosophers: I have promised to take my children for a picnic on the river at Oxford, and then a lifelong friend turns up from Australia and is in Oxford for the afternoon, and wants to be shown round the colleges with his wife. Clearly I ought to show them the colleges, and clearly I ought to keep my promise to my children. Not only do I think these things, but in some sense I am clearly right.

If I am in this dilemma, I may decide on reflection, and in spite of thinking, and *going on* thinking, that I ought to keep my promise to my children, that what I ought, all things considered, to do is to take my friend round the colleges; and this involves a decision that *in some sense* I ought not to take my children for their picnic, because it would preclude my doing what, all things considered, I ought to do, namely take my friend round the colleges. In general, it seems that we think that, if I ought to do A, and doing B would preclude my doing A, I ought not to do B. I rely here on our linguistic and logical, not our moral, intuitions. And if this is so, it looks as if I both ought, and ought not, to take my children for their picnic. And it is a small step from this to concluding that I ought to both take them for their picnic and not take them. This, obviously, runs counter to the claim that 'ought' implies 'can'; for I cannot both take them and not take them. And, even if we do not make the move from saying that I ought to do A to saying that I ought not to do B because it would preclude doing A, we can still get a breach of the dictum that 'ought' implies 'can' by going from the statement that I ought to do A and ought to do B to the statement that I ought to do A and B; for I cannot, in this imagined case, do both A and B.

Faced with these difficulties, some have taken the heroic course of saying that from the proposition that I ought to do A and ought to do B it does not follow that I ought to do A and B. And others might take the equally heroic course of saying that it is possible for it to be the case that I ought to do A and ought not to do A, but that this does not entail that I ought to both do A and not do A. Others, again, might abandon the dictum that 'ought' implies 'can'.

There is indeed some case on other grounds for limiting the application of this dictum (*FR* 4.1). But even its complete abandonment would remove only one, and that not the most awkward, of the difficulties presented by cases of moral conflict.

It is not very helpful to try to sort out these difficulties by some relatively minor tinkering with the calculus of deontic logic. The linguistic and logical intuitions which give rise to them are all right so far as they go. We may suspect, rather, that there is some ambiguity, or at least difference of use, affecting 'ought' as it occurs in different contexts; and this is the suggestion which I shall in effect be making. What is required is an understanding of the two levels of moral thinking and of the different ways that 'ought' is used in each of them. I say this, because, if we have this understanding, the difficulties disappear, and because there are many independent reasons for taking this step.

2.2 It will be illuminating at this point to take a look at the phenomena of moral conflict and ask why philosophers, and indeed most of us, are so certain that we sometimes ought to do two things of which we cannot do both. One clue is to be found in an argument sometimes advanced. It is said that, whichever of the things we do, we shall, if we are morally upright people, experience *remorse*, and that this is inseparable from thinking that we ought not to have done what we did. If, it is said, we just stopped having a duty to do one of the things because of the duty to do the other (as on the wayside pulpit) whence comes the remorse?

This might be questioned. It might be said that, though *regret* is in place (for my children, after all, have had to miss their picnic, and that is a pity), remorse is not; just because it implies the thought that I ought not to have done what I did (a thought which I do not have; I do not reject my decision that, all things considered, I ought to do what I did), it is irrational to feel remorse. On this account, the philosophers in question have just confused remorse with regret. Or they might be said to have confused either of these things with a third thing, which we might call, following Sir David Ross (1930:28), *compunction*. This feeling is not easily distinguishable from fear; and it afflicts us during or before the doing of an act, unlike remorse, which only occurs afterwards. Compunction is also not normally so strong a feeling as remorse; but, like remorse, it *can* be irrational. It would be a very hardened intuitionist who maintained that we never have these feelings in situations in which it is wholly absurd to have them. So perhaps, on the occasion I have been describing, regret would be in place (just as it would be if the picnic or the tour of the colleges had to be cancelled because of the weather), but remorse and compunction are not.

We may, however, feel a lingering unease at this reply. Would not the man who could break his promise to his children without a twinge of compunction be, not a better, because more rational, person, but a morally worse one than most of us who are afflicted in this way? It is time we came to more serious examples. The following kind of case is often cited. A person falls overboard from a ship in a wartime convoy; if the master of the ship leaves his place in the convoy to pick him up, he puts the ship and all on board at risk from submarine attack; if he does not, the person will drown. In the film *The Cruel Sea* (adapted from Monsarrat, 1951) a somewhat similar case occurs; the commander of a corvette is faced with a situation in which if he does not drop depth-charges the enemy submarine will get away to sink more ships and kill more people; but if he does drop them he will kill the survivors in the water. In fact he drops them, and is depicted in the film as suffering anguish of mind. And we should think worse of him if he did not. The former case is perhaps the better one to take, because it avoids some irrelevant features of the second; it too would cause anguish. Although we might feel tempted to say that this anguish is just extreme regret and not remorse, because the master has decided that he ought to leave the person to drown, and remorse would imply his thinking that he ought not to have left him to drown, which, *ex hypothesi*, he does not think—all the same we may also feel that there is some residuum of *moral* sentiment in his state of mind which is not mere non-moral regret. This, at any rate, is the source of the intuitionist view that we are discussing, that there are irresoluble moral conflicts.

Reverting to the case of promising: let us suppose that I have been well brought up; I shall then think, let us say, that one ought not to break promises. And suppose that I get into a situation in which I think that, in the circumstances, I ought to break a promise. I cannot then just abolish my past good upbringing and its effects; nor should I wish to. If I have been well brought up, I shall, when I break the promise, experience this feeling of compunction (no doubt 'remorse' would be too strong a word in this case), which could certainly be described, *in a sense*, as 'thinking that I ought not to be doing what I am doing, namely breaking a promise'. This is even clearer in the case of lying. Suppose that I have been brought up to think that one ought not to tell lies, as most of us have been. And suppose that I get into a situation in which I decide that I ought, in the circumstances, to tell a lie. It does not follow in the least that I shall be able to tell the lie without compunction. That is how lie-detectors work (on people who have been to this minimal extent well brought up). Even if I do not blush, something happens to the electrical properties of my skin. And for my part, I am very glad that this happens to my skin; for if it did not I should be a morally worse educated person.

When we bring up our children, as both Plato and Aristotle (1104^b12) agreed, one of the things we are trying to do is to cause them to have reactions of this kind: 'to like and dislike the things they ought to like and dislike'. It is not by any means the whole of moral education, although some people speak as if it were; indeed, since one can do this sort of thing even to a dog, it may not be part of a typically human moral education at all, or at any rate not the distinctive part. People who think that it is the whole of moral education, and call it 'teaching children the difference between right and wrong', do not have my support, though they are very numerous (which explains why intuitionism is such a popular view in moral philosophy). But there is no doubt that most of us have, during our upbringing, acquired these sentiments, and not much doubt that this is, on the whole, a good thing, for reasons which will shortly become evident.

I recently visited Prague to talk to some philosophers there. If, when I was crossing into Czechoslovakia, the officials had asked me the purpose of my visit, I should certainly have told them a lie, because if they had known they would most probably have expelled me, as they have some of my colleagues, these visits being frowned upon by the Czech government. And, just as certainly, I should have felt, not merely fear of being found out and getting into trouble, but a feeling of *guilt* at telling the lie (although I should have been in no doubt that I ought to tell it). A lie-detector would certainly have exposed my deception. And I should be a morally worse man if I were not affected in that way. So then, if I felt guilty, it looks as if there is a sense of 'thinking that I ought' in which I could have been correctly described as 'thinking that I ought not to be telling the lie'. Feeling guilty is inseparable from, in this sense, thinking that I ought not. Only those with some philosophical sophistication are able to distinguish them even in thought (2.4; *LM* 11.2). Yet in another sense I should certainly have been thinking that I ought to tell the lie.

2.3 Nobody who actually uses moral language in his practical life will be content with a mere dismissal of the paradox that we can feel guilty for doing what we think we ought to do. It will not do to say 'There just are situations in which, whatever you do, you will be doing what you ought not, i.e. doing wrong'. There are, it is true, some people who like there to be what they call 'tragic situations'; the world would be less enjoyable without them, for the rest of us: we could have much less fun writing and reading novels and watching films, in which such situations are a much sought after ingredient. The trouble is that, if one is enough of an ethical descriptivist (4.1) to make the view that there are such situations tenable, they stop being tragic. If, that is to say, it just is the case that both the acts open to a person have the moral property of wrongness, one of their many descriptive properties, why should he be troubled by that? What makes the situation tragic is that he is using moral thinking to help him to decide what he ought to *do*; and when he does this with no more enlightenment than that provided by those 'absolutist' thinkers who believe in very simple and utterly inviolable principles, it leads to an impasse. He is like a rat in an insoluble maze, and that is tragic. But the very tragedy of it may make more humane philosophers look for an alternative to the theory which puts him there. In such a conflict between intuitions, it is time to call in reason.

However, it is not immediately obvious that a rational approach to such predicaments requires the complete separation of levels of moral thinking which I am going to postulate. Let us try to do without it. One expedient might be to seek to qualify or modify one of the principles which seem to apply to the situation, introducing some saving clause which will make the two principles no longer conflict, even *per accidens* in this situation. (Two principles conflict *per accidens* when, although the conjunction of the two is not self-contradictory, which would be a conflict *per se*, they cannot, as things happen to be, both be complied with.) In order to display the logic of the conflict briefly, I shall have to be formal and use letters for the features of situations which figure in the conflicting principles.

Let us then suppose that I start off with principles that one ought never to do an act which is F (some property of acts, e.g. being an instance of promise-breaking), and that one ought never to do an act which is G (some other property), and that I find myself in a situation in which I cannot avoid doing either an F act or a G act. And suppose that I decide, all things considered, that I ought to do the G act, to escape the (worse) F act. We might then try supposing that, as a result of this piece of moral thinking (however it was done), one of my moral principles has *changed*. Instead of reading 'One ought never to do an act which is G', it now reads 'One ought never to do an act which is G, unless it is necessary in order to avoid an act which is F'. This principle, then, which was only ten words long (counting 'G' as one word, though in fact it stands for many words), has now attained a length of twenty-three words. This is important, because the philosophers I have in mind seem often to be speaking as if moral principles ought to be very simple and general, and if one were required to quantify simplicity or generality, one crude way of doing it would be in terms of the number of words in a principle; and they do sometimes talk as if no decent moral principle would contain more than, say, a dozen words.

But obviously this lengthening-process has only just begun. By the time we have been in, or even considered without actually being in them, a few such dilemmas, we shall be getting very long principles indeed. Very early on we shall get principles like 'One ought never to do an act which is G, except that one may when it is necessary in order to avoid an act which is F, and the act is also H; but if the act is not H, one may not' (43 words). For reasons of space I shall not pursue this process further (see Nozick, 1968), but shall assume that it will soon get out of hand, if what we are after are simple principles. And that certainly seems to be what the philosophers I am thinking of are after, because those are the principles which they like appealing to in their examples, and the making of exceptions to which they resist.

Another expedient would be to say that neither of the two rival principles is qualified, but that I adopt a superior or second-order principle which says, for example, 'The principle that one ought never to do an act which is G ought to be obeyed in all cases except where obeying it involves a breach of the principle that one ought never to do an act which is F; in such cases one ought to break it', plus, of course, additional complications to deal with the 'H'-factor just mentioned. Even without these additional complications the new principle contains 49 words. It is obvious that this expedient, though it yields a longer and more cumbrous principle, is no different in substance from the first one. It is also obvious that any attempt to set up what is called a hierarchy of principles, telling us which is to override which, and when, will, if it is to do justice to the moral judgements which we actually make in cases of conflict, soon become extremely complicated; for the instructions for operating the hierarchy will mostly be in the form of the 49-word principle just mentioned. There is the additional problem, brought out by the 'H'-factor in the 43-word principle of the preceding paragraph, that we are unlikely to be able always to put principles in the same order of priority; shall we not want to say that we ought to tell lies to avoid giving pain in *some* circumstances, but that we ought to give pain in order to avoid telling lies in *other* circumstances (for example when the pain is not great)?

Some may wish to introduce God on his traditional machine to ensure that there are no real conflicts of duties even in a one-level system. I shall not discuss this view, because I do not think that even many Christians will believe that God has fixed things in this way, but rather that God has, and we have to a much more limited degree, the means (rational moral thinking) wherewith to resolve at the critical level conflicts which arise at the intuitive. I later profess a less extravagant faith about how the world has to be ordered if morality is to be viable (11.8).

I shall also not discuss a fourth expedient, which has been quite popular: that of saying that when two principles or two duties conflict *per accidens*, the conflict is to be settled by a judging or weighing process to determine which ought, in the particular case, to be conformed to. This is less a method than an evasion of the problem; we are not told *how* to weigh or judge the rival principles. It is, further, not a one-level but a two-level procedure, without any explanation of what is supposed to happen at the second level. The procedure can, however, be made viable within an adequate two-level system (2.4).

I can think of no other way of registering what happens in cases where conflicts of principles are decided that is open to the user of a one-level structure of moral thinking. Since, therefore, a one-level structure seems condemned either to having no determinate procedure for settling moral conflicts, or to having principles of ever increasing complexity, we can only be content with it if we are happy with the complexity or the indeterminacy. I am not yet taking sides on the question of how simple moral principles have to be. As we shall see, it depends on the purposes for which the principles are to be used; different sorts of principles are appropriate to different roles in our moral thinking.

2.4 Let us then look at some of these roles and purposes. One very important one is in *learning* (*LM* 4.3 f., 8.3, 10.3). If principles reach more than a certain degree of complexity, it will be impossible to formulate them verbally in sentences of manageable length; but it might still be possible, even after that, to learn them—i.e., to come to know them in some more Rylean sense which does not involve being able to recite them (Ryle, 1949:27). Assuredly there are many things we know without being able to say in words what we know. All the same, there is a degree of complexity, higher than this, beyond which we are unable to learn principles even in this other sense which does not require that we be able to recite them. So principles which are to be learnt for use on subsequent occasions have to be of a certain degree of simplicity, although the degree has been exaggerated by some people.

In addition to this psychological reason for a limit to the complexity of principles, there is also a practical reason related to the circumstances of their use. Situations in which we find ourselves are not going to be minutely

similar to one another. A principle which is going to be
useful as a practical guide will have to be unspecific enough
to cover a variety of situations all of which have certain
salient features in common. What is wrong about situational ethics and certain extreme forms of existentialism
(we shall see in a moment what is right about them) is that
they make impossible what is in fact an indispensable help
in coping with the world (whether we are speaking of moral
decisions or of prudential or technical ones, which in this
are similar), namely the formation in ourselves of relatively
simple reaction-patterns (whose expression in words, if
they had one, would be relatively simple prescriptive
principles) which prepare us to meet new contingencies
resembling in their important features contingencies in
which we have found ourselves in the past. The same
trouble afflicts the crude caricature of act-utilitarianism
which is the only version of it that many philosophers seem
to be acquainted with. If it were not possible to form such
dispositions, any kind of learning of behaviour would be
ruled out, and we should have to meet each new situation
entirely unprepared, and perform an 'existential' choice or
a cost-benefit analysis on the spot. Let anybody who is
tempted by doctrines of this kind think what it would be
like to drive a car without having *learnt* how to drive a car,
or having totally forgotten everything that one had ever
learnt—to drive it, that is, deciding *ab initio* at each
moment what to do with the steering wheel, brake and
other controls.

   This point can also be illustrated by the practice of good
chess-players and by the experience of those who have
designed computers to play this and other games. Even the
best chess-players cannot explore more than a few moves
ahead. It is therefore rare for them, until late in the game,
to win games by working out all the branching alternative
moves up to the end of the game, i.e. by calculating which
of the available moves will put them in a position which,
whatever the opponent does, enables them to make a
further move which will put them in a position which,

whatever the opponent does, will put them in a position which . . . (after a very large number of such calculated moves) . . . enables them to check-mate the opponent. Nor can any computers so far developed complete such calculations up to the check-mate in the time allowed at chess tournaments.

The point is even clearer with games like backgammon, in which the use of dice introduces an element of chance, thereby vastly multiplying the alternative possibilities that have to be considered at each move. Backgammon is actually a better analogue of our ordinary human problems than chess; that is why its simpler analogues among children's games are such a good moral preparation for facing 'the changes and chances of this mortal life'. The designer of a computer which recently beat the world champion at backgammon makes it clear that the way he did it was not by exploiting the power of the computer to explore beyond human limits the consequences of alternative moves, but rather by programming the computer with relatively simple principles for selecting promising moves (i.e. those most likely to improve the strength of one's position, as assessed by another set of principles picking out general features of positions which are important in *those* kinds of positions) and for selecting *which* of the many alternative future courses of the game to explore more fully, and for how far. 'Unlike the best programmes for playing chess, BKG 9.8 does well more by positional judgment than by brute calculation. This means that it plays backgammon much as human experts do' (Berliner, 1980:64). Obviously judgement that can be programmed into a computer is not open to the strictures I made in 2.3 against 'judging or weighing'. It is governed by principles or rules; a method has been given. No doubt good military commanders and good politicians operate in the same way as the good backgammon-players whom this computer emulates, and so do good moralists.

It by no means follows from this that *who wins* a game of backgammon, a battle, or an election is defined by reference to these rules of good play. The winner of a game of backgammon is the player who first bears off all his pieces in accordance with the rules of the game, not the one who follows the best strategies. Similarly in morals, the principles which we have to follow if we are to give ourselves the best chance of acting rightly are not definitive of 'the right act'; but if we wish to act rightly we shall do well, all the same, to follow them. A wise act-utilitarian, unlike his caricature mentioned earlier, will agree with this, so he is not vulnerable to objections based on it.

A further reason for relying in much of our moral conduct on relatively general principles is that, if we do not, we expose ourselves to constant temptation to special pleading (*FR* 3.6). In practice, especially when in haste or under stress, we may easily, being human, 'cook' our moral thinking to suit our own interest. For example, it is only too easy to persuade ourselves that the act of telling a lie in order to get ourselves out of a hole does a great deal of good to ourselves at relatively small cost to anybody else; whereas in fact, if we view the situation impartially, the indirect costs are much greater than the total gains. It is partly to avoid such cooking that we have intuitions or dispositions firmly built into our characters and motivations.

The term 'rules of thumb' is sometimes used in this connexion, but should be avoided as thoroughly misleading. I regret having once used it myself (*LM* 4.4). Some philosophers use it in a quite different way from engineers, gunners, navigators and the like, whose expression it really is, and in whose use a rule of thumb is a mere time- and thought-saving device, the breach of which, unlike the breach of the moral principles we are discussing, excites no compunction. A much better expression is 'prima facie principles'. Such principles express 'prima facie duties' (Ross, 1930:19), and, although formally speaking they are just universal prescriptions, are associated, owing to our upbringing, with very firm and deep dispositions and feelings. Any attempt to drive a wedge between the principles and the feelings will falsify the facts about our intuitive thinking. *Having* the principles, in the usual sense of the word, is having the disposition to experience the feelings, though it is not, as some intuitionists would have us believe, incompatible with submitting the principles to critical thought when that is appropriate and safe.

There are, then, both practical and psychological reasons for having relatively simple principles of action if we are to learn to behave either morally or skilfully or with prudence. The situational ethicists have rejected this obvious truth because they have grasped another obvious truth which they think to be incompatible with it, though it will seem to be so only to someone who has failed to make the distinction between the two levels of moral thinking which I shall be postulating. The situations in which we find ourselves are like one another, sometimes, in some important respects, but not like one another in all respects; and the differences may be important too. 'No two situations and no two people are ever exactly like each other': this will be recognized as one of the battle-cries of the school of thought that I am speaking of.

It follows from this that, although the relatively simple principles that are used at the intuitive level are necessary for human moral thinking, they are not sufficient. Since any new situation will be unlike any previous situation in *some* respects, the question immediately arises whether the differences are relevant to its appraisal, moral or other. If they are relevant, the principles which we have learnt in dealing with past situations may not be appropriate to the new one. So the further question arises of how we are to decide whether they are appropriate. The question obtrudes itself most in cases were there is a conflict between the principles we have learnt—i.e. where, as things contingently are, we cannot obey them both. But if it arises in those cases, it can arise in any case, and it is mere intellectual sloth to pretend otherwise.

2.5 The most fundamental objection to the one-level

account of moral thinking called intuitionism is that it yields no way of answering such a question. The intuitive level of moral thinking certainly exists and is (humanly speaking) an essential part of the whole structure; but however well equipped we are with these relatively simple, prima facie, intuitive principles or dispositions, we are bound to find ourselves in situations in which they conflict and in which, therefore, some other, non-intuitive kind of thinking is called for, to resolve the conflict. The intuitions which give rise to the conflict are the product of our upbringings and past experience of decision-making. They are not self-justifying; we can always ask whether the upbringing was the best we could have, or whether the past decisions were the right ones, or, even if so, whether the principles then formed should be applied to a new situation, or, if they cannot all be applied, *which* should be applied. To use intuition itself to answer such questions is a viciously circular procedure; if the dispositions formed by our upbringing are called into question, we cannot appeal to them to settle the question.

What will settle the question is a type of thinking which makes no appeal to intuitions other than linguistic. I stress that in this other kind of thinking, which I am calling *critical* thinking, no moral intuitions of substance can be appealed to. It proceeds in accordance with canons estab-lished by philosophical logic and thus based on linguistic intuitions only. To introduce substantial moral in-tuitions at the critical level would be to incorporate in critical thinking the very same weakness which it was designed to remedy. A philosopher will not be content with the intuitive props on which most moral philosophers rely, if he wishes his work to last.

Critical thinking consists in making a choice under the constraints imposed by the logical properties of the moral concepts and by the non-moral facts, and by nothing else. This choice is what I used to call a decision of principle (*LM* ch. 4). But the principles involved here are of a different kind from the prima facie principles considered so far. Since some people have been misled by the term 'principle', I have asked myself whether I should avoid it altogether; but I have in the end retained it in order to mark an important logical similarity between the two kinds of principles. Both are universal prescriptions; the difference lies in the generality–specificity dimension. To explain this: a prima facie principle has, for reasons I have just given, in order to fulfil its function, to be relatively simple and general (i.e. unspecific). But a principle of the kind used in critical thinking (let us call it a critical moral principle) can be of unlimited specificity.

There is not space here to explain at length the difference between universality and generality. It is very important, and it is a pity that these words are still often used as if there were no distinction (H 1972a:2). My own terminology in *LM* 10.3 was slovenly. Briefly, generality is the opposite of specificity, whereas universality is compatible with specificity, and means merely the logical property of being governed by a universal quantifier and not containing individual constants. The two principles 'Never kill people' and 'Never kill people except in self-defence or in cases of adultery or judicial execution' are both equally universal, but the first is more general (less specific) than the second. Critical principles and prima facie principles, then, are both universal prescriptions; but whereas the former can be, and for their purposes have to be, highly specific, the latter can be, and for *their* purposes have to be, relatively general. Just *how* general they should be will depend on the circumstances and temperaments of individuals. I have discussed this question more fully elsewhere (H 1972a:8).

2.6 Let us, after these preliminaries, return to our conflict-situation, in which two prima facie principles require two incompatible actions. This will be because one of the principles picks out certain features of the situation as relevant (e.g. that a promise has been made), and the other picks out certain others (e.g. that the failure to show my friend the colleges would bitterly disappoint him). The

problem is to determine which of these principles should
be applied to yield a prescription for this specific situation.
The method to be employed in critical thinking can only be
briefly sketched here, in anticipation of the full account I
shall be giving in Part II.

Notice first that in theory it is not necessary (though it
usually is in practice), in order to describe a situation fully,
or as fully as we need, to mention individuals. We can
describe it in universal terms, including in the description
the alternative actions that are open and their respective
consequences. We can, however, without omitting any
descriptive information, omit all individual references, so
that the description will apply equally to any precisely
similar situation involving precisely similar people, places,
etc. Individual references preceded by 'like', 'similar', and
equivalent expressions are exempted from this ban; they
can be treated as universal in the required sense (H
1955:30).

The thesis of universalizability requires that if we make
any moral judgement about this situation, we must be prepared to make it about any of the other precisely similar
situations. Note that these do not have to be *actual*
situations; they can be precisely similar logically possible
hypothetical situations (*FR* 6.4; 6.4). Therefore the battle-
cry referred to earlier, 'No two situations and no two
people are ever exactly like each other', is not relevant in
this part of moral thinking, and the thought that it is
relevant is due only to confusion with other parts. What
critical thinking has to do is to find a moral judgement
which the thinker is prepared to make about this conflict-
situation and is also prepared to make about all the other
similar situations. Since these will include situations in
which he occupies, respectively, the positions of all the
other parties in the actual situation, no judgement will be
acceptable to him which does not do the best, all in all, for
all the parties. Thus the logical apparatus of universal
prescriptivism, if we understand what we are saying when
we make moral judgements, will lead us in critical thinking

(without relying on any substantial moral intuitions) to make judgements which are the same as a careful act-utilitarian would make. We see here, and shall see in much greater detail in Part II, how the utilitarians and Kant get synthesized.

Much of the controversy about act-utilitarianism and rule-utilitarianism has been conducted in terms which ignore the difference between the critical and intuitive levels of moral thinking. Once the levels are distinguished, a form of utilitarianism becomes available which combines the merits of both varieties (H 1972a:13 ff.; 1976a). The conformity (for the most part) to received opinion which rule-utilitarianism is designed to provide is provided by the prima facie principles used at the intuitive level; but critical moral thinking, which selects these principles and adjudicates between them in cases of conflict, is act-utilitarian in that, in considering cases, actual or hypothetical, it can be completely specific, leaving out no feature of an act that could be alleged to be relevant. But since, although quite specific, it takes no cognizance of individual identities, it is also rule-utilitarian in that version of the rule-utilitarian doctrine which allows its rules to be of unlimited specificity, and which therefore is in effect not distinguishable from act-utilitarianism (*FR* 7.6; H 1972c:170; Lyons, 1965:ch.iii). The two kinds of utilitarianism, therefore, can coexist at their respective levels; the critical thinker considers cases in an act-utilitarian or specific rule-utilitarian way, and on the basis of these he selects, as I shall shortly be explaining, general prima facie principles for use, in a general rule-utilitarian way, at the intuitive level.

3

THE ARCHANGEL AND THE PROLE

3.1 We have next to ask, what the relation is between the two levels of moral thinking, and how we know when to think at one level, and when at the other. Let us be clear, first of all, that critical and intuitive moral thinking are not *rival* procedures, as much of the dispute between utilitarians and intuitionists seems to presuppose. They are elements in a common structure, each with its part to play. But how are they related?

Let us consider two extreme cases of people, or beings, one of whom would use *only* critical moral thinking and the other *only* intuitive. First, consider a being with superhuman powers of thought, superhuman knowledge and no human weaknesses. I am going to call him the archangel (H 1976a:124, cf. Godwin, 1793: II, 2). This 'ideal observer' or 'ideal prescriber' (*FR* 6.4; H 1972a:18; 1972c:168) resembles the 'clairvoyant' of *LM* 4.2 in his powers of prediction but adds to these the other superhuman qualities just mentioned. He will need to use only critical thinking. When presented with a novel situation, he will be able at once to scan all its properties, including the consequences of alternative actions, and frame a universal principle (perhaps a highly specific one) which he can accept for action in that situation, no matter what role he himself were to occupy in it. Lacking, among other human weaknesses, that of partiality to self, he will act on that principle, if it bids him act. The same will apply to other partialities (e.g. to our own friends and relations) which are hardly weaknesses, but which are, for reasons which I shall later explain, excluded from critical thinking, though they play a large part in intuitive thinking (H 1979b; 8.3). Such an archangel would not need intuitive thinking; everything would be done by reason in a moment of time. Nor, therefore, would he need the sound general principles, the good dispositions, the intuitions which guide the rest of us.

On the other hand, consider a person who has these human weaknesses to an extreme degree. Not only does he, like most of us, have to rely on intuitions and sound prima facie principles and good dispositions for most of the time; he is totally incapable of critical thinking (let alone safe or sound critical thinking) even when there is leisure for it. Such a person, if he is to have the prima facie principles he needs, will have to get them from other people by education or imitation. Let us call him the *prole* (after George Orwell in *1984*). Although the archangel and the prole are exaggerated versions of the top and bottom classes in Plato's Republic, it is far from my intention to divide up the human race into archangels and proles; we all share the characteristics of both to limited and varying degrees and at different times.

Our question then is, 'When ought we to think like archangels and when like proles?' Once we have posed the question in this way, the answer is obvious: it depends on how much each one of us, on some particular occasion or in general, resembles one or the other of these two characters. There is no philosophical answer to the question; it depends on what powers of thought and character each one of us, for the time being, thinks he possesses. We have to know ourselves in order to tell how much we can trust ourselves to play the archangel without ending up in the wrong Miltonic camp as *fallen* archangels.

One thing, however, is certain: that we cannot all of us, all the time, behave like proles (as the intuitionists would have us do) if there is to be a system of prima facie principles at all. For the selection of prima facie principles, and for the resolution of conflicts between them, critical thinking is necessary. If we do not think that men can do it, we shall have to invoke a Butlerian God to do it for us, and reveal the results through our consciences. But how then would we distinguish between the voice of God and the voices of our nursemaids (if we had them)?

3.2   I have, then, sidestepped the issue of when we should engage in these two kinds of thinking; it is not a philosophical question. The other question however is; for unless we can say how the two kinds of thinking are related to each other, we shall not have given a complete account of the structure of moral thinking.

Aristotle, in a famous metaphor, says that the relation of the intellect to the character (which is what we have been talking about in other words) has to be a paternal one: in so far as a man's motives and dispositions are rational, it is because they 'listen to reason as to a father' (1103ᵃ3). Because intuitive moral thinking cannot be self-supporting, whereas critical thinking can be and is, the latter is epistemologically prior. *If* we were archangels, we could by critical thinking alone decide what we ought to do on each occasion; on the other hand, if we were proles, we could not do this, at least beyond the possibility of question, by intuitive thinking.

Provided that we do not give it a 'subjectivist' or 'relativist' interpretation (12.1), there is no harm in saying that the right or best way for us to live or act either in general or on a particular occasion is what the archangel would pronounce to be so if he addressed himself to the question. This is not 'subjectivist' in any bad sense, and is certainly a highly rationalist thesis, because, as we shall see, archangels, at the end of their critical thinking, will all say the same thing (6.2, 12.3), on all questions on which moral argument is possible (*FR* 8.1 f.; 3.5); and so shall we, to the extent that we manage to think like archangels. Intuitive thinking has the function of yielding a working approximation to this for those of us who cannot think like archangels on a particular occasion. If we wish to ensure the greatest possible conformity to what an archangel would pronounce, we have to try to implant in ourselves and in others whom we influence a set of dispositions, motivations, intuitions, prima facie principles (call them what we will) which will have this effect. We are on the whole more likely to succeed in this way than by aiming to think like archangels on occasions when we have neither the time nor the capacity for it. The prima facie principles themselves, however, have to be selected by critical thinking; if not by our own critical thinking, by that of people whom we trust to be able to do it.

Let us suppose that we are thus criticizing a proposed prima facie principle. What, as legislating members of this kingdom of ends (Kant, 1785:75), do we actually think about? The principle is for use in our actual world. One thing, therefore, that we do *not* do is to call to mind the improbable or unusual cases that novelists, or philosophers with axes to grind, can dream up, and ask whether in *those* cases the outcome of inculcating the principle would be for the best. To take an analogous example from the prudential field: suppose that we are wondering whether to adopt the principle of always wearing our seat belts when driving. We have to balance the minor inconvenience of fastening our belts every time we drive against the serious harm we shall come to on those rare occasions, if any, on which we have collisions. Here the rarity of the occurrence is compensated for by the gravity of its consequences, and so we may well decide that it is right to adopt the principle. But then suppose somebody alleges, perhaps truly, that in *some* collisions the risk of injury or death is increased by wearing belts (for instance, when an unconscious driver would otherwise have been thrown clear of a vehicle which caught fire). There are people who fix their attention on such cases and use them as a reason for rejecting the rule to wear seat belts; and many people argue similarly in ethics, using the mere possibility or even mere conceivability of some unusual case, in which a principle would enjoin an obviously unacceptable action, as an argument for rejecting the principle. The method is unsound. Disregarding, for simplicity's sake, the difference in severity between injuries: if, say, in 95 per cent of all collisions the risk of injury is reduced by wearing belts, and in 5 per cent it is increased, it will be rational to wear them if we want to reduce our expectation of injury more than we want to avoid the inconvenience of wearing them.

To generalize: if we are criticizing prima facie principles, we have to look at the consequences of inculcating them in ourselves and others; and, in examining these consequences, we have to balance the size of the good and bad effects in cases which we consider against the probability or improbability of such cases occurring in our actual experience. It seems to be the case that popular morality has actually been caused to change without sufficient reason by failure to do this. It is very easy for a novelist (D. H. Lawrence for example) to depict with great verisimilitude, as if they were everyday occurrences, cases in which the acceptance by society of the traditional principle of, say, fidelity in marriage leads to unhappy results. The public is thus persuaded that the principle ought to be rejected. But in order for such a rejection to be rational, it would have to be the case, not merely that situations *can* occur or be conceived in which the results of the acceptance of the principle are not for the best, but that these situations are common enough to outweigh those others in which they are for the best. It is of course a matter for dispute what principle about fidelity in marriage would, on a more rational evaluation, be the one to adopt; but the evaluation has to be done. If it turned out that more suffering was caused by the breakdown of the marriage conventions than by their preservation, then an archangel, following our method (6.1), and giving equal weight to the interests of each in his impartial critical thinking, would favour their preservation.

A similar, or complementary, mistake is often made by opponents of utilitarianism when they produce unusual examples (such as the sheriff who knows—who can say how?—that the innocence of the man whom he hangs in the general interest will never be exposed, 9.7). More such examples will confront us in ch. 8. The purpose of them is to convince us that utilitarianism, when applied in these unusual situations, yields precepts which are at variance with our common intuitions. But this ought not to be surprising. Our common intuitions are sound ones, if they are, just because they yield acceptable precepts in common cases. For this reason, it is highly desirable that we should all have these intuitions and that our consciences should give us a bad time if we go against them. Therefore all well brought up people can be got to gang up against the utilitarian (if they can somehow be inhibited from any deep philosophical reflection) by citing some *un*common case, which is undoubtedly subsumable under a prima facie principle which we have all absorbed, and in which therefore we shall accept the utilitarian precept, which requires a breach of the principle, only with the greatest repugnance.

These anti-utilitarians sometimes overreach themselves. Professor Bernard Williams, in his elaboration of a well-known example (1973:98), thinks that he can score against the utilitarians by showing that in this far-fetched case they would have to prescribe the killing of one innocent man, the alternative being that he and nineteen others would die by another hand. We all have qualms about prescribing this—very naturally, because we have rightly been brought up to condemn the killing of innocent people, and also to condemn succumbing to blackmail threats of this sort, and good utilitarian reasons can be given to justify such an upbringing. But when we come to consider what actually ought to be done in this bizarre situation, even Williams seems at least to contemplate the possibility of its being right to shoot the innocent man to save the nineteen other innocent men (ib.:117). All he has shown is that we shall reach this conclusion with the greatest repugnance if we are 'decent' people; yet there is nothing to stop the utilitarian agreeing with this. But we shall have to return to these manoeuvres later (8.1 ff).

3.3   To sum up, then, the relation between the two kinds of thinking is this. Critical thinking aims to select the best set of prima facie principles for use in intuitive thinking. It can also be employed when principles from the set conflict *per accidens*. Such employment may lead to the improvement of the principles themselves, but it need not; a principle may be overridden without being altered (3.6). The best set is that whose acceptance yields actions, dispositions, etc. most nearly approximating to those which would be chosen if we were able to use critical thinking all the time. This answer can be given in terms of acceptance-utility, if one is a utilitarian; if one is not a utilitarian but a Kantian, one can say in effect the same thing by advocating the adoption of a set of maxims for general use whose acceptance yields actions, etc., most approximating to those which would be chosen if the categorical imperative were applied direct on each occasion by an archangel. Thus a clear-headed Kantian and a clear-headed utilitarian would find themselves in agreement, once they distinguished between the two kinds of thinking.

But besides the role of *selecting* prima facie principles, critical thinking has also the role of *resolving conflicts* between them. If the principles have been well chosen, conflicts will arise only in exceptional situations; but they will be agonizing in proportion as the principles are deeply held (as they should be). Though in general it is bad policy to question one's prima facie principles in situations of stress, because of the danger of 'cooking' already referred to, the conflicts we are speaking of force us to do this (hence the anguish). There can be different outcomes. In simpler cases we may 'feel sure' that some principle or some feature of a situation is *in that situation* more important than others (compare the backgammon parallel, 2.4). We shall then be able to sort the matter out intuitively, letting one principle override the other in this case, without recourse to critical thinking. This might well be best in the promise-breaking example with which we started. But though this intuitive sorting out may seem to offer a straw at which intuitionists can clutch, it is obvious that it will not be available in more serious conflicts.

At the other extreme, a conflict may force us to examine the prima facie principles themselves, and perhaps, instead of overriding one, qualify them from then on. People who have been through such crises often think differently thereafter about some fundamental moral questions—a sign that some critical thinking has been done, however inarticulate. This qualification of the principles will have brought with it a resolution of the conflict, because the principles as qualified are no longer inconsistent even *per accidens*. There is also a middle way: the person in the conflict-situation may come to be fairly sure that one or both of the principles ought to be qualified, but not be sure how, except that the qualification would allow such and such an accommodation in this particular case; he can then decide about the particular case, overriding one of the principles, and leave reflection on the principles themselves for another time when he is in a better position to do it rationally. Only when he has done it can he be sure that he was right.

Another version of this middle way is to say 'The principles, since they are in conflict, cannot be altogether relied on; I am compelled to depart from one or the other, and do not know which. So let me put the principles aside for the time being and examine carefully the particular case to see what critical thinking would say about it.' This is possible for critical thinking, in so far as humans can do it, and it is what the situational ethicists and crude act-utilitarians might recommend in all cases. It is, as we have seen, a dangerous procedure; but sometimes we may be driven to it. Anti-utilitarians make it their business to produce examples in which this is the only recourse, and then charge utilitarians with taking it (which is unavoidable) and with taking it light-heartedly (which is a slander, 8.1 ff.). The good utilitarian will reach such decisions, but reach them with great reluctance because of his ingrained good principles; and he may agonize, and will certainly reflect, about them till he has sorted out by critical thinking, not only what he ought to have done in the particular case, but what his prima facie principles ought to be.

It may be said that one cannot compartmentalize one's moral thinking in the way the two-level account seems to require (Williams, 1976:230). I can only reply by asking whether those who raise this objection have ever faced such situations. I do my own moral thinking in the way described in this book (not like an archangel, for I am not one, nor like a prole, but doing my best to employ critical and intuitive thinking as appropriate). In difficult situations one's intuitions, reinforced by the dispositions that go with them, pull one in different directions, and critical thinking, perhaps, in another. A person with any deep experience of such situations will have acquired some *methodological* prima facie principles which tell him when to launch into critical thinking and when not; they too would be justified by critical thinking in a cool hour. To say that it is impossible to keep intuitive and critical thinking going in the same thought-process is like saying that in a battle a commander cannot at the same time be thinking of the details of tactics, the overall aim of victory, and the principles (economy of force, concentration of force, offensive action, etc.) which he has learnt when learning his trade. Good generals do it. The good general is one who wins his battles, not one who has the best prima facie principles; but the best prima facie principles are those which, on the whole, win battles.

3.4 We have now to recur to a problem which was postponed at the end of ch. 1, and has been rendered more acute, but also easier of solution, by what we have said since. This is the problem of differentiating moral from other evaluative judgements. I said that the differentia I should be using was that of overridingness; and this notion must therefore now be explained. This will give me an occasion to say something more about the problem of weakness of will, which has been such a crux for moral philosophers, especially for those of a prescriptivist persuasion like myself (*FR* 5.1). It becomes much clearer when we see it as a particular case of the problem of conflicts between prescriptions, of which the moral conflicts dealt with in the last chapter were another different, though analogous, case. It became obvious, after the levels of moral thinking were distinguished, how moral conflicts are to be accounted for; and much the same treatment helps with some important kinds of weakness of will. Those who insist that there can be conflicts of duties are quite right as regards the intuitive level; for there can indeed be conflicts of duties which are irresoluble *at that level*, and they can cause all the anguish that anybody desires. What these thinkers do not see is that there is another level, the critical, which exists for the purpose of resolving these conflicts, and also of so ordering our choice of moral principles that they will arise as infrequently as is consistent with the other purposes of moral thinking.

Both the problem of weakness of will, and that of conflicts of duties, arise because the ordinary man is firmly convinced that he ought to do certain things; and he is convinced of this because his intuitions, embodied in prima facie principles, assure him that this is so. So it is very easy for a philosopher to set up cases which will convince the ordinary man that he ought to do both of two incompatible things, or that he knows he ought not to be doing something which he is doing. The first of these cases is the one we have been dealing with; the second is one kind of weakness of will.

3.5 We have to examine the second case in more detail. But first let us take up the question of the definition of 'moral'. The two properties of universalizability and prescriptivity did not suffice to define the class of moral judgements, since at least some other, and indeed in a strict sense all, evaluative judgements have these properties (*FR* 2.8, 8.2; 1.6). In order to distinguish moral judgements within the larger genus, a differentia is required. The name I shall use for this distinguishing property is 'overridingness'. Though it is important that moral judgements, in one sense of that ambiguous word, have this property or (as we shall see) a property closely related to it, it will not play a very large part in our argument. Nor will the word 'moral' itself.

There are two reasons for this. The first is that we do not need this property in order to construct our account of moral reasoning. The canons of moral argument are based on the other two properties of 'ought' and 'must', which they share with all evaluative words. This is possible because moral judgements, though they are not confined to situations where the interests of others are affected, have their predominant use in such situations. For cases where the interests of others are not affected, I make no claim to provide canons of moral reasoning. But for cases where they are, the two properties of universalizability and prescriptivity suffice to govern the reasoning, and no other properties were appealed to in my account in *FR*. The reason why this account cannot be extended to argument about, e.g., aesthetic questions is that arguments about them do not turn on other people's interests, but only on the sensory and affective qualities of the aesthetic object; the reason why it cannot be extended to moral questions not affecting others' interests is the same: argument based on these two properties cannot get a grip on such questions (*FR* 8.1).

A second reason for avoiding, if we can, bringing the word 'moral' into our account of moral reasoning is that it is so ambiguous. It has, not even a variety of well-defined uses, but a very vague spectrum of uses which shade into one another and are hard to distinguish. This is nothing unusual; Wittgenstein seems to have thought that words were typically like this (1953 secs. 65 ff.), and though he was exaggerating (dictionary-making is a feasible and useful activity), there are indeed many such words and 'moral' is one of them. 'Ought' and 'must' are less Protean; I feel safer with them, though they too have various uses. But I have regretfully decided that, although it is possible to base an account of moral reasoning on a certain distinguishable use of 'ought' and of 'must' (the universalizable prescriptive use), whose rules determine what we can and cannot say without self-contradiction when using the words, nothing so definite is possible with the word 'moral'.

However, we do need a concept which will delimit those uses of the universalizable prescriptive 'ought' and 'must' with which we, as moral philosophers, are concerned; and it seems to me that 'moral', in one of its uses, is the word, or a possible word, for that concept. So the best policy will be to admit that the word is ambiguous and even vague, and to define a use of it which will mark out those uses of 'ought' and 'must' in which we are primarily interested.

3.6 We might suggest as a first approximation that a use of 'ought' or 'must' is a moral use in this sense if the judgement containing it is (1) prescriptive; (2) universalizable; and (3) overriding. Before we come to the inadequacies in this definition let us try to make the third element more precise. I may say in passing that, if the attempt to define 'moral' in these terms, or in a more developed version of them, were successful, I should not mind *substituting* the expression 'overriding-prescriptive-universalizable' for the expression 'moral', in this sense, if it were not so cumbrous. Then I could happily make a present of the word 'moral' to those who wish to use it in other of its meanings.

But what is it for one prescription to override another? I gave a brief account of this notion in *FR* 9.3. The example I used was that of the conflict between the aesthetic principle that one ought not to juxtapose scarlet with magenta, and the moral principle that one ought not to hurt one's wife's feelings, in a case in which my wife has given me a magenta cushion to put on my scarlet sofa in my room in college. I said that I would allow the moral principle or judgement to override the aesthetic one; and this means at least that, although both are prescriptive, I would think that I ought to act, and accordingly would act, on the moral one and thus not act on the aesthetic one. This, I said, was quite different from *qualifying* the aesthetic one to admit of an exception in such a case; the aesthetic judgement remains quite unqualified and is prescriptive, but is simply over-ridden in this case. I do not, thereafter, hold the aesthetic principle in the form 'One ought not to juxtapose scarlet and magenta, except when it is necessary in order to avoid hurting one's wife's feelings'.

Note that if I were to treat the principle forbidding colour-clashes as overriding, and thus think that I ought to throw away the cushion at whatever cost to my wife's feelings, I should be, on a definition of 'moral' in terms of overridingness, elevating it into a moral principle; whereas many definitions of 'moral' in terms of the contents that principles called 'moral' can have would bar this. This shows that there are two senses of 'moral' involved, as I have already allowed; it does not show that mine is not a possible or useful sense, provided that it is distinguished from others.

To treat a principle as overriding, then, is to let it always override other principles when they conflict with it and, in the same way, let it override all other prescriptions, including non-universalizable ones (e.g. plain desires). Note that I say 'treat as'. It might be thought a defect in my account that I do not try to say what it is for a principle to *be* overriding, but only what it is to *treat* a principle as overriding. But this is a necessary feature of the definitions of many such terms. Suppose, for example, that we were to define in part the expression 'sign of conjunction' by saying that a person is treating a word (for example 'and') as a sign of conjunction if, whenever this word occurs between two sentences, he thinks it inconsistent to affirm the whole proposition expressed by the two sentences with 'and' between them, but deny a proposition expressed by one of the two sentences by itself. It would not be a valid objection to this definition to say that it only tells us what it is to *treat* 'and' as a sign of conjunction, and not what it is for it to *be* a sign of conjunction. If it is used in that way, it is, as so used, a sign of conjunction. And similarly, if someone treats a principle as overriding all others, but does not let any other override it, then the words he uses in expressing the principle are so used that they express for him an overriding principle.[1] This statement of the position does not involve us in the subjectivist view that one can make moral judgements true simply by adopting them (12.1). Whether he *ought* to be treating this principle as an overriding one is another question; but it is clear that he *is*; what he means when he utters the principle is something overriding. And if it were possible to define 'moral' in terms of overridingness, we could go on to say that, if the definition were satisfied by somebody's use of an expression, what he meant to express by it was a moral principle.

But, though this difficulty is not a real one, there are others which are. The account I have just sketched would make it impossible for a moral principle to be overridden by another moral principle, or by any other prescription. But both of these cases occur. There are both moral conflicts, which are resolved by allowing one moral principle to override another, and cases where, to use a somewhat revolting expression which I once heard a colleague use, we 'take a moral holiday'. Some cases of weakness of will are examples of this; and so also are such cases as that described by Austin in a famous passage (1956:24n.), where I deliberately, and not through weakness, when dining at High Table, help myself to two portions though there are only enough for one apiece. Our account so far is too simple to deal with these cases. But its inadequacies can be remedied by invoking our two-level structure of moral thinking. This will enable us to adjust our account of the word 'moral', and of the moral words, to their actual human uses (3.8).

3.7 Returning, then, to the problem of weakness of

---

[1] It will make no difference to the argument whether we say that 'ought', as used in a principle, means the same whether or not the principle is treated as overriding, but that the person accepting the principle may, without change of meaning, treat it as overriding or as not overriding; or whether we say that if he treats it as overriding he is using 'ought' in a different way. I have assumed that the latter is the case.

will, let us see what use can be made of the concept of overridingness, which must not be confused with that of prescriptivity. In *LM* 11.2, in a very preliminary look at the problem of weakness of will, I did indeed say that some of the cases of this were cases in which the moral judgement in question lacked prescriptivity. These cases certainly occur. Sometimes, when someone says 'I ought, but I am not going to', his moral judgement is of the 'So what?' variety (4.2 *s.f.*). But it would be unsubtle to suppose, and I did not even then suppose, that all cases of weakness of will were of this sort.

I mentioned, in fact, even at that early stage, two sorts of non-prescriptive moral judgements that might be involved (and the fact that there can be non-prescriptive moral judgements (*FR* 2.8) is another sign of the inadequacy of our first definition of 'moral'). The first was the 'inverted commas' moral judgement, implying merely that a certain act is required in order to conform to the moral standards current in society. The second was the moral judgement incorporated in our moral feelings. This notion was not very fully explained; but its connexion with what I said in the preceding chapter about intuitive moral thinking will be obvious. There are two elements in this judgement which need to be distinguished: the judgement *that we have* the feeling, and the judgement which is the *expression* of the feeling. If we have been well brought up in the way that I have described, we shall both have a feeling of moral repugnance against lying, for example, and know that we have this feeling. These two factors are often jumbled up under the term 'moral intuition'.

In *FR* 5.9 I gave a list of possible types of weakness of will, and explicitly admitted that the list might not be exhaustive. I will not now repeat it. But two of the important items on it were, first, the case in which a man cannot resist the temptation to do what he thinks he ought not to do; secondly, the case in which he departs from what I called 'the rigour of pure prescriptive universality' such as would characterize 'a holy or angelic moral language'. I have nothing further to say here about the first of these cases; but what I have been saying in this chapter will be recognized as an expansion of the second (*FR* 5.5; 1.6).

Because we are human beings and not angels we have adopted or inherited what I called the intuitive level of moral thinking with its prima facie principles, backed up by powerful moral feelings, and attached to rather general characteristics of actions and situations. In our predicament, this is not vicious; we need this device, as I have amply explained. The prima facie principles are general in two connected senses; they are rather simple and unspecific, and they admit of exceptions, in the sense that it is possible to go on holding them while allowing that in particular cases one may break them. This possibility was not mentioned in *LM* 3.6, and should have been. In other words, they are overridable. Again, though in the sense in which I have been using the term they are universal (they contain no individual constants and start with a universal quantifier), in another sense they are not universal (they are not universally binding; one may make exceptions to them). It would be impossible for prima facie principles to fulfil their practical function unless they had these features, which may seem from the theoretical point of view to be faults. In order to be of use in moral education and character-formation, they have to be to a certain degree simple and general; but if they are, then we shall encounter cases (the world being so various) in which to obey them (even if two of them did not conflict) would run counter to the prescriptions of an angelic moral thinking.

This fully explains why prima facie principles have to be overridable—why, that is to say, it is possible to go on holding them even when one does not obey them in a particular case. I repeat that this overridability does not mean that they are not prescriptive; *if* applied, they would require a certain action, but we just do not apply them in a certain case. Moreover, although I have so far considered cases in which one such prima facie moral principle is overridden in favour of another prima facie moral principle, it is likely that a principle which has this feature of overridability will also be open to being overridden by other, non-moral, prescriptions, as when we take 'moral holidays'. That is why the whole problem becomes clearer when one sees the kind of conflict which we call weakness of will as just one example of conflicts between prescriptions. What happens when I decide that I ought to break a promise in order not to disappoint my Australian friend of his tour of Oxford has quite close affinities with what happens when I decide to break one in order not to disappoint my own appetites.

3.8 In the light of this admission that some moral principles can be overridden without ceasing to be held as moral principles, the reader will reasonably expect me to qualify the suggestion about the meaning of 'moral' made earlier (3.6). We cannot simply say that someone is treating a universal prescriptive principle as a moral principle if and only if he does not let it be overridden by any other principles; for we have seen that prima facie moral principles can be overridden, not only by other moral principles, but by non-moral prescriptions, without ceasing to be held as moral principles.

But the separation of levels, which is the cause of this difficulty, also provides its solution. If we think of the whole structure of moral thinking with its two levels, 'moral' can be defined, in the sense in which we are using it (as I said, not the only sense), as follows. The class of a man's moral principles consists of two sub-classes: (1) those universal prescriptive principles which he does not allow to be overridden; these will all be what I called 'critical moral principles' (2.5), and are therefore capable of being made so specific and so adapted to particular cases that they do not need to be overridden; (2) those prima facie principles which, although they can be overridden, are selected in the way above described, by critical thinking, in the course of which use is made of moral principles of the first sub-class. So, if we want to know whether someone is treating a principle as a moral principle, we have first to ask whether he would ever, in any circumstances, let it be overridden. If he says that he would not, then he is treating it as a moral principle. But even if he says that there are some circumstances in which he would let it be overridden, it might be a moral principle of the second sub-class. We have to ask him, therefore, in that case, how he would justify his selection of this as one of his principles; and if he says that it would be on the basis of critical thinking, in that this was a principle whose general acceptance would lead to people's actions and dispositions approximating to the greatest extent to the deliverances of a perfectly conducted critical thinking (i.e. to the moral principles of the first sort that such critical thinking would arrive at), then this principle too will count as a moral principle, but of the second sub-class.

It may be objected to this definition that it makes it impossible for proles and intuitionist philosophers, who know of only the intuitive level of moral thinking, to have any moral principles; for they cannot justify their 'moral principles' by appeal to critical thinking. It would be more correct to say that such people have no way of distinguishing their moral from their other principles. Can *we*, who know about the two levels, make the distinction on their behalf? We can, by saying that a principle is for them a moral principle if, either (1) it is treated by them as overriding (and such people may well so treat even prima facie principles, though it will put them in familiar straits if ever the principles conflict); or (2) *if* they were constrained (perhaps by such a conflict-situation) to do some critical thinking, however primitive, they would justify the principle by appeal to some higher principle treated as overriding. But it may be best simply to say that there is a difficulty, in the case of such people, in distinguishing their moral principles in the sense we are after; this is a sign of a gap in their thinking rather than ours.

It will be noticed that such a more complex definition of 'moral' brings us somewhat nearer to the point of view of some (e.g. Warnock, 1967:52 ff.) who think of themselves as my opponents. They wish to insist that no purely formal definition of 'moral' can be given; it has to be defined either in terms of possible contents of moral principles, or in terms of possible reasons for or justifications of them. I am not for a moment abandoning my formalist position; but in spite of it (i.e. without making any other than formal moves) I have allowed that a principle is being treated as moral (of the second sub-class) if the justification for it, in the mind of the person who holds it, is of a certain sort. And when we have worked out the implications of the method of critical thinking, as we shall be doing in Part II, we shall see that the justifications which it provides will be of the same general sort as these writers are after. For well conducted critical thought will justify the selection of prima facie principles on the ground that the general acceptance of them will lead to actions which do as much good, and as little harm, as possible.

This is another illustration, which can stand alongside that provided in an earlier article of mine (H 1972b:92), of how purely formal moves can lead, by a more indirect route, to conclusions to which it is tempting to take a too hasty naturalistic short cut by writing some substance into the definition of 'moral' or of the moral words. How the more indirect route arrives at this destination will become clear in Part II.

3.9 This is perhaps the most convenient point at which to add a note on another concept which will play little part in my argument but which it is important to understand: that of *relevance*. I shall do no more than summarize what I have written elsewhere about it (H 1978b:73). I did indeed use this concept in *FR* 2.3, in one alternative definition of descriptive meaning, and thus of universalizability, which is a concept very central to my argument. I said 'we cannot without inconsistency apply a descriptive term to one thing, and refuse to apply it to another similar thing (either exactly similar or similar in the relevant respects)'. But our present argument has no need of a definition of universalizability in terms of relevant similarity. In this book we shall be appealing, in our account of critical thinking, only to exact similarity, and shall not need, therefore, to say, before the argument begins, what is and what is not relevantly similar. The argument itself will provide criteria of relevance *pari passu* with the selection of principles, both critical and prima facie, as we shall see. In critical thinking the principles used can be as specific as required, and therefore we can use hypothetical cases exactly similar in their universal properties, and differing only in the roles played by individuals. It is only when we come to intuitive thinking, guided by relatively general prima facie principles, that we need to be able to pick out the morally relevant features of situations, so as to leave out of consideration all the other features. But this is done for us by the prima facie principles themselves, which critical thinking is equipped to select.

In general, to treat a feature of a situation as morally relevant is to apply to that situation a moral principle which mentions the feature. It is a mistake to suppose that we could *first* pick out the morally relevant features of a situation and only *then* start asking what moral principles to apply to the situation. It is the principles which determine what is relevant. There are, it is true, certain formal restrictions on what features of situations can figure in moral principles: individual references are excluded by the requirement of universality, and the making of demands to do the impossible by the requirement of prescriptivity (*FR* 4.3). But substantial restrictions on relevance have all to be justified by appeal to substantial moral principles; it is a method of selecting *these* that we need.

Philosophers who have not understood this have sometimes sought to establish substantial criteria of relevance as a preliminary to selecting moral principles; but this is to get things the wrong way round. To treat the fact that an action was one of clasping the hands three times in an hour as irrelevant to an assessment of its goodness (Foot, 1958a:92) is to reject principles of the type 'Good actions are, among others, those consisting in clasping, etc.' (H 1978b:74). We need reasons for rejecting such principles, and critical thinking is able to provide them. It is also able to provide reasons for selecting principles which forbid us to discriminate between people purely on grounds of skin colour; and that is why we are able to treat skin colour as irrelevant to moral judgement (except in cases where it *is* relevant, as where I have a duty to take a faithful photograph of a man's face and must get the exposure right).

Another mistake often made is to think that because individual constants are formally excluded from moral principles, so are 'rigged definite descriptions' (Rawls, 1971:131). No secure definition of 'rigged' can be given; appeals to intuition will not help. The way to exclude such devices (e.g. treating the fact that I am the only man with eleven toes as morally relevant) is not by any formal restriction, which would drive out the good principles with the bad (H 1962:353), but by asking the man who advocates such a principle whether he accepts it for hypothetical cases where he lacks the extra toe (*FR* 6.8). Critical thinking, as will be explained later (6.4), has no difficulty with such manoeuvres.

Another too common mistake, that of supposing that because individual constants are excluded from moral principles, so likewise are bound individual variables, is dealt with later (8.5; cf. H 1978b:76).

4

DESCRIPTIVISM AND
THE ERROR THEORY

4.1 Nothing is so difficult in philosophical writing as to get people to be sympathetic enough to what one is saying to understand what it is. Perhaps nobody will ever understand a philosophical book of any depth without, initially, believing it, or at least suspending his disbelief. Otherwise he will never grasp what the writer is trying to convey. And that is what I am going to ask the reader to do, in order that we may examine the consequences for ethical theory of the separation of levels of moral thinking, suggested in ch. 2. The method I am going to follow is hypothetico-deductive, and was sketched in 1.3. I am going to put forward the hypothesis that the meanings of the moral words, and their logic, are as I have stated: that moral judgements are universal or universalizable prescriptions which are either overriding or related to overriding principles in the way suggested in 3.8. I am going to add to it the hypothesis that in moral thinking we operate at the two levels we have distinguished, the intuitive and the critical. And then I am going to test these hypotheses jointly by asking what is likely to happen once people start to ask *philosophical* questions about moral thinking. I hope to show that what is likely to happen, on those hypotheses, is what actually has happened. The mistaken theories which have arisen in moral philosophy are readily explicable, with hindsight, once we have understood the true situation. If so, the hypothesis that this is indeed the true situation will have stood up to at least some of the facts.

Let us imagine a society that has as yet done no moral philosophy. It has done plenty of moral thinking, mostly intuitive, but sometimes critical—though inarticulately, so as never to distinguish clearly between the two. Further, it has not inquired into the meanings of its moral words or the nature or logical properties of its moral concepts. And then let us suppose that someone does start such an inquiry. What sort of theory is he likely to come up with? The facts about moral thinking which will most obviously confront him are facts about intuitive moral thinking. He will observe that people do react in consistent ways, in their verbal and other behaviour, to certain types of action in certain types of situation. For example, they react with admiration and approval to acts of courage in the face of danger, and with reprobation and indignation to acts of leaving other people in the lurch when one has promised not to, or to acts of gratuitous cruelty.

I am not intending in what follows to claim historical accuracy, especially in regard to the chronological order in which philosophical theories arise, which is bound to be to some extent fortuitous. All I am claiming is that, if the situation were as I have described it, these theories would have in turn arisen; they are the easiest mistakes to make, if moral thinking functions as I have said it does.

If people in such a society start to ask what their moral terms mean, a resemblance will inevitably strike them between our verbal behaviour in relation to the moral concepts and in relation to other concepts of an apparently more straightforward kind. If we take almost any descriptive word, such as, for example, 'red' or 'rectangular', and observe people using it, we find that when they are confronted with objects of certain kinds, they say, if asked, that they are red (or rectangular), and when they are confronted with objects of other kinds, they say that they are not. If they fail to react in these ways, they are made to realize, particularly if they are children, that they are somehow at fault. It is very natural to assume that, when one learns the meaning of one of these words, what one learns is to react in these ways to objects of these kinds. We can detect a misuse of a descriptive word by observing that the word is used of an object of a certain kind, when the descriptive rule which determines its meaning excludes its use of objects of that kind (*FR* 2.1—our incipient philosophers are not likely to have yet thought of the complications which I warned against in that section, so we can ignore them).

It is likely that the view will become current that what seems to be true of words like 'red' and 'rectangular' is true of all words. As I have tried to show in that section and elsewhere (H 1963b), this is a mistake—the mistake which was called by Austin (1961:234; 1962:3) 'the descriptive fallacy', and for which we may conveniently use the name 'descriptivism'. Our philosophers will very naturally fall into this error, and will therefore think that to know the meaning of a *moral* word is to know to what we may or may not apply it.[1] They will thus, in their moral philosophy, look for properties of actions, people, etc., to which the moral words are tied in this way by the rules for their use, so that to misuse them is to apply them to objects which do not have the required properties.

The question will then be, what these properties are. We have imagined that in this society, as in our own, people do most of their moral thinking at the intuitive level, and that their intuitive reactions are fairly constant throughout the society. What more natural, then, than to go on to assume that actions, people, etc., do have certain properties which, according to the rules for the use of the moral words, entitle one to apply the various moral words to them? So, for example, it will be natural to suppose that there are properties which, when an action has them, entitle us to

---

[1] Mr. David Wiggins, in a difficult lecture (1976), in which he says many true things and some false, vitiates his entire argument by resting it on a similar question-begging assumption, that meanings can all be explained in terms of assertion conditions (ib. 352). This can be said of prescriptions only if one assumes that they are like pure descriptive statements. How would we say under what conditions 'Shut the door' may be asserted? He also (ib. 349n.) neglects the familiar point that in the ordinary commendatory sense of 'good' it is self-contradictory to say 'It is a good one, but that is no reason for preferring it', but that in the ordinary sense of 'yellow' it is never self-contradictory to say 'It is a yellow one, but that is no reason for preferring it'.

call the action wrong. And, since people are fairly consistent in what actions they call wrong, it ought to be easy
to say what these properties are. At any rate, it would seem
that they must include the property of being an act of
promise-breaking, or of being an act of gratuitous cruelty.

So we can see that the prevalence of intuitive thinking,
coupled with the natural temptation to suppose that all
words get their meaning in the same descriptive way, will
lead to the view that the moral words too are descriptive
words, and that an exhaustive account of their meaning can
be given by saying what things we may or may not apply
them to. No doubt attempts will be made to systematize. It
looks inelegant to say that 'wrong' means a disjunction of a
rag-bag of unrelated properties of actions: so it will be
attractive to suggest that there is some more general, but
still empirically observable, property which all wrong acts
have, and which entitles us to call them all wrong. That the
particular kinds of act are wrong can be shown, it will be
claimed, by showing that the more down-to-earth properties which they have entitle us to subsume them under
this more general property. But what the more general
property is, is likely to remain mysterious.

4.2   Is it an error to suppose what we have said they
would naturally suppose? To answer this question we have
to become rather more sophisticated. In one way it is not an
error; there is truth in it. According to the conventions of
the society, one *is* entitled to call acts of these sorts wrong,
and to deny the name to other sorts. Someone who had
thoroughly absorbed the conventions would not misuse
the word, in the sense of applying it to acts which he is not
entitled to apply it to. Thus this form of descriptivism,
which at the present stage has picked out certain non-moral
properties of acts as those which entitle us to call them
wrong, has, *up to a point*, given a true account of the
meaning of the word. This is the form of descriptivism
known as 'naturalism'.

Naturalism has a great deal to be said for it, especially as
an account of the intuitive level of moral thinking and of

the moral concepts as used at that level. Let us list some of its merits. First of all, a moral philosopher who wanted to give an account of moral reasoning, and took to naturalism with this aim in view, would, in one way, be on the right lines; for he would have had the insight that the way to discover the canons of moral reasoning is to study the meanings of the moral words. But he would be taking too short a cut. It is not possible to treat the following as the single canon of moral reasoning: find out what sorts of things the moral predicates can properly be applied to according to the conventions of our language, and apply them only to those things. For this would be to treat the conventions as merely linguistic conventions, and as binding, therefore, on anybody who wishes to speak the language correctly. The mistake of confusing moral with linguistic conventions is analogous to the mistake of confusing moral with linguistic intuitions (1.3). Both have the effect of tying our moral reasoning to the received opinions of our society. It is an important feature of moral language, neglected by naturalists, that we can go on using the moral words with their same meanings to express moral opinions at variance with the received ones, as moral reformers do. This would be impossible if the moral words were tied by virtue of their very meanings to fixed properties of actions, etc.

Suppose that such a moral reformer is arguing with a supporter of received moral opinions (for example, perhaps he is saying that there is nothing wrong with sex outside marriage). We must not fail to notice that the two disputants have to be using the word 'wrong' with the same meaning if they are to be in real dispute. If they meant different things by it, they could both be right in what they said, in their own senses of 'wrong'; extra-marital sex could be wrong in one sense but not in the other (*LM* 3.5 *s.f.*). 'No substantial disagreement without verbal agreement' is a useful slogan by which to remember this important point, which is fatal to naturalism and to most other kinds of descriptivism.

The meanings of the moral words cannot tie them to fixed properties of actions, etc., if they are not to tie us, their users, to the moral views fixed by received opinion. There is therefore a danger in applying to moral philosophy the dictum of Wittgenstein (1953: sec. 242, applauded by Wiggins, 1976:359) that 'if language is to be a means of communication there must be agreement not only in definitions but, queer as this may sound, agreement in judgements also'. Descriptivists, because of their preconceptions, often find it hard to see the point that you and I can be using the word 'wrong' in the same sense but disagree fundamentally on what properties of actions make them wrong. This is possible because 'wrong', unlike descriptive words, does not have its meaning fixed for it by descriptive criteria. Otherwise it could not be used to voice these disagreements. It is a mistake to suppose that all words have to have commonly accepted descriptive criteria of application before they can be used for communication. Try this out with the word 'it' or the command 'Don't do it.' Their meaning is known prior to any inkling of *what*, or even what *kind* of thing, may be referred to or prohibited by means of these locutions on some future occasion.

However, the naturalists are not wholly mistaken even here. For the moral conventions, which tell us what we can and cannot call wrong, are *very like* linguistic conventions. That was my reason for taking over from Stevenson the term 'descriptive meaning', which has got me into a certain amount of trouble through being misinterpreted (*LM* 7.3; *FR* 2.1 ff.). The current standards or criteria for applying the moral words are very like linguistic conventions, except that to observe them is to adopt substantial moral opinions, which adopting a merely linguistic convention would not be. Even the moral reformer who is recommending a new moral convention is a bit like somebody who is recommending a new linguistic convention; to suggest that we should no longer call extra-marital sex wrong is *in some ways* like suggesting that we should no longer call whales fish.

There is, however, another reason why even somebody who has confined his moral thinking to the intuitive level would reject naturalism, once he had become philosophically sophisticated. This is that moral words have, even at that level, a commendatory or condemnatory or in general prescriptive force which ordinary descriptive words lack (*LM* 5.4). The person who thinks that the fact that an act would be wrong is no reason at all for not doing it shows thereby that he has not fully grasped the meaning of the word. He may have grasped its descriptive meaning, so that he is able to apply it infallibly to the right actions, according to the current moral conventions; but there is another part of its meaning, the prescriptive or evaluative, which he has not grasped. Descriptivism of any sort, if absorbed and practised by any section of society, will lead to the adoption by them of a 'So what?' morality; they will be able to say 'Yes, I know it would be wrong: so what?' (H 1971c:113).

4.3   There are, then, good reasons for rejecting naturalism as an account of our moral language even as used at the intuitive level. But I have said enough to show how tempting a view naturalism is for one who has never done much critical thinking, and has not looked very carefully at the little he has done. Naturalism draws attention to the important truths that the way to understand moral reasoning is to understand the meanings of the moral words, and that these meanings do include a descriptive element. Our incipient moral philosopher, if he rejects naturalism for the reasons I have just given, is likely to look for a way of retaining these insights; and if, as is to be expected, he remains a descriptivist, the next theory he is likely to try is some form of intuitionism. We have already glanced at this kind of theory (1.3); but more must now be said.

There are in fact, in the situation we have described, not one but two temptations to 'objectivize' the moral properties or, as I should prefer to put it, 'descriptivize' the moral words. The first temptation lay in the fact that there really are objective properties of actions (e.g. the property of being an act of killing someone just for one's own financial gain) which entitle us to call them wrong, according to the current conventions. The second temptation lies not in these objective properties of acts, but in their subjective properties (their tendencies to evoke certain reactions in us) which, though subjective, are consistently enough manifested to tempt us to call them objective. We nearly all recoil in horror when we hear that somebody has killed somebody else for financial gain. It is very easy to take these feelings of 'outrage or shock', as Sir Stuart Hampshire (1972) calls them, for perceptions of objective properties in the action.

If all our thinking were done at the intuitive level, we might never feel the need to dispute the intuitionist account of the meanings of the moral words and of moral epistemology. The 'So what?' objection would remain which applies to all forms of descriptivism; but in this case it might not be felt as damaging. For if people are outraged or shocked by an act, they will tend to avoid doing such acts themselves; so it is quite easy to represent the subjective feeling as, at one and the same time, both a perception of a quality in the action, and a tendency in the percipient to behaviour of a certain kind.

We sometimes find philosophers maintaining that the evaluative–descriptive distinction breaks down in such cases. To view an act as cruel, for example, is, they say, at one and the same time to describe it and to take up an adverse moral attitude to it. Sometimes this is put in a more 'ontological' way by saying that some properties of actions are *in themselves* motivative. This last expression would be quite acceptable if all that it meant were that there are some properties of actions which do, as a matter of fact, repel (or attract) nearly all of us. But more is meant than that. It is being suggested that this kind of action is somehow *inherently* motivative; if it did not motivate us in this way, or otherwise touch our feelings, it would not be *that* kind of action (not, for example, cruel). So there are properties which are in themselves evil, and moral words which are inseparably both descriptive and prescriptive. If we look at our ordinary intuitive moral thinking, in which no questions are asked about whether we *have* to, or *ought* to, react in the way that we do to, e.g., cruelty, it is easy to see the plausibility of such a view.

It is, however, mistaken, as anybody will recognize who has done some critical thinking and seen it for what it was. As in the case of naturalism, we can expose its weakness if we examine cases where people are in dispute about the morality of some action. Here critical thinking is likely to be required. Suppose, for example, that one man sees an act as cruel, and another does not, though they know just what is being done and know how much the victim is suffering. A rather extreme practical joke, say, has been perpetrated at Sandhurst or West Point; its victim is having to suffer at the same time extreme discomfort and general derision, and his feelings are badly hurt. Some of the spectators are shocked by what has been done. Others just find it hilarious. Although they realize how upset the victim is, they think that he would not be if he had a more robust sense of humour; and this gives them a feeling of superiority over him which adds to their enjoyment.

We shall be returning much later on to situations in which moral thought requires us to put ourselves in the place of somebody who is suffering (5.3). In our example, the second lot of people are not doing this, and to that extent their moral thinking is at fault. But in order to see why it is at fault we have to look deeper into the matter than the philosophers I am now criticizing. That what they say is wrong can be seen quite easily by noticing that the statement that the victim is suffering, and the statement that the act which made him suffer was wrong, are two distinct statements. One can believe one but not the other. It may be that the *word* 'cruel' (an example of what we called a secondarily evaluative word, 1.5) carries with it an evaluative meaning which it does not readily give up (though it can: we can say 'Yes, cruel certainly, but that's just what made it such fun'). But the fact that *if* we use this word we are almost committed to the evaluation does not entail that we have got to use the word at all in order to describe the action fully. We can say 'He was caused to suffer deeply', but add, 'All the same, there was nothing wrong in it; it happens all the time in good military academies, and that's the way to produce officers with moral fibre'. I have discussed this question many times with proponents of this view (the view that the evaluative and descriptive meanings of some terms are inseparable, and that therefore the description brings with it an inescapable evaluation); and without exception, the examples they have produced have succumbed to this kind of treatment. I am sure that the same will be true of any examples that may be produced in the future (as, no doubt, many will be, for it is an attractive view).

Perhaps it is worth while quoting just one more, from a paper by Professor Lawrence Kohlberg (1970:61). It neatly shows how weak is a famous argument of Mrs. Foot's (1958b:507), in which she tried to show that, because 'rude' is an evaluative word, and yet has quite clear descriptive conditions for its use, we can derive the evaluation from the descriptive statement that the conditions are satisfied. Kohlberg says:

Let me cite an example from my observation of an enlightened and effective fourth-grade teacher. The teacher was in the back of the room working with a project group, the rest of the class engaged with their workbooks. In the front row, a boy said something to his neighbor, who retaliated by quietly spitting in his face. The first boy equally quietly slugged the other without leaving his seat, by which time the teacher noted the disturbance. She said calmly, 'Stop that and get back to your workbooks.' The boy who had done the slugging said, 'Teacher, I hit him because he spit in my face.' The teacher replied, 'That wasn't polite; it was rude. Now get back to work, you're supposed to be doing your workbooks.' As they went back to work, the boy who had done the spitting said to his opponent with a grin, 'I will grant you that; it was rude.'

I hope that this case will convince Mrs. Foot that it is

possible to accept that an act satisfied the descriptive conditions for being called 'rude' without being committed to evaluating it adversely, even though 'rude' is normally an adjective of adverse evaluation.

4.4 The intuitionists, however, are not so sophisticated as the proponents of the view we have just been discussing. Their view is not so much that there are words which are simultaneously and inseparably evaluative and descriptive, or properties which are inherently motivative. They fail, rather, to pay attention to the distinction at all. For them, moral properties are just like any other properties, and moral words just like any other predicates.

It may be asked at this point why I keep going on about intuitionism. Is it not a long-exploded doctrine which nobody now supports? This, regrettably, is not the case. True, few philosophers are prepared to own to the *name* 'intuitionist'; but the great majority use arguments which would have no cogency unless intuitionist assumptions were made. Professor Rawls (1971) is a good example. Having (like Professor Urmson, 1975) diverted the name 'intuitionism' into a new meaning, in which it means something like 'pluralism', and signifies the belief that there are moral principles which are logically independent of one another (a belief which could be held by many besides intuitionists, and which intuitionists who are monists and believe in a single all-sufficient moral principle could deny), Rawls then proceeds, although disclaiming the name, to use appeals to intuition at all the crucial points in his arguments, which he would not do unless he believed that this was a valid method of reasoning (H 1973a). It therefore needs to be shown that it is not valid, as I have tried to do in 1.3. All I wish to show at this point is how natural a mistake intuitionism is, if moral thinking is structured in the way I have suggested. Intuitions are certainly used in our moral thinking, and this is highly desirable; how easy it is, therefore, to attribute to intuitions an epistemological status which they do not have!

Undoubtedly the reaction of many intuitionists (including crypto-intuitionists) to this book will be to accept the division of moral thinking into two levels, but claim that they are observing it. Do they not reflect, and criticize their own and others' moral principles? The question however is whether the reflection and the criticism has any probative, or even, to anybody who understands the position, any persuasive power, if the screws which hold the argument together are substantial moral intuitions, which are themselves not criticized. If one goes through such writings and discounts all the arguments which rest on undefended moral intuitions of substance, nothing is left but the mere moral opinions of the authors with which they hope we will agree.

4.5 Naturalism and intuitionism exhaust the varieties of descriptivism, if they are taken in sufficiently comprehensive senses. For example, we have to follow Moore (1903:39) in treating what he called 'Metaphysical Ethics' as committing essentially the same error as naturalistic ethics. There remains, however, a sub-species of naturalism which requires a special mention because of its affinities with intuitionism. This is what is sometimes called 'old-fashioned subjectivism'. It could rightly be said of this, unlike intuitionism, that hardly anybody now holds it. Indeed, perhaps hardly anybody ever did, though it has been attributed to Hume, and there are traces of it in Stevenson, perhaps due to the influence on him of Westermarck, who has also been said to have held the view, though this may be unfair (Stroup, 1981). This is the view that moral judgements are equivalent in meaning to *reports* that somebody (normally the speaker) is in a certain psychological state (for example of disapproval of the act that is being judged). The objection of Sidgwick (1907:26) and Moore (1912:91) to this view is well known and conclusive; and indeed it was Stevenson's attempt to circumvent Moore's arguments which led him to espouse his variety of emotivism (1942). This latter is not equivalent to old-fashioned subjectivism. It is a non-descriptivist view, and it is one of the commonest mistakes made by inexpert moral philosophers to confuse the two sorts of theory (H 1976b:191; 12.1). The objection is that, if old-fashioned subjectivism were true, two people who had different moral opinions about the same act (e.g. that it was, and that it was not, wrong) would not really be disagreeing with each other; each would be stating that *he* had a certain attitude or feeling (of approval and disapproval respectively), and these statements would be mutually consistent. So the effect of old-fashioned subjectivism is to make impossible the moral disagreements which we all know exist.

However, it is interesting to notice that this view, which is generally recognized to be absurd, has marked affinities with intuitionism, which retains fairly wide support. The difference between the two views is that the subjectivist rightly recognizes, what the intuitionist fails to see, namely the essentially subjective character of the data to which they say we should appeal to support our moral judgements. The subjectivist allows that these are mere feelings or attitudes of our own. The intuitionist, though he has in fact nothing to appeal to but the feelings, supposes that these represent objective properties in the actions he is judging. Thus old-fashioned subjectivism, for all its absurdity, is a superior view to intuitionism, because more self-aware.

One final remark must be made about the two main varieties of descriptivism. It may be asked, what is the essential difference between them. The clearest way of stating the difference appeals to the distinction between analytic and synthetic statements. According to naturalism, it is analytically true that if actions have certain non-moral descriptive properties, they have, in consequence, certain moral properties. According to intuitionism, this is not so; the proposition that if the actions have the descriptive properties they have the moral properties, though true, is synthetic, and non-empirical. It has to be known to be true by the special faculty of moral intuition, by which we are able to discern the moral properties of actions. Philosophers who follow Professor Quine (1951) in denying the viability of the analytic–synthetic distinction will not be able to distinguish naturalism from intuitionism in this way, nor perhaps in any way. But since both positions are mistaken, this need not trouble us, especially if we are not Quineans.

4.6 I have been maintaining that descriptivism is an error, albeit one into which, in our circumstances, it is very easy to fall, and one which even grasps certain aspects of the truth. This seems therefore an appropriate point at which to discuss the so-called 'Error Theory' of ethics, which has been put forward by Mr. John Mackie (1946, 1977) and Mr. Richard Robinson (1948), notably in the former's recent book *Ethics: Inventing Right and Wrong*, to which I shall be mainly referring. It may be asked, since both Mackie and I think the same sort of views erroneous, what differences there are between us.

Mackie espouses a form of what he calls 'subjectivism'; but it is important not to think that this is the same view as we have just been calling 'old-fashioned subjectivism'. Unlike that, it is not a view about the meanings of moral words at all. His view (1977:35) is that in ordinary use these words connote objective properties of actions, etc.; the error, which he thinks is almost universal among ordinary people, does not consist in any misunderstanding of the words they use. It is not a conceptual error, but a factual one; people think that actions have these moral properties, but they do not have them, since there are no such properties (not in the sense that the words connote nothing, but in the sense that nothing actually has the properties which they connote).

Mackie plausibly maintains that many philosophers, from Plato onwards, have thought that moral words connoted such objective, but at the same time prescriptive, properties, and that the properties existed *in rerum natura* to make some of our moral judgements true. He also maintains, much less plausibly, that ordinary people, innocent of any philosophy, are the whole time committing the same error. Our two-level account of moral thinking will help to make clear how Mackie's view, though in the end mistaken, captures some important truths. We saw that ordinary moral thinkers, whose thinking had been confined in the main to the intuitive level, and who had not noticed the distinction between that and the critical level, would naturally, if they started to philosophize, first embrace some form of descriptivism. Whether it would be a naturalistic or an intuitionistic form we need not ask—perhaps each by turns, and without distinguishing clearly between them.

If they did this, it would certainly be an error. But it would be a philosophical error, akin to that committed by ordinary people if, starting in a naive way to ask philosophical questions in the theory of knowledge, they very naturally come out first with some theory like that called 'naive realism' (e.g. about colours). Many people, if forced (perhaps as beginner students of philosophy) to say what the sentence 'The curtain is red' means, will reply that it attributes a property, redness, which really does reside upon the surface of the curtain. We do not need to enquire what is right or wrong about saying this; they probably will not go on saying just this after they have been put by their tutors through a few philosophical hoops. But all the same it was not *completely* wrong. I wish merely to point out that, although it is very natural for a beginner in philosophy to say this, it is not necessary, *before* asking philosophical questions, to say this *or anything else* about the meaning of the sentence 'The curtain is red'; and for all that, philosophically innocent people are able to use it correctly and without hesitation.

The same is true of words like 'wrong'. Any ordinary moral thinker who keeps off philosophy may be using the words quite correctly without asking any questions about what he means by them. This does not prevent us, as philosophers, asking what he does mean by them; and the answer may be disputed. We saw how tempting it was to say that what he means by them is that actions, etc., have an objective property of which 'wrong' is the name. We may agree with Mackie that many great philosophers have committed just this objectivist error; that is to say, they have thought that when they said that an action was wrong, they were attributing to it an objective property of wrongness somehow residing *in rerum natura*, and also thought that they were often speaking truly in making this attribution. But from the fact that philosophers have thought this it does not in the least follow that ordinary people have thought it, or anything else philosophical, however easy it is for philosophers, once ordinary people do ask philosophical questions, to get them to say things like this.

4.7   If we want to find out what ordinary people mean, it is seldom safe just to ask them. They will come out with a variety of answers, few of which, perhaps, will withstand a philosophical scrutiny or elenchus, conducted in the light of the ordinary people's *own* linguistic behaviour (for example what they treat as self-contradictory). That is what is wrong with such arguments as, for example, Brandt's (1979:6 ff.), who counts it an objection to the linguistic method that a religious person may say that he means by 'wrong', 'prohibited by God', and can then be confuted by arguments such as those in Plato's *Euthyphro* (esp. 10d); and that therefore appeals to people's linguistic intuitions are always unreliable. In order to do the conceptual analysis of expressions in ordinary language, it is not sufficient to ask people what they mean; it is necessary after that to do some dialectic in much the Platonic sense; we have to put up proposed analyses, and draw consequences from them concerning what it would be self-contradictory, or logically consistent, or analytically true, to say. Then we have to find out whether, as the ordinary man uses the words, they have (i.e. are treated by him as having) these properties; and if not, the analyses have to be rejected. Since the ordinary man's use, in the relevant sense, is determined by the logical properties he gives the words, this is the only method we can employ. It helps if we can teach the ordinary man what these technical expressions of philosophical logic mean, so that we can ask him, for example, whether such and such a statement would be self-contradictory. But even this may not be necessary, if we think we can recognize from his behaviour whether he is treating a statement as self-contradictory or merely as false. And no doubt we can sometimes recognize this (Grice and Strawson, 1956).

A case in point is the question of whether ordinary people use the word 'ought' universalizably. What will settle this question is the test of whether when confronted with a statement like 'Jack did just the same as Jim, in just the same circumstances, and they are just the same sort of people, but Jack did what he ought and Jim did what he ought not', they will react to it in the same way as they will to 'The two figures are exactly the same shape, but one is triangular and the other not'.

It is my contention, not that the ordinary man, if asked, 'What do you mean by "ought"?', would come right out with an answer consonant with my ethical theory; but rather that the theory makes predictions as to what the ordinary man would treat as self-contradictory, etc., which accord with the facts of his behaviour. As we have seen (1.3, 5), it does not follow, from the fact that ordinary people do not use their words in the way (that is with the logical properties) that the theory claims, that the theory has to be abandoned as a *proposal* about how the words should be used; innovation is permissible. But it does follow that the theory has to be rejected as a *description* of ordinary use. Since I am interested in finding rational ways of answering the questions which the ordinary man is asking, I am happy that I have not yet come across any consequences of my theory which would compel me to reject it as a description. Our distinction between the levels of moral thinking helps a great deal to square the theory with the facts of linguistic behaviour. The theory predicts that the moral words will be used, especially at the intuitive

level, with a fairly constant descriptive meaning; that this
will lead to their use having properties which are well
reflected in various descriptivist theories; but that,
nevertheless, the words also have other properties
(connected with their prescriptivity) which escape these
theories; the theories have therefore to be rejected, not as
wrong, but as incomplete. My own more complex theory,
which tries to do justice to both the descriptive and the
prescriptive meanings of these words, is therefore a more
adequate account of their meaning.

It also has the advantage over Mackie's of not accusing
the ordinary man of being systematically and consistently
in error about facts which, on the theory, it should be easy
for the ordinary man to discover. Why has the error not
been corrected long ago, on this view? On the other hand
my own theory, which makes it a conceptual, or, if one likes
the expression, metaphysical error, committed by only
those relatively few people who ask philosophical questions (and not even by all of them), seems more plausible,
especially since its two-level account of moral thinking
reveals clearly how tempting the conceptual error is. On
the whole, conceptual errors are more insidious than
factual ones, and more difficult to escape. True, there are
optical illusions; but they do not deceive us for long. We
learn, for example, to allow for refraction when estimating
the depth of a swimming pool. Mackie has to suppose that
in morals we have been the victims of a long-standing
'optical illusion' which nobody saw through clearly until
he and Mr. Robinson came on the scene.

4.8   Moreover, the means of exposing the error taken by
Mackie himself are appropriate to exposing a conceptual,
not a factual error. He uses two arguments, which he calls
the argument from relativity and the argument from
queerness. I will start with the latter. It is hard to believe
that such an argument could prove the *falsity* of common
moral opinions, or of the alleged common opinion that
these moral opinions are objectively true. For the argument consists, in effect, in asking the ordinary man what on
earth he thinks he is looking for.

What is the connection between the natural fact that an action is a piece of deliberate cruelty . . . and the moral fact that it is wrong? It cannot be an entailment, a logical or semantic necessity. Yet it is not merely that the two features occur together. The wrongness must somehow be 'consequential' or 'supervenient'; it is wrong because it is a piece of deliberate cruelty. But just what *in the world* is signified by this 'because'? And how do we know the relation that it signifies, if this is something more than such actions being socially condemned, and condemned by us too, perhaps through our having absorbed attitudes from our social environment? (1977:41)

This passage smells heavily of conceptual analysis; the very words 'consequential' and 'supervenient' are reminiscent of *LM* 5.2, where I investigated the same conceptual difficulty. It is not at all like somebody's saying to the ordinary man 'You know what you mean by "It's wrong because it's cruel"; you mean that its cruelty gives it the objective property of wrongness, and you and I understand perfectly what this property would be if anything had it; but if you look you will see that nothing has it'. Rather, it is as if Mackie is saying to the ordinary man 'Before we can talk about how cruelty makes acts wrong, you will have to tell me where to turn my mind's eye, and what kind of spectacles to put on, in order to be able to discern the causal relation (or whatever kind of relation it is) between the cruelty of the act and its wrongness'. And of course the ordinary man, when he is thus addressed by the Socratic philosopher, will suffer the paralysing perplexity described by Meno (Plato, *Meno* 80a). They may then be able jointly to undertake the *conceptual* inquiry that is needed to remove the perplexity.

But even if the passage I have quoted were not plainly an introduction to a conceptual inquiry, it is obvious that what is wrong with a claim that there exist authoritative objective prescriptions is incoherence, not falsity. There can certainly be prescriptions issued by an authority (God, for example, or the collective conscience). But what is then objective (in one sense of that ambiguous word (12.1)—i.e. is a fact) is *the fact that* they are issued, not the prescriptions themselves. These are imperatives, and it does not make sense to ask whether an imperative (for example 'Thou shalt not commit adultery', said by God), states an objective fact, since it does not state any fact. It may also be a fact that God or the collective conscience possesses authority in some sense (though we should have to ask in what sense); but the prescription itself, though issued *with* authority, still does not become a *statement that* it is issued with authority. The notion of an objective prescription is an incoherent conflation of the notions (each in itself coherent) of a prescription and the factual statement that it is issued.[2]

It may be that the only factual error that Mackie is seeking to expose is the error of thinking that there *exists* an authoritative prescriber. I should agree that, if God does not exist, it is, on most common interpretations of the statement that he exists (though not on my own, H 1973b), a factual error to suppose that he does; and so is it to suppose that there exists some more spectral authority sitting crowned on his grave. However, I do not think that Mackie intended his theory merely as an affirmation of atheism.

4.9 We may now turn to his 'argument from relativity'. As he himself allows, mere differences of opinion on moral questions, however wide and widespread, do nothing by themselves to show that there are not objective moral facts. It might simply be that there was great ignorance about the moral truth. What does cast doubt on the existence of objective moral facts is the way we handle such differences. As Mackie says,

Disagreement about moral codes seems to reflect people's adherence to and participation in different ways of life . . . In short, the argument from relativity has some force simply because the actual variations in the moral codes are more readily explained by the hypothesis that they reflect ways of life than by the hypothesis that they express perceptions, most of them

---

[2] It is surprising how often this confusion is made (e.g. Moore, 1903:128).

seriously inadequate, and badly distorted, of objective values (1977:36 f.).

Why is this the better explanation? It is because it is more natural to suppose that people *mean* by the moral words something to do with commitments to ways of life, than that they mean by them to express alleged perceptions. It may seem rather obvious that variations in moral codes reflect primarily different ways of life rather than different perceptions (which is not to deny that, if we have different ways of life, we may come to 'see' and certainly to describe things differently); but it runs counter to Mackie's main contention that, according to the opinion and use of ordinary people, moral statements do express, or purport to express, perceptions of objective values (all illusory).

The agreements and differences between Mackie and myself, so far as the present argument is concerned, can thus be summed up as follows. (1) We agree that there are no objective prescriptive properties, in the sense of 'objective' in which it means 'factual' and in which a word ascribing such a property would be a descriptive word. But whereas I think it incoherent to posit such properties (simply because the words, or the properties, would have to be descriptive and prescriptive at once, which nobody who understood these expressions could suppose them to be), he thinks that it is coherent but false. (2) We agree that 'old-fashioned subjectivism' (the view that the moral words ascribe subjective properties) is false; but whereas I think that the words are not (purely) descriptive (and thus call myself a non-descriptivist), he is, so far as the meaning of the words in ordinary use goes, a descriptivist: he thinks that the words are used to ascribe to actions, people, etc., objective prescriptive properties existing *in rerum natura*. (3) These two divergencies of view have the consequence that, whereas he has to say that ordinary people when they use these words are universally in factual error (they are ascribing to actions, etc., properties which they do not have), I can hold a position which seems on the face of it more acceptable: that ordinary people when they use these words are not intending to ascribe objective prescriptive properties to actions, etc.; in so far as they are intending (in virtue of the descriptive meaning of the words, 4.1 f.) to ascribe objective properties, these are ordinary descriptive properties like the property of being the breaking of a promise; in so far as they are saying something prescriptive, they are not thereby ascribing any property. However, the combination of these two functions in their utterances has the result that, if they once start asking, in a philosophical way, what they mean, they will very easily fall into the conceptual (not factual) error of thinking that there are objective prescriptive properties—an error in which they have been encouraged by a number of distinguished philosophers.

PART II
METHOD

The voice of howling, who has suffered knows;
The assaying of pure gold, experience knows;
Come, burning souls, and howl we all together;
What 'tis to burn the burning soul well knows.

TAHIR[1]

5

ANOTHER'S SORROW

5.1 It is now time to set out in more detail how the logical properties of the moral concepts help us to construct moral arguments. I have already done this in a preliminary way in *FR* 6.3 ff. The method I shall be outlining here will be the same in essentials; but much has been written on the subject since then, and I have myself seen some of the moves more clearly (H 1976a, 1978b). In order to avoid repeating myself, I shall adopt a quite different manner of exposition; instead of an extended example of a moral argument, I shall present the metaethical argument step by step and illustrate it with appropriate examples as we go along.

We shall be concerned here with the method of *critical* thinking; our aim is to find a way of thinking about moral questions critically and rationally. We shall return to this word 'rational' later; but for now it suffices to mention just one point: that any rational thinking about them has to be done in the light of the facts. This is because of the kind of question they are. As we shall see (12.4), rationality is a quality of thought directed to the answering of questions, and what procedures are rational will depend on what the questions are. If we were seeking to answer factual

[1] *The Lament of Bābā Tāhir*, ed. E. Heron-Allen (Quaritch, 1902), 9. Tahir was writing for his fellow-Sufis about his (evidently disagreeable) mystical experiences; but his words have a wider application.

questions, it is obvious that rationality would require us to ascertain the facts, just because the *questions* are factual. It has therefore to be asked why, when answering *moral* questions, which are not entirely factual but partly prescriptive, we have to do the same. The reason is connected with the universalizability of moral judgements; this, as I have shown at length elsewhere, results in their having, like purely factual or descriptive statements, a descriptive meaning (*FR* 2.1 ff.; *LM* 7.1 ff.). In making moral judgements we are purporting to commend or condemn actions or people *because* they have some properties which make them right or wrong, good or bad; and therefore it would be obviously irrational to make the judgements without ascertaining whether or not they in fact had the properties. This requirement is unaffected by the other element in the meaning of moral judgements, the prescriptive or evaluative (1.6).

We are required to ascertain the facts before making factual statements, because a statement is a truth-claim; that is the kind of speech act it is. Even if moral judgements cannot be called truth-claims without qualification (H 1976b: sec. 6; 4.2, 12.3), they are subject to a similar requirement to ascertain the facts before pronouncing morally upon them. It is the function of moral principles to provide universal guidance for actions in all situations of a certain *kind* (whether minutely specified or, as in the case of intuitive principles, more generally characterized); and one of the most important functions of singular moral judgements is to make clear what our principles are (e.g. in teaching them, *LM* 10.3 ff.). All this would come to nothing if our moral judgements were unrelated to the facts about the situations on which we were commenting. Nobody would know what our moral principles might be, because our judgements could apparently be made regardless of what the actions and situations were like (H 1978b *s.f.*).

It is possible to go further and claim that the requirement to make our moral judgements in the light of the facts is related to a requirement of rationality that governs *any* prescriptions that we issue, even singular ones. I have discussed this requirement elsewhere (H 1979a). It is irrational to prescribe anything without regard to what, concretely, we are prescribing; and this involves cognizance of what our prescription means, and of what its execution in this concrete situation would entail. Obviously we cannot be cognizant of this without attention to the facts of the situation (12.4). If this is right, then it can be shown that rationality in prescriptions depends on cognizance of facts, without bringing universalizability into the argument. When the prescription is universal or universalizable, however, the requirement in consequence becomes stronger; we are required to satisfy ourselves that we can accept the *universal* application of the prescription; and this includes its application were we in the other's position. So the facts we need to be cognizant of will include facts about his position as it affects him with his preferences, as we shall shortly see.

We cannot, when making a moral judgement, be expected to ascertain all the facts that there are (though an archangel would know them, and therefore what I am going to say applies only to human critical thinking, not to critical thinking as such). We need some way of selecting those facts to which we are going to attend. We need, that is to say, to make judgements of relevance. As we have seen (3.9), to treat a feature of an action or situation as morally relevant is to apply to the action or situation a moral principle which mentions the feature. If we are beginning our moral thinking, however, we are clearly not in a position to assess moral relevance in this way, because we have not yet decided what moral principles are to be applied. We have therefore to proceed initially by guesswork. If we think that a feature of a situation *might* be relevant, we experiment with principles mentioning the feature; to accept the principles will be to accept the relevance of the feature, and to reject them will be to reject *those* reasons why it might be relevant, though there may yet be *other* principles which make it relevant.

This procedure is no more circular than that of a chess-player who says 'Any feature of the present position *might* be relevant to my decision on the best move to make next; so I'll look first at such and such a feature: ah, yes, it means that I shall lose my queen if I take his bishop; so, since it is a good principle (in general) not to sacrifice one's queen for a bishop, that feature is relevant'. He selects the relevant features by looking for features which will bring the present position, and the moves possible in it, under principles which he can accept; and the moralist has to do the same.

The procedure is not circular, because it consists not in *assuming* that these facts are relevant, but in asking whether they are relevant. Once the question is asked, and gone into, it turns out that they *are* relevant, because we find ourselves constrained by our reasoning to accept principles in which they figure. The question of *which* principles to accept is logically prior, but may be confronted only after an initial, tentative, sorting out of features of an action or situation which are *likely* to figure in principles which we ultimately accept. In ordinary moral thinking we have our intuitive or prima facie principles to start from, and shall normally treat as prima facie relevant the features that figure in them; but because we cannot take our prima facie principles for granted in critical thinking (which is what we are now trying to find a method for), we must be prepared to consider other features besides these as candidates for relevancy.

5.2 I am now going to propose as obvious candidates for such relevancy one class of features of actions and situations. We may characterize this class provisionally as the likely effects of possible actions in those situations on people (ourselves and others); that is to say, on their experiences, and on whether those experiences are such as the people prefer to have, or the reverse. Vegetarians will wish to say, instead of 'people', 'sentient beings', in order to include other animals within the scope of morality; I am happy to accept this amendment, but shall continue to say 'people' for brevity's sake.

A clear example of such a relevant feature would be the fact that, if I now drove at an interval of less than so many cars' lengths from the vehicle in front (given the speed at which we are travelling), and it had to stop abruptly, we should have a collision and several people, dogs, etc., would be hurt. The candidacy of such a feature will be amply supported and confirmed in what follows, when we discuss how we are to decide what moral principles to accept. We shall see that the method of critical thinking which is imposed on us by the logical properties of the moral concepts requires us to pay attention to the satisfaction of the preferences of people (because moral judgements are prescriptive, and to have a preference is to accept a prescription); and to pay attention equally to the equal preferences of all those affected (because moral principles have to be universal and therefore cannot pick out individuals). All this will come later; for the moment all I am proposing is that we consider probable effects on preference-satisfactions as *candidates* for the status of relevant features of actions.

If such features are or may be relevant, then rationality will require us to try to obtain knowledge of whether actions have them or not. If we are wondering how close we ought to drive to the vehicle in front, we shall need to know how this will affect the probability of collisions, and how collisions will affect the occupants of the vehicles. The relevance of all this will depend in the last reckoning on what it is like to be one of those occupants in a collision, and how they will like it, i.e. how it will affect the satisfaction of their preferences as to the experiences they should undergo. If they would all very much prefer not to have the experience of being in a collision, that, on the proposal I am making, is what makes the fact that to drive closer than a certain distance would greatly increase the probability of collisions relevant to a decision on how close to drive.

But what exactly is it that we have to know? The answer

is 'What it is like to be those people in that situation'. It is important to dwell for a moment on the conditions which have to be fulfilled before we can know this. In so far as they will *suffer* if they are in the collision (it will *hurt* to have one's neck broken), I shall not know what it will be like for them (or for me if I am one of them) unless I know what it is like to suffer like that. It will not do to know that someone's neck will be broken in the sense that the X-ray will show a fracture. I have to know what it will be *like* for the patient. In what follows we shall have to keep carefully in mind the distinction between merely knowing that something is happening to someone, and knowing *what it is like for him*. It is the latter kind of knowledge which, I am proposing, we should treat as relevant, and as required for the full information which rationality in making moral judgements demands.

This brings us to a further point about the relation between affective and cognitive states, and in particular between suffering, and knowing that I am suffering. This is that I cannot have either of these states without the other. If I am suffering, I know that I am suffering, and if I know that I am suffering, I am suffering. That this is true of perception in general was understood by Aristotle (1170ᵃ 29). These are conceptual truths, and the latter is true not just because (necessarily in virtue of the meaning of 'know') if I know anything it is so. Rather, if the experience of suffering were absent, both the object and the means of knowledge would be absent. It must be understood that by 'suffering' I mean an actual experience; I could be being *harmed* in some way without knowing anything about it (for example, if somebody were at this moment stealing my apples). I am not speaking here of harm in general.

Out of caution I will make two qualifications to this claim about knowledge of suffering which do not affect the argument. It has to be admitted that a being, if there were such, who lacked *self*-consciousness, might suffer without knowing that it was *he* who suffered. To avoid this difficulty, let us confine our attention to beings who have self-consciousness. And it has to be admitted that one might suffer without being able to specify the precise nature of the suffering (whether, for example, it was resentment that made me feel so bad or fear of a repetition of the injury). This will not affect the argument either; it is however necessary for me to claim that if I am suffering to a certain degree or with a certain intensity, I must know that I am suffering to that degree and with that intensity, and vice versa.

These related cognitive and affective states bring with them also a conative state. If I am suffering, I have a motive for ending the suffering. This also is a conceptual truth, which holds in virtue of the meanings of the words. I do not, for our present purposes, need to take a position on whether these three states (cognitive, affective and conative) are distinct, given that if we have the first two, we must, as a conceptual necessity, have the third. Some may wish all the same to call them distinct states.

The thesis just put forward must not be confused with a similar, but false, thesis about *pain* (H 1964; Brandt 1979:131). In unusual cases it is possible to have pain without suffering, and without having a motive for ending or avoiding the pain, even *ceteris paribus*. Though 'pain' can be, and often is, used evaluatively in the same way as 'suffering', so that to experience pain is *eo ipso* to have a motive for ending or avoiding the pain, it is also sometimes used descriptively as the name of a recognizable sensation or class of them; and there are well attested instances of people who report pain but say that they do not mind it. However, it would be self-contradictory to report suffering but claim that one did not mind it, and had no motive for ending or avoiding it, even *ceteris paribus*. If there were no such motive, there would be no suffering. Other motives might outweigh this one, or we would never submit ourselves to the dentist; but it must be there.

The same applies to knowledge of the degree of our own suffering, and its quality. Kipling, indeed, was exaggerating when he wrote

The toad beneath the harrow knows
Exactly where each toothpoint goes;[2]

for even if the toad spoke English and knew anatomy and
were far more capable of accurate observation than, in that
situation, it would be likely to be, it might not be able to say
with confidence 'One of the points went through my
seventh vertebra from the top, another is now going
through my right lung'. But at any rate we are the
authorities on what it is like to be ourselves in a suffering
state.

5.3 Now consider our knowledge of what it is like to be
somebody else who is suffering (e.g. because his neck is
being broken). Can I properly be said to know what it is
like for him (not just to know that his neck is being broken),
unless I myself have an equal aversion to having that done
to me, were I in his position with his preferences? Here
again there is an intimate conceptual relation between the
cognitive, affective and conative states, but the last have as
their objects hypothetical, not actual states of affairs.
Suppose that I said 'Yes, I know just how you feel, but I
don't mind in the least if somebody now does it to me':
should I not show that I did not really know, or even
believe, that it was like *that*? Would not my lack of
knowledge, or else my insincerity, be exposed if somebody
said 'All right, if you don't mind, let's try'?

I emphasize that the imagined situation must be one in
which I have *his* preferences. If, by some quirk of nature, I
were a person who knew that he did not feel pain in that
situation, or if I knew that I was going to become such a
person by being anaesthetized, then I might indeed
sincerely say that I did not mind being subjected to the
experience (ignoring for the sake of argument its
consequences). But this would be irrelevant; and so would
it be if I knew that I would feel pain, but for some reason
would not mind it. For I am to imagine myself in his

---

[2] 'Pagett: M. P.', in *Departmental Ditties and Other Verses*. The main part of
the poem is about the harrowing experience of living in the Indian climate.

situation with *his* preferences. Unless I have an equal
aversion to myself suffering, forthwith, what he is suffering
or going to suffer, I cannot really be knowing, or even
believing, that being in his situation with his preferences
will be like *that*.

I do not wish to be taken as claiming that we can ever in
fact have full knowledge of other people's experiences. The
epistemological puzzles that arise here I shall postpone
until ch. 7. It would be wrong to claim that our imagin-
ations somehow *inform* us of what the experiences of others
are like. Imagination is a very common source of error; it
can just as well be of experiences and preferences which
they do not have as of those which they have. But if we do
know what it is like to be the other person in that situation,
we shall be (correctly) imagining having those experiences
and preferences, in the sense of knowing or representing to
ourselves[3] what it would be like to have them; and this, I
have been claiming, involves having equal motivations
with regard to possible similar situations, were we in them.

It is important to emphasize the distinction between the
two propositions:

(1) I now prefer with strength S that if I were in that
situation x should happen rather than not;[4]
(2) If I were in that situation, I would prefer with strength
S that x should happen rather than not.

Confusion between these statements, or pairs like them, is

[3] See the very useful discussion of adequacy of representation in Brandt
(1979:58 ff.). Plato's discussion in *Prot.* 357d is relevant, and so are Spinoza's
remarks in 1677:III, 18, though both relate to knowledge or belief about our own
future experiences, as does Brandt's discussion. It seems that Brandt does not
commit himself to a view which I am inclined to hold, that full representation of
future preferences entails the replication of them in the present.

[4] The last three words raise a problem which has been acutely discussed by
Professor Bergström (1971): how to say exactly *between what alternatives* a choice
or preference is being exercised. Since this is a problem which has to be faced by
any theory of rational choice, and not merely by utilitarianism, those who clutch
at it as an argument against utilitarianism in particular reveal only their own lack
of interest in rational choice between alternatives. But it has to be faced all the
same.

very common, and has been made commoner by misunderstandings or even mistranslations of the scriptural
versions of the Golden Rule.[5] What I am claiming is not
that these propositions are identical, but that I cannot
know that (2), and what that would be like, without (1)
being true, and that this is a conceptual truth, in the sense
of 'know' that moral thinking demands.

5.4 There is another possible way in which it might be
thought that I could know what it was like to suffer as this
man is, without myself having as strong a preference that it
should not forthwith happen to me. It might be thought
that I could do it by failing to 'identify', as it is said, with
the 'myself' who would be suffering. I do not think that
this actually makes sense, but to ask whether it does may
shed some light on our problem. Puzzles about personal
identity are extremely vexed and complex, and I have no
wish to enter into them here. But there is one suggestion
about it which, if true, would support the account of moral
thinking I am giving. It is a commonplace to say that there
are certain criteria of personal identity—bodily continuity,
continuity of personal characteristics, and linked memories—which are normally all satisfied by those whom we
identify as the same person; but that examples can be
invented, and perhaps even occur, in which these criteria
'come apart'—that is to say, some are satisfied and some
not. The difficulty we then have in saying whether it is the
same person or not is used by philosophers for various
argumentative purposes into which we need not go. I wish
merely to suggest here (not entirely originally) that there
may be another element in personal identity which has to
be added to these.

The suggestion is that 'I' is not wholly a descriptive
word but in part prescriptive.[6] In identifying myself with

---

[5] e.g. Luke VI, 31. The King James version is correct though archaic; the New
English Bible is incorrect and the Vulgate correct, as may be seen by consulting
the Greek (H 1975d:44).

[6] I do not know the source of this idea. Without attributing it to these writers, I
have found the following suggestive: Williams, 1970; Parfit, 1971:26; Locke,
1690:II, xxvii, 9, secs. 18, 26; Royce, 1908: IV, sec. 4, *ap.* Rawls, 1971:408. The

some person either actually or hypothetically, I identify with his prescriptions. In plainer terms, to think of the person who is about to go to the dentist as myself is to have now the preference that he should not suffer as I believe he is going to suffer. In so far as I think it will be myself, I now have in anticipation the same aversion as I think he will have. If this view were accepted, it would solve what has seemed a difficulty, that of why deterrent punishments deter. If thinking of the person who would be punished as myself entails having now an aversion to his being punished equal to his then aversion, that explains why I avoid committing the crime for which he would be punished.

There are difficulties in this view, of which the chief is that it makes personal identity no longer an all-or-nothing affair, as it is commonly held to be. I can identify to a greater or less extent with the prescriptions of the future inhabitant of my body (if I may be allowed that seriously misleading metaphor); and I can identify with the prescriptions of other people (my children for example). It would support our present argument, however, if it were impossible, even hypothetically, to identify fully with somebody else, in his situation with his preferences, without sharing those preferences (i.e. if to say 'If it were *myself* in that situation. . . ', with full representation of the situation including the preferences of the person in it, were already to accept prescriptions about what should be done to oneself, were one in that situation, which correspond with those of the person actually in it).

A further difficulty is that it might be only contingently true that we identify with the prescriptions of the future inhabitants of our own bodies; it is easy to see how such a propensity could have been selected for in evolution to a certain extent, though balanced by altruistic propensities which also favour the survival of the genes producing them (Singer, 1981).

---

idea that 'I' is in one of its senses not a descriptive word (7.3) I owe to Professor Vendler, but not the idea that it is prescriptive. A kindred idea is probably to be found in some existentialist writers. I have also learnt much from discussion on this subject with John Perry.

Probably we have here an example of a familiar phenome-
non in philosophy. A contingent correlation between
different things, which has a causal explanation, is,
however, so firm that it has proved convenient to adopt a
way of speaking which will only be viable if the correlation
is practically universal. Thus, we happily use terms like 'I'
and 'same person' in ordinary life, in which people do not
acquire one another's brains or memories or personalities.
But if we are asked what we would say if my brain were
divided down the middle and each half put in a different
body, whose inhabitant then had all of my characteristics
and memories (would both of them be me, or only one, and
if so which one?), then our linguistic intuitions fail us. Like
our moral intuitions, they were formed to cope with
ordinary cases, and break down in this extraordinary case.
In particular, the all-or-nothing character of personal
identity can be made to break down for any of the
identifying features, as the case just cited shows.

As applied in ordinary cases, it is probable that the word
'I' is attached to all the identifying properties above-
mentioned in varying degrees. I wish merely to suggest
that to these we should add, not another identifying
property, but another feature of the word 'I', namely that,
by calling some person 'I', I express at least a considerably
greater concern for the satisfaction of his preferences than
for those of people whom I do not so designate. Thus, in a
normal clear-cut case, if I were asked, when somebody is
being maltreated and dislikes it, 'How do you feel about
being put yourself forthwith in that position with his
preferences?', I shall reply that if it would be *me*, I do now
have the same aversion to having it done as he now has. If
the person in front of me has fallen into the boiling dye vat,
and I fully realize how much he is wishing that he had not, I
shall myself desire with equal intensity not to fall in, and thus
shall take good care not to, assuming that I expect my
mental state if I do to be the same as his. The critical
thinking of a perfect moral thinker manifests this full
representation and identification. Archangels can do it,

and of course God, as Blake well brings out in the poem from which I have borrowed the title of this chapter.[7] We human beings are not gifted with so much sensitivity or sympathy, and for that reason have to make do for the most part with intuitive thinking; but we have to try, if we are to do the critical thinking which would validate our intuitions.

We might be tempted, as some have been, to go further and say that unless, when someone is suffering, I have an aversion to *his* suffering as he is suffering, I cannot be fully representing to myself how he is suffering. I am not making any such claim, which is not necessary to my argument. I am only saying that having an aversion to *my* forthwith suffering like that is a condition of full representation. A talented torturer or single-minded sadist may understand very well the quality of the suffering he is inflicting, and be spurred on by that very understanding to go on inflicting it. The friend of Camus's hero in *L'Étranger* (1942: ch. 4), who had the habit of beating his mistress, was perhaps like this: 'The woman went on screaming, and Raymond went on hitting.' The answer to Blake's question,

Can I see another's woe
And not be in sorrow too?
Can I see another's grief
And not seek for kind relief?

is regrettably, so far as such people are concerned, 'Yes'. However, it suffices for our argument that I cannot know the extent and quality of others' sufferings and, in general, motivations and preferences without having equal motivations with regard to what should happen to me, were I in their places, with their motivations and preferences.

5.5 Before proceeding further, it may be helpful to point out that I have, in the above argument, taken a direct route from knowledge of, and preferences regarding, my own present experiences, to knowledge of, and preferences regarding, what should happen to me in the hypothetical

---

[7] 'On Another's Sorrow', in *Songs of Innocence and Experience*.

case in which I am to be, forthwith, put into the position of somebody else. Other philosophers have thought it more persuasive to take an indirect route, going first from my own present preferences and experiences to my present preferences regarding my own *future* experiences, and thence to my present preferences regarding *other people's* experiences, in the hypothetical case in which I should have to experience them. I have myself been attracted by this alternative route, and indeed used it in an earlier draft of this chapter. But I have avoided it because it entails several complications whose unravelling would have made the book longer than I or the reader would wish it to be. I have to thank Mr. Parfit for suggesting to me that the shorter route is more secure.

The longer route proceeds by first showing that it is rational to choose prudently, i.e. to treat one's own future preferences as of equal weight to one's present; and then exhibiting morality as universalized prudence—i.e. using the universalizability of moral judgements to show that, if we are thinking morally, we must pay as much regard to the preferences of other people as to our own. I will mention only some of the difficulties that beset this route, in order to explain why I have not taken it. I think that they can probably be overcome, but I doubt my ability, within a reasonable compass, to convince all readers that they can be.

The first difficulty concerns the pure discounting of the future. By 'discounting', I mean our tendency to give less weight to future preferences, because they are future. By 'pure' discounting, I mean that this tendency (as some suppose) has nothing essentially to do with the unpredictability of the future, and would persist, even if we were certain what the future would bring; we would give less weight to our future preferences just because of their futurity. It is a matter of dispute whether this pure discounting occurs (i.e. whether there is discounting which cannot be explained by mere unpredictability), and whether it is rational for it to occur. My own view is that it does occur but is not rational (though discounting because of unpredictability is rational); but argument for this view is one thing that I wish to spare the reader. I have done so by always supposing that, when we are asked, in moral thinking, to put ourselves in somebody's shoes (even his future shoes), we are asked to do so now and forthwith. There is thus no possibility of discounting the future, because we have to imagine it as present. This is a necessity for critical moral thinking, because, as we shall shortly see, the universalizability of moral judgements puts a prohibition on the occurrence of time-references in moral principles; mere dates, by themselves, cannot have moral relevance (6.4). Some may wish to maintain that the same is true of prudential thinking; but I do not need to argue the question.

5.6 The second difficulty is one which we cannot altogether avoid, but can at least postpone. It is perhaps worth mentioning that this is not a difficulty peculiarly for utilitarianism; it would have to be overcome by any theory which included an account of prudence, as any complete theory of practical thinking surely must.

When we are talking about rational choice at a given time, it is important to distinguish between two different questions which we might be seeking rationally to answer. The difference may be illustrated by means of a schematic example. Suppose that I now prefer that at some later time (then, for short), x should happen, but that I shall then prefer that x not happen. Let us also suppose that the second, or future, preference is the weaker. In that case, I might be seeking to make my present preference as rational as possible by exposing it, as Professor Brandt bids, to 'cognitive psychotherapy', i.e. to logic and the facts (1979:111 ff.). There are, however, two ways in which I might proceed, and which are not obviously destined to lead to the same result.

It will simplify the example if we suppose that the second preference (the preference then), is what I shall call a then-for-then preference. By this I mean that it is a preference then for what should happen then. I shall ignore for the purpose of this brief exposition preferences at one future time for what should happen at some other future time. The first preference in the preceding paragraph is a now-for-then preference; and we have supposed that the second, then-for-then, preference is opposite, and weaker.

One way of proceeding, in order to achieve a rational choice, would be for the chooser to ask the question 'What would my *present* preferences be, if I exposed them to logic and the facts?' 'My present preferences' will include now-for-now and now-for-then preferences. Let us suppose that the result of this exposure is that, having fully represented to himself the future then-for-then preference, without discounting the future, he has ac-quired an equal now-for-then preference with the same object, which opposes his original now-for-then preference. He now, therefore, has two now-for-then preferences, the original one a preference that x should then happen, and the new one a preference that x should not then happen. Since the original preference is, and remains, stronger, it will prevail, and the chooser will rationally answer his question by saying that his present preferences, all things considered, after exposure to logic and the facts, come down in favour of x then happening.

On the other hand, the chooser might proceed differently. He might remind himself that, when the time comes for x to happen or not happen, his present now-for-then preferences will all be things of the past. He might, accordingly, ask himself a *different* question, namely 'What would maximize the satisfaction of my now-for-now and then-for-then preferences—i.e. what will result in the maximal satisfaction of my preferences at all times for what should happen at those times, ignoring preferences for what should happen at other times?' The rational answer to this question will be 'That x should not then happen'. The reason is that the now-for-then preference that x should then happen is excluded from consideration by the form of the question.

If we now ask, 'Which of these two questions would it be rational to ask?', the answer will depend on what we are after. Those who are seeking rationally to maximize their own now-for-now and then-for-then preferences will opt for the second question. Those who, in contrast, are seeking rationally to maximize the satisfaction of their present preferences after they have been adjusted in the light of full exposure to logic and the facts, will opt for the first. Both can be stated in terms of the satisfaction of preferences; but it is a question of *which* preferences. The second method admits only now-for-now and then-for-then preferences; the first admits now-for-now and now-for-then preferences, and is prepared to adjust the latter in the light of information about what the then-for-then preferences will be, but not to the exclusion of any antecedent now-for-then preferences which may survive the exposure. We have for simplicity ignored then-for-later-thens preferences; but clearly they would have to be discussed in a full account.

A distinction is often made between *happiness* and *preference* versions of utilitarianism. It seems to me that the distinction I have just made enables us to locate the essential difference between the versions. It is possible to define 'greatest happiness', in the restricted sense used by some utilitarians, as the maximal satisfaction of now-for-now and then-for-then preferences. The happiest man is then, in this sense, the man who most has, at all times, what he prefers to have *at those times*. The difference between the two versions will then lie in whether only this restricted class of preferences is considered, or all preferences. That a happiness-utilitarianism can be formulated in terms of the satisfaction of a restricted class of preferences is important; for it enables us to retain the link between it and prescriptions, and thus relate it to our present theory. The simplifying assumption which I shall shortly be making will turn my theory, in effect, into a happiness theory of this kind; I make it in order to avoid the sort of complications which Brandt ably brings out (1979:247 ff.). But it is still my belief that a full account of the matter would assign weight to *all* preferences. I must confess, however, that such a general theory of preferences is beyond my grasp at the moment.

It has also to be asked whether the class of preferences to be considered ought to be restricted in another respect too. So far we have allowed into our reckoning all now-for-now and then-for-then preferences. But some of these will be for states of affairs which are not presently within the experience of the person having the preference. I may for example prefer that my apples not be stolen, but not know whether they are being stolen or not. In the examples we have been considering so far, we have been concentrating on preferences with regard to experiences which the preferrer is currently having. Ought we to extend our account to cover what have been called 'external' preferences (Dworkin, 1977a:234)? I am inclined to think that we ought, but that I cannot at present do so. There is obviously unfinished business here. But for the present I shall exclude such preferences.

Suppose, next, that we are trying to answer rationally the practical question 'What shall I now do?', i.e. that we are asking what the rational action for us in this situation would be. Since we shall in any case do what the balance of our present preferences requires—in other words, act on the prescription which results when the prescriptions we are now disposed to accept have been balanced against one another in proportion to the strengths with which we accept them—the rational action will be determined by what our present preferences are when we have submitted them to logic and the facts. And in this process we shall (since it is now that we are making the decision) rationally consider   only   our   now-for-now   and   now-for-then preferences; our then-for-then preferences will figure only in that, when fully now represented, they engender surrogate now-for-then preferences which are equal to them.

I agree, therefore, with what I take to be Brandt's view, but put into my own words, that the rational action will be

what is preferred when our *present* preferences have been
exposed to facts and logic. This may not be the action
which leads to our own maximal welfare, in the sense of the
maximal satisfaction, in sum, of all our now-for-now and
then-for-then preferences; for we may have strong antecedent now-for-then preferences which lead to actions
which, then, we would very much prefer not to have been
taken, because they led to the non-satisfaction of our then-
for-then preferences. This conflict will be resolved if we
add to our present preferences what we may call the
requirement of prudence. This is that we should always have
a dominant or overriding preference now that the satisfaction of our now-for-now and then-for-then preferences
should be maximized. If this requirement is complied
with, then we shall always prefer to maximize our own
happiness, in the restricted sense above defined, and shall
be entitled to the name 'prudent' in one of its senses. On
the other hand, somebody who allows strong antecedent
now-for-then preferences to override fully represented
then-for-then preferences manifests one (not the only)
kind of imprudence. We might call him an *autofanatic*,
because of his similarity, in the sphere of prudence, to the
fanatic in the sphere of morality (H 1972b:103; 10.1 ff.).

It is interesting that Brandt, whose account of rational
action, if I have got him right, relies only on now-for-now
and now-for-then preferences (albeit adjusted in the light
of information about then-for-then preferences), when he
comes to the rational choice of a morality opts for a method
which seeks to maximize happiness, and not preference- or
desire-satisfaction in general. The term 'happiness' here
could be defined in the restricted way suggested above,
though this is not quite Brandt's definition. He takes this
step primarily in order to avoid the complications I have
mentioned. I am going to do the same, though, as I said,
with a sense of leaving unfinished business.

I propose, then, the following simplifying assumption.
We are to assume, when we come to universalize our
prescriptions, as morality demands, that we have to

consider only those prescriptions and preferences of others which they would retain if they were always prudent in the sense just defined. Our knowledge of the facts, so far as we manage to emulate the archangel in attaining it, will enable us to say what others would prefer if they were prudent; for it will inform us about their then-for-then preferences, even those of which they are now ignorant. I should guess that this simplification of the argument will not make an enormous difference when it comes to the selection of prima facie principles for use in intuitive thinking; the autofanatical now-for-then and external preferences which we have excluded from consideration will turn out, in practice and generally speaking, to have become so weak relatively to other preferences, after 'cognitive psychotherapy', as not to influence our selection of prima facie principles. But I shall not here attempt to show this. The demonstration, if it could be achieved, that *imprudent* preferences would not in the end affect the selection of prima facie principles would take much the same form as our later attempt to show that *evil* desires would not in the end affect it (though full critical thinking would take them into consideration initially, 8.6 ff.).

UNIVERSALIZATION

6.1 We have now reached the point at which we can apply the ideas of the preceding chapter in order to construct our theory of moral reasoning. It will be convenient if we continue sometimes to speak, not in terms of motivational states, nor even of preferences, but in terms of the prescriptions which are their expressions in language. This will enable us to display the logical relations between them. In the case of all intentional states, as they are called, like belief and desire, which require a linguistic form for their full description (as when we speak of the belief *that* the world is round or of the desire *that* x not happen) we often, in order to display the logical relations that they have, use the linguistic form. Thus we say that the belief that the world is round is inconsistent with the belief that it is flat, because the statement that it is round is inconsistent with the statement that it is flat. And similarly the desire that x not happen would be inconsistent with a desire that it should happen, because the corresponding prescriptions 'Let x happen' and 'Let x not happen' are mutually inconsistent. It is therefore much more convenient, and does not alter the argument in any essential respect, to speak in terms of logical relations between prescriptions.

Note that in both cases the inconsistency is between the states of mind (beliefs or desires) and between their expressions, not between the *statements that* these states of mind are present. We must carefully distinguish between the expressions of two desires and the statements that I have them. 'Let x happen' could be, and is, inconsistent with 'Let x not happen' without 'Hare desires that x happen' being inconsistent with 'Hare desires that x not happen'. We therefore do not need to discuss whether the last two statements are mutually inconsistent, and if so in what sense.

It must also be noted that the thesis that moral judgements are universalizable has not yet played a crucial role in the argument. Mentions of it in the preceding chapter were all mere anticipations of what is going to be said in this, except for its use to show that rational moral thinking requires cognizance of the facts; and even that, as we saw, could be dispensed with if we accept the view that all prescriptions, universal and singular, have to be made in cognizance of the facts if they are to be rational (5.1). But in what follows universalizability will begin to play a crucial role.

I wish to stress that there are not, strictly speaking, as Mr. Mackie claims that there are, different *stages* of universalization (1977:83 ff.). Moral judgements are, I claim, universalizable in only one sense, namely that they entail identical judgements about all cases identical in their universal properties. There is, however, as Mackie sees, a progression in the use we make of this single logical property as we develop our theory of moral reasoning. The effect of the argument of the preceding chapter is to facilitate one step in this progression, namely the step from prescriptions which I accept for my own experiences to prescriptions which I must accept for experiences I should have, were I to be in someone else's position with his preferences. In establishing the possibility of this step, we appealed to universalizability only to the limited extent mentioned in the preceding paragraph, and that did not require any special sense of universalizability beyond the one just defined.

It follows from universalizability that if I now say that I ought to do a certain thing to a certain person, I am committed to the view that the very same thing ought to be done to me, were I in exactly his situation, including having the same personal characteristics and in particular the same motivational states. But the motivational states he actually now has may run quite counter to my own present ones. For example, he may very much want not to have done to him what I am saying I ought to do to him (which involves prescribing that I do it). But we have seen that if I fully represent to myself his situation, including his motivations, I shall myself acquire a corresponding motivation, which would be expressed in the prescription that the same thing *not be* done to me, were I to be forthwith in just that situation. But this prescription is inconsistent with my original 'ought'-statement, if that was, as we have been assuming, prescriptive. For, as we have just seen, the statement that I ought to do it to him commits me to the view that it ought to be done to me, were I in his situation. And this, since 'ought' is prescriptive, entails the prescription that the same *be* done to me in that situation. So, if I have this full knowledge of his situation, I am left with two inconsistent prescriptions. I can avoid this 'contradiction in the will' (cf. Kant, 1785:58) only by abandoning my original 'ought'-statement, given my present knowledge of my proposed victim's situation.

6.2 A problem arises here, however, about this conflict between my own and my victim's preferences. There is first of all the difficulty, which we shall be dealing with in the next chapter, of comparing his preferences with mine in respect of intensity. How am I to say which is the greater, and by how much? But even if we assume that this difficulty can be overcome, the problem remains of why my preferences, even if they are less intense, should be subordinated to his. And if mine are more intense than his, ought they to be subordinated at all? Suppose, for example, that all I think I ought to do to him is move his bicycle so that I can park my car, and he has a mild aversion to my doing this (not because he dislikes someone else interfering with his property, but simply because he wants it to stay where it is). This problem seems even more pressing in multilateral cases in which the preferences of many people are affected; but it will do no harm to deal with it in this simple bilateral case first.

I can see no reason for not adopting the same solution

here as we do in cases where our own preferences conflict
with one another. For example, let us change the case and
suppose that it is my own bicycle, and that it is moderately
inconvenient to move it, but highly inconvenient not to be
able to park my car; I shall then naturally move the bicycle,
thinking that that is what, prudentially speaking, I ought to
do, or what I most want, all in all, to do. Reverting now to
the bilateral case: we have established that, if I have full
knowledge of the other person's preferences, I shall myself
have acquired preferences equal to his regarding what
should be done to me were I in his situation; and these are
the preferences which are now conflicting with my original
prescription. So we have in effect not an interpersonal
conflict of preferences or prescriptions, but an intrapersonal one; both the conflicting preferences are mine. I
shall therefore deal with the conflict in exactly the same
way as with that between two original preferences of my
own.

Multilateral cases now present less difficulty than at first
appeared. For in them too the interpersonal conflicts,
however complex and however many persons are involved,
will reduce themselves, given full knowledge of the preferences of others, to intrapersonal ones. And since we are
able, in our everyday life, to deal with quite complex
intrapersonal conflicts of preferences, I can see no reason
why we should not in the same way deal with conflicts of
this special sort, which have arisen through our awareness
of the preferences of others combined with the requirement that we universalize our moral prescriptions.

Let us apply this to our simple bilateral car–bicycle case.
The other party wants me not to move his bicycle, but I
want more to move it in order to park my car. I am fully
aware of the strength of his desire, and therefore have a
desire of equal strength that, were I in his situation, the
bicycle should stay where it is. But I also have my original
desire to move it in order to park my car. This latter desire
wins by superior strength. On the other hand, if the
positions were reversed (the bicycle mine, the car his), and

I could somehow prevent the bicycle being moved, the case would be from my individual point of view different (though not different in its universal properties). Suppose that, in this different case, my desire not to have the bicycle moved is far weaker than the other party's desire to park his car; and suppose that I am fully aware of the strength of his desire and therefore have an equal desire that, were I in his position, I should be able to park my car. I shall then, in this different situation, have again two desires: the original desire to leave my bicycle where it is, and my acquired desire that were I the other party I should be able to park my car; and the latter will be the stronger. So in this different situation I shall think that the bicycle ought to be moved.

Note that, although the situations are different, they differ only in what *individuals* occupy the two roles; their *universal* properties are all the same. That is why (and this is interesting and significant) in both cases the conclusion is that the bicycle ought to be moved; this is because in each case its owner's desire to leave it where it is is less than the car-owner's desire to park his car. We see here in miniature how the requirement to universalize our prescriptions generates utilitarianism. And we see also how in principle unanimity can be reached by our method of reasoning, once each fully represents to himself the situation of the other. And there is in principle no difficulty in extending the method to multilateral cases; the difficulties are all practical ones of acquiring the necessary knowledge and correctly performing some very complex thought-processes. In difficult cases it would take an archangel to do it.

6.3 I shall mention here three further difficulties, of which the first two will be left for consideration in ch. 10. The first is that raised by an objector who says 'What is all this talk about preferences and desires and motivations? What we are supposed to be talking about is *morality*. Granted, if we put the whole conflict in terms of mere preferences, the stronger preference will win; but moral duties are higher and more authoritative than mere pre-ferences (have you not yourself said that moral judgements are overriding?) and cannot be weighed in the same scales. In setting up your "preference-utilitarianism" have you not in effect thrown morality out of the window, not given it a basis?' This objection will be dealt with in 10.5.

The second is this: even if it be granted that I have given grounds for *rejecting* certain moral judgements, can I claim that I have given grounds for *accepting* any, even negative ones like 'I ought not to do this'? To revert to our earlier schematic case (6.1), in which I withdrew the statement that I ought to do something to some person in the face of my desire that it not be done to me in a like situation: we notice that I only had to withdraw the moral statement, which could be done by saying 'It is not the case that I ought'; I was not compelled to accept the contrary statement, 'I ought not'. But the latter seems to be what we were after. To put it another way: the following three prescriptions, or negations of prescriptions, are mutually consistent:

(1) Let me do it to him;
(2) Let it not be done to me in like circumstances;
(3) It is not the case that I ought to do it to him.

An amoralist, as we shall call him, could assent to all three, and do the act without further hesitation; it is only somebody who feels a need to embrace some universal prescription for situations just like this who will be forced to choose between the prescriptions 'I ought to do it' and 'I ought not to do it'. This objection I shall be considering in 10.7.

The third objection, which I shall deal with in the next section, is the following. We have been assuming that we are constrained to apply our moral principles, because they are universal, to all identical situations, whether actual or hypothetical. Since there are not likely to be any identical actual situations (2.4), the application to hypothetical ones is crucial. It might be objected that someone who wanted to escape our argument might just refuse to consider the application of the moral principle, to which his moral judgement about the present case commits him, to any but actual situations. If we allow him to get away with this, we shall be unable to pursue the above argument, because that depended on asking him to prescribe for the hypothetical case in which he occupied the position of his victim—a case which, we may suppose, will never actually arise (*FR* 6.4; H 1978a:78).

6.4 There is implicit in what I have said (5.3) an answer to this objection. I have maintained that in so far as I know what it is like to be the other person, I have already acquired motivations, equal to his, with regard to the hypothetical case in which I should be in his position. So the prescription which is going to conflict with my proposed moral judgement is already there. But the objector might retort that this judgement, in committing me to a universal principle (viz. that the same ought to be done in all identical cases) commits me only to judgements about cases which are or will be actual, not to hypothetical ones. The question which arises, therefore, is whether moral principles, in order to be universal, have to apply to all cases both actual and hypothetical, or only to actual cases. To use the fashionable terminology, do we have to be able to apply our moral principles to all logically possible worlds, or only to the actual world?

We shall certainly become confused here unless we observe carefully the distinction between intuitive and critical thinking. What we are concerned with here is critical thinking; the principle to which the proposed moral judgement will commit its author is a highly specific one, namely that in all cases just like this a certain thing should be done. I have in other places, and elsewhere in this book (2.9, 8.2, 9.7, 9.9), insisted that intuitive or prima facie principles have to be selected for their acceptance-utility in the actual world; and that therefore it should not be held against them that in hypothetical cases, *different* in their universal properties from what would be likely to occur in the actual world, they would yield unhappy results, nor should it be held against utilitarianism that in such cases it could conflict with these intuitions. The incautious might therefore expect me to say here too that what results a principle will produce in hypothetical cases is irrelevant to the argument. But actually I am going to say the opposite, and must therefore explain why.

The point is that what we are concerned with in this kind of critical thinking are hypothetical cases *not different* in their universal properties from the actual (*FR* 3.6). It follows from this that any properly universal principle will apply to them too. There is no way of framing a properly universal principle which prescribes for actual cases but does not similarly prescribe for non-actual cases which resemble the actual cases in all their universal properties and differ from them only in the roles played in them by particular individuals. Given two cases differing solely in that in one of them individuals A and B occupy certain roles, and in the other the roles are reversed, any universal principle must yield the same prescriptions about them both. In order to yield different prescriptions about the two cases, the principle would have to contain the names of the individuals, and would therefore not be universal.

To this it might be objected that the actual case does differ from the non-actual case in one universal property, that of being *actual*, and that this property could be treated as morally relevant without breaching the universalizability requirement. This objection brings us into a very difficult area of metaphysical dispute, in which, also, the analogous question is argued of whether *existence* is a property. Without entering the argument, I think it worth while to mention the view of those who say that actual cases or worlds cannot be distinguished from merely possible cases or worlds without referring to the fact that the actual world is the one in which *we* (these individuals) are. It would not do to say that the (or an) actual world is that in which *any* individual is; for this must mean 'any *actual* individual' (a merely possible individual would not do), and so the definition would become circular. I would reject this view if it committed me to the thesis that all the cases and worlds, both actual and merely possible, somehow exist or subsist simultaneously to be discriminated in this way; for the possible ones exist only as objects of thought. It is not clear to me, however, that it would so commit me, if I abjured 'ontology' of any kind, except in so far as it is a *Doppelgänger* of conceptual analysis. Why cannot I say that I distinguish *in thought* between worlds A and B by calling A actual, and that this means that it is the world in which I am, without being committed to saying that B is in some shadowy sense actual too? I should only be committed to this absurdity if to *think about B* already presupposed its actuality; but does it presuppose this? Into this question, however, I shall not go; for ethics can be done without ontology, and is more simply so done (1.2).

If this move were rejected, I should have a further recourse. The thesis of universalizability itself was established by arguments of a philosophical-logical sort (1.2, 1.6, 4.7; *FR* 2.2 ff.; *LM* 8.2, 10.3 f.). The most important of these consists in showing that a person who makes different moral judgements about cases which he admits to be identical in their non-moral universal properties encounters the same kind of incomprehension as is encountered by a logical inconsistency (for example a self-contradiction). If any dispute arises about precisely what properties are to count as universal for the purposes of the thesis, the same test can be applied again. For example, it is usually held that spatial and temporal properties do not count (because they cannot be defined without reference to an individual point of origin of the coordinate system); and they can be shown not to count by pointing out that the sort of logical incomprehension just described would arise if somebody treated the date (irrespective of what sorts of things happened on that or on related dates) as morally relevant; and similarly for the grid map reference (irrespective of what was at that or at related locations).

The same move can be made in the present case. If somebody says 'I ought to do it to him, but nobody ought to do it to me if I were in precisely his position with his preferences', and gives as his reason, not that he is he, nor that today is today, but that this is the actual case and that merely hypothetical, then, I claim, the same logical incomprehension would arise as if he had said either of those two other things. I am here appealing to our *linguistic* intuitions, being confident of my own, and confident that they are linguistic not moral (because they must be shared by anybody who understands the use of 'ought', whatever his moral opinions).

INTERPERSONAL COMPARISON

7.1 I hope in this chapter to set at rest some epistemological worries which will certainly have affected the reader in the course of the preceding chapters. Several of them have been the subject of a vast literature, and I shall not be so ambitious as to try to solve all the problems involved—only to indicate why I think they are soluble, at any rate to the extent of no longer being an obstacle to the acceptance of my argument. None of the epistemology required is moral epistemology; it is, rather, part of general epistemology. If there were problems that arose within moral epistemology (e.g. problems about how, *given* knowledge of the non-moral facts, we could then reason morally with assurance), then they would have to be dealt with much more fully, as forming part of the main subject matter of moral philosophy. But the problems I shall now be dealing with are not problems in moral philosophy at all; I am happy to leave them to my colleagues who know about them, provided that doubts about them do not impede the understanding of my own views.

All these problems concern our knowledge about other people's experiences. It is commonly objected to utilitarianism that it requires us to make comparisons between utilities to different people. The method I have myself been advocating may seem to be open to the same objection. It could be debated whether the comparison required is cardinal or merely ordinal; whether it needs to be quantifiable at all; and what precisely we are trying to compare. I shall answer the last question by fiat: what I am going to discuss is the interpersonal comparison of *degrees or strengths of preference*, because that is the kind of comparison I need for my own argument. I do not need to discuss anything else but this, because the method we are after turns out to be formulable in those terms, and does not need to mention pleasures or any other kind of utilities. The answers to the other questions will become apparent as we proceed.

It is worth saying right at the beginning that this is not a problem peculiarly for utilitarians. Those who think it is an easy objection to utilitarianism have not examined their own consciences. Any method of moral reasoning which gives any weight whatever to beneficence or non-maleficence has to cope with this problem. For example, Mr. Warnock (1971:30) and Sir David Ross (1930:21) are not utilitarians; but both admit duties or virtues of beneficence. To that extent, they ought, in their accounts of moral reasoning, to say how we would tell which of two acts would do the more good to other people. How else could we know that we were fulfilling the duty or exhibiting the virtue? The fact, if it is one, that there are other independent virtues and duties as well makes no difference to this requirement. Only a theory which allowed no place at all to beneficence or to respect for the interests of others could escape this demand. Anybody, therefore, who is tempted to bring up this objection against utilitarians should ask himself whether he is himself attracted by a theory which leaves out such considerations entirely?

7.2   It will be useful next to distinguish a number of elements within the problem of interpersonal comparison; for, as we shall see, the solution lies in dealing with these elements piecemeal, which is much more difficult if they are confused with one another. There is, first, the old philosophical problem of scepticism about other minds. How do I know there are any conscious experiences but my own and, if so, what they are? I shall obviously not be expected to deal with this here. It is sad that the vast amount of writing that has been devoted to the problem during this century has not produced any generally accepted solution. Many of his disciples think that Wittgenstein solved the problem; but I have not met any who could make clear to me what the solution was. I think it much more probable that we shall be driven back to some form of the old 'argument from analogy'; for, after all, it is tempting to say that we reasonably guess that beings so like us in all other respects are also like us in having similar conscious experiences under similar conditions. I shall not discuss the question further, but shall merely take it that its solution is so crucial to almost all parts of philosophy that it will not be held against my own theory in particular if I just *assume* that it can be solved.

A more pressing problem for me is that of how it is possible for me to speak meaningfully of my being in somebody else's situation to the extent required by the argument of ch. 5. For if all the properties of the situation in which I had to imagine myself, including the properties of the person in whose shoes I was putting myself, were so unlike those of myself and my present situation, would it any longer be *me*? (Taylor, 1965.) This problem has been solved, I think, by Professor Zeno Vendler in a very illuminating paper (1976). I will therefore do no more than restate briefly in my own words what I take to be his view.

We may start by admitting, but only for the sake of argument, that a lot of what would be said by an objector who raised this problem is correct. Let us concede, then, that it involves a contradiction to suppose that Jones, the torturer, might become, or turn into, the same person as Smith, his victim. Actually, since we have many different ways of identifying people, it makes perfectly good sense to say in such a case 'If Jones were Smith he would be suffering horribly'; but suppose that it does not. Perhaps, it might be said, Jones has an 'essence', and so has Smith, and if either lost his essence he would cease to be the same person, or even cease to be altogether. What these essences would consist in we need not inquire; perhaps being born at those times of those parents, perhaps in other conjunctions of properties. Admitting this does not stop us admitting that there are also non-essential properties of people: Jones might have had red hair instead of black, and been a foot taller than he is, and still have been Jones. But what we have to understand is that our argument does not require us to say, when reasoning with Jones in order to convince him that he ought to leave off torturing Smith, 'Suppose that Jones were Smith'. That, we may admit for the sake of argument, is to suppose something logically impossible.

We can even admit for the sake of argument that it is self-contradictory to suppose that Jones might be in Smith's precise situation (this being understood to include having precisely his personal characteristics and preferences). Rather, we ask him to suppose that *he* were, or to imagine *being*, in Smith's precise situation.

But can there be any difference between Jones imagining Jones being in Smith's precise situation, and Jones imagining being in Smith's precise situation; or between Jones saying 'If Jones were in Smith's precise situation, he would be suffering horribly', and his saying 'If I were in Smith's precise situation, I should be suffering horribly'? It is important to see that there is, although certainly 'I' and 'Jones' refer to the same person. It is not, that is to say, legitimate to argue that, since 'I' in Jones' mouth and 'Jones' in anybody's mouth refer to the same person, and since 'Jones might be in Smith's precise situation' is self-contradictory (as we have conceded), therefore 'I might be in Smith's precise situation', said by Jones, is self-contradictory. For, although Jones and Smith may have essences, I have none (*qua* myself, though I may have, on some views, an 'essence' *qua* Richard Hare), and Jones also could similarly and truly say 'I have none'. We may notice in passing the related, though not identical, linguistic fact that the bringing into use of the expression 'Jones' involves the ascription to Jones of some properties (not necessarily the same properties for all those who use them to identify Jones); but the bringing into use of the expression 'I' involves the ascription of no essential properties beyond that of being a person (and perhaps not even that, for one could put on one's stove as a warning 'I am hot' and the 'I' be readily understood as referring to the stove). So when

Jones and Smith both use the expression 'I' to refer to themselves, they use it synonymously, though with different references. 'I' is tied to no 'essence'.

So, as Vendler elegantly illustrates, putting myself in somebody else's shoes does not involve supposing myself to have simultaneously two incompatible sets of properties; it involves merely supposing that I might lose one set and acquire the other. But I doubt whether many will be convinced of this by my bald and brief explanation. Vendler's article should be read by anybody who is attracted by any objection of this sort to my method.

7.3　We may now turn from problems which have been discussed mainly by philosophers to some which have been of more interest to economists, and which I, as a philosopher, take up with some diffidence, because much of the literature on the subject is highly technical (see Baker, 1977: VI, 3.4; Arrow, 1963; Sen, 1970; Harsanyi, 1953, 1955). This group of problems is known under the name of 'the interpersonal commensurability of utilities'; and I advisedly say 'group', because there are more than one problem. And it is important to distinguish those with which it is incumbent on someone who thinks as I do to deal, from those which need not, so far as my contentions and arguments go, trouble me.

The distinction I have made between levels of thinking will help here. Some critics of utilitarianism have supposed that the utilitarian is committed, whenever faced with a particular moral problem, to doing an elaborate calculation of utilities, involving interpersonal comparisons, in order to arrive at the optimum choice. I have adopted the view that such calculations are in practice usually impossible and that to undertake them would often be dangerous. We do better to stick to well tried and fairly general principles. At the intuitive level of moral thinking, then, interpersonal comparisons are no great problem. Admittedly, if our prima facie principles include, as they certainly should, a principle of beneficence, we shall have in our intuitive thinking to estimate the amount of good or harm we are doing to various people; but this too can be, and is, done by appeal to fairly general predictive principles (also intuitive) about how much who will be hurt by what. We do not need to employ any felicific calculus to determine that knocking somebody over with a car will hurt him.

For the critical level of thinking the problem is greater. But we are not claiming that human beings can do that at all well. To archangels, who can do it perfectly, I have ascribed superhuman powers and superhuman knowledge, and there is no reason why this should not include knowledge of other people's states of mind. The most that human beings can ask for, when they are trying to do the best critical thinking they can, is some way of approximating, perhaps not at all fully, to the thought-processes of an archangel. And there is the further point that in selecting our prima facie principles by critical thinking, the first stage of the process needs to use only hypothetical cases, and we can assume as much knowledge as we need to about those without asking how we could get it. It is only when our archangel comes to the second stage, that of assigning probabilities to the occurrence of the cases in the actual world, that he will have to exercise his superior knowledge.

However, economists who have concerned themselves with this problem have treated it as a theoretical and not a practical one. Nobody supposes that in practice human beings will be able to find out all the facts about other people's preferences and their strengths which would be necessary for a secure answer to all moral questions. The problem has been seen as one of giving a *sense* to statements about others' preferences; and it has been thought that this cannot be done unless the truth-conditions of the statements are known. And this has been seen as involving the possession of some 'method of verification' of them. If we were facing philosophical sceptics about other minds, we should have at this point to ask whether and in what sense the 'verification theory of meaning' (now in such bad odour) is true. But we have excused ourselves already from the task of confronting the philosophical sceptics. Actually, the short answer to the problem about the *meaning* of statements about other people's states of mind is that terms like 'I' and 'you' have no *descriptive* content in the strict sense; that is to say, if you and I just changed places, the world would be no different in its universal properties. So the meaning of the *predicate* in 'You are in pain' is exactly the same as in 'I am in pain'; there is no difficulty in knowing what it means, and this sameness of meaning is indeed the reason why it is possible to teach the use of this predicate. I owe this point to an unpublished paper by Professor Vendler.

The problem of ordinality versus cardinality is more difficult. On the face of it it looks as if our method does not require us to be able to measure utilities in constant units or with a constant zero point. For it is enough if I, who am making a moral decision by critical thinking, can say 'Jones prefers outcome J_1 to outcome J_2 more than Smith prefers outcome S_2 to outcome S_1'. We do not have to be able to say how much more. This is because in our method of critical thinking we are not summing utilities, but, from an impartial point of view, which treats Jones' and Smith's equal preferences as of equal weight, forming our *own* preferences between the outcomes.

But, as Mr. Griffin and Professor Harsanyi have made clear to me, this way of proceeding introduces cardinality by the back door. It also makes possible the introduction of units of strength of preference. For if I can compare preferences in respect of strength, it is open to me to find pairs of preferences which are neither greater nor less than each other, i.e. which are equal. But if the preference for A over B is equal to that for B over C, it looks plausible to say that the preference for A over C is twice that for A over B; and then by using the preference for A over B as a unit of strength of preference, we shall be able, by more complex repetitions of the same sort of comparisons, to be able to set up a cardinal scale of strengths of preference, and a zero point (no preference either way).

If this were so, it would not trouble me. For objections to utilitarian theories which rely on the allegation that they require cardinal interpersonal comparisons all take the following form: utilitarianism requires cardinal comparisons; but these are impossible; so out with utilitarianism! But if the comparisons of strengths of preferences that I hope to justify sufficed in themselves to generate cardinal comparisons, then the second premiss of this argument would have to be abandoned, and utilitarianism would survive the assault. The same applies if any other method of cardinalization is independently shown to be viable. All we *require* for our method are comparisons of strengths of preferences. We do not have to be able to sum units of pleasure or happiness.

7.4 There are obvious analogies between other people's preferences and our own preferences in the future (i.e. those which *in* the future we *shall* or may have, not those which we *now* have *for* the future—in our previous terminology, then-for-then, not now-for-then preferences (5.6)). Even our own past preferences generate difficulties of the same sort. Suppose, for example, that I ask in retrospect, on returning from my holiday in Italy, whether I enjoyed the concert on Tuesday night more than I enjoyed the dinner on Wednesday night. This looks like an inquiry into summable pleasures, of the sort which I have said we do not require. So let us approach the question in a less ambitious way by asking whether, if I were going to have my time over again, I prefer that I should have the dinner or the concert, given that I cannot have both. I am not, needless to say, allowed to bring in extraneous considerations, such as the after-effects of the dinner, or the improvement in my musical education; I have to confine my attention to the actual experiences. Still, it does seem that, even in order to answer this simple question, I have to be able to think myself back into the states of mind I was in on the successive evenings. No amount of evidence about other choices to eat or to hear music would be *logically* sufficient (though it might be practically sufficient) to establish a preference now for one replayed scenario over another; for my tastes can, and do, change from one day to the next. And the same considerations will apply to the more complicated question of whether I prefer that dinner to that concert more than I prefer (also in retrospect) the walk up the mountain on Thursday to the visit to the mediaeval city on Friday.

Even in the case of experiences that we have actually had, and which we should surely be able to compare in this way if we can compare anything, it looks as if it can be done only by reducing past preferences to present ones. We imaginatively suppose that we could have the choice of having one of these experiences or the other, and form a preference *now*. But even in this simple case difficulties arise which have been noticed in the more troublesome cases of our own future preferences and other people's preferences.

One such difficulty is perhaps not a real one. This is the problem of how we can discount our own present values or tastes in making such a judgement about the past. It might be objected that if I form my present preference for the dinner over the concert in the light of my present values, tastes, or dispositions-to-prefer, the resulting preference will tell me nothing about my past states of mind; for even if I have these vividly before me, my present taste (perhaps I have got tired of Vivaldi) may tilt the balance and make me say that I prefer the dinner to the concert although in fact the concert was at the time enjoyed more. On the other hand, it might be said, if we seek to avoid this difficulty by banning all appeal to our own present tastes, how can we form a preference at all? For are not all preferences formed on the basis of tastes existing at the time? This objection, however, is easily seen to be mistaken. For in order to *form* preferences it is not necessary to have them already. We can acquire new tastes, coming to prefer things that we did not previously prefer; we can fall in love for the first time, and the second, and the *n*th, on each occasion *changing* our order of preference between companions; and we could not do this if we were stuck with our existing dispositions-to-prefer. If we were, we could never *start* having preferences.

The problem remains, however, of how we can be sure that our present preference correctly represents our past states of mind. Let us take an even simpler case. I always take sugar in my coffee, because I prefer it sweet. Presumably my lack of hesitation each morning at breakfast in putting half a teaspoon of sugar in my coffee owes something to my confidence that I shall like it that way; and this in turn must owe something to my recollection that I liked it that way on previous occasions. In terms of preferences, I predict that I shall prefer that amount of sugar to any other amount on the strength of remembering that I did prefer it so in the past. But if I cannot have any knowledge of my past preferences, how can I make such a prediction?

Without further labouring this point, I am going to take it that, even if we say nothing about other people's preferences, our whole governance of our lives depends on the solution of a problem of which knowledge of other people's preferences is a special case: the problem of truly and with confidence representing to ourselves experiences which are now absent; for all or nearly all preferences are between experiences, etc., at least one of which is absent. And there is no doubt that, philosophical scepticism aside, we have this confidence. However, I am not going, by relying just on this, to lay myself open to the sort of reproaches that I have been accustomed with tedious repetition to level against my intuitionist opponents. As I mentioned just now, there are levels of thinking in factual reasoning as well as in moral, and from the premiss that at the intuitive level we confidently make factual statements about absent experiences, it does not follow that we have any good reason for our confidence. There is need, here too, for critical thinking; and that, no doubt, is what the economists and others are engaged in.

Nevertheless, if we assume, as we are assuming, that philosophical scepticism about other minds can be disregarded, we may perhaps also assume, as part of the solution of that as yet unsolved problem, and of other unsolved problems raised by philosophical sceptics, that we are entitled sometimes to be confident in representing to ourselves the states of mind, including the preferences, of ourselves in the past, ourselves in the future, and other people. In the first case, we say that we do it by memory. In the second case, we do it by a combination of memory and induction, making the assumption that future experiences will be like those we remember having under similar conditions. Or (and this brings us to the third case) we may predict our own experiences on the basis of what others tell us about theirs. But more commonly and more basically we represent to ourselves the experiences of others by analogy with our own, judging that their situations are similar (someone has just hit his head on a low beam), their physiologies are similar (his skull has about the same dimensions as ours and his nerves are in roughly the same places), and that therefore their experiences will be similar (he will be liking it just about as much as we did).

I have used a simplified example to illustrate the theoretical point. There are, it need hardly be said, practical difficulties in getting to know the states of mind of other sentient beings, which increase with the remoteness of their experiences from ours. These difficulties are to be overcome by getting as closely acquainted as we can with their circumstances, verbal and other behaviour, anatomies, etc., and comparing them with our own; and this, in ordinary cases such as the one just sketched, we do not find difficult. But we are here concerned not with the practical, but with the theoretical problem. This is soluble, given a rejection of philosophical scepticism about other minds, in the way just outlined.

I do not feel obliged here, as I said, to argue for the validity of this kind of reasoning. I shall merely assume that it, or something like it, is in order, and shall go on to point out a consequence that follows from it, in conjunction with a thesis argued for in ch. 5. There we saw that to have knowledge of somebody else's motivations is *eo ipso* to

form the same motivations oneself with regard to hypothetical situations in which one would forthwith be in the
others' positions. To the extent that we lack such motivations of our own, we lack full knowledge of those of the
other people. If these two premises be granted, further
light can be shed on the problem of comparison. For they
enable us to reduce comparisons between other people's
preferences to comparisons between our own. Professor
Arrow (1977) has named this device 'extended sympathy'
and Professor Harsanyi 'extended preferences' (1977:54).
In a sense what I have said is a *petitio principii*, because we
have merely assumed the existence of a solution to the
philosophical problem about other minds, and are now
saying that *if* it were solved, its solution would bring with
it, without further premises beyond that argued for in ch.
5, a solution to the comparison-problem. But it may all the
same be helpful to point out this consequence.

7.5   If all this be granted, then we can say that in so far
as I fully represent to myself the strengths of other people's
preferences, I have preferences, myself now, regarding
what should happen to me were I in their positions with
their preferences. If I do this with two other people or
more, I can then compare the strengths of their preferences
by comparing the strengths of my own corresponding
ones. Thus, on these assumptions, the comparison problem would be solved. As before, I have to disregard entirely
my own antecedent preferences; the preferences which I
form have to consist entirely of replicas of the other
people's preferences.

A schematic illustration may help. I have to give a bun
either to Jones or to Smith, and Jones wants it more than
Smith. Let us call Jones-with-bun J_1, Smith-without-bun
S_1, Jones-without-bun J_2, and Smith-with-bun S_2. Jones
prefers J_1 to J_2 more than Smith prefers S_2 to S_1. Suppose
then that I put myself in their two positions in the two
outcomes, four positions in all. My choice is going to be
between J_1 plus S_1 (Jones-with-bun plus Smith-without-
bun) and J_2 plus S_2 (Jones-without-bun plus Smith-with-
bun). It is not necessary to imagine myself occupying the

four positions simultaneously; that would be asking too much. We might follow a suggestion of C. I. Lewis (1946:546 f.) and suppose that I have a choice between occupying J_1 and S_1 in random order and occupying J_2 and S_2 in random order. Clearly, given the assumed strengths of Smith's and Jones' preferences, my own preference will be for the first of these alternatives, and I shall, in accordance with the method of ch. 6, say that that is the one I ought to choose. An alternative would be to suppose myself to have a choice between having an equal chance of being in J_1 and S_1, and having an equal chance of being in J_2 and S_2. This has the advantage that we do not have to consider any effects which might arise from the fact that I am to be in *both* positions (though these effects are not hard to discount).

In estimating the preferences of others, and my own future preferences, I have, then, to keep my own antecedent present preferences out of the reckoning. This does not mean that my own preferences play no part in moral thinking. The argument of ch. 6 required us to be impartial between our own and other people's preferences, not altruistic in its correct sense of giving *more* weight to the preferences of others. We have to treat everybody as one, including ourselves: to do unto others *as* we wish they should do to us (sc. in their situations with their preferences), and love our neighbours *as* (not more than) ourselves. We get no extra weight for our own preferences because we are doing the moral thinking, but they get equal weight with those of others in so far as we are affected parties (H 1976a:120). This applies, as before, to *critical* thinking; for our intuitive thinking we might well select some altruistic principles, because they will keep us away from the more seductive vice of selfishness (Aristotle, 1107^{b}1). We may also select some principles requiring partiality to those near to us (8.3). But critical thinking, which will favour the inculcation of intuitions incorporating these departures from impartiality, is itself impartial; it favours them because their inculcation will be for the best for all considered impartially.

8

LOYALTY AND EVIL DESIRES

8.1 The two remaining chapters of this part will be devoted to answering some objections commonly made against utilitarianism, which might also be, and have been, encountered by my own theory. Since nearly all these objections employ the same basic move, originating in the same misunderstanding, it may be helpful if I first explain the move and the answer to it in quite general terms. I shall do this in the form of some simple instructions to students, first on how to manufacture objections of this sort, and then on how to demolish them. I hope thereby to forewarn and forearm them against anybody who tries to waste too much of their time with such objections; the answer to them all is the same, and one exercise in dealing with them is enough.

Suppose then that you are in a disputation with a utilitarian. Your object should be to enlist the sympathies of your audience on your side by showing that the utilitarian is committed to views which nearly everybody finds counterintuitive. What you have to do, therefore, is to find some moral opinion which nearly everybody will agree with, and bring utilitarianism into conflict with it. It is not necessary to choose for this purpose an opinion that can be defended by argument; any widely held prejudice will do. I have heard this kind of objection based on premises like 'Surely any theory is absurd which makes cruelty to animals as wicked as the same degree of cruelty to humans'; and no doubt in earlier centuries 'blacks' and 'whites' would have done as well. But obviously it is better if the opinion is a defensible one; the objection will then seem even more plausible.

Having selected your favoured received opinion, you can then proceed to bring utilitarianism into conflict with it in the following way. You find some example, rather simply described, in which, on an obvious interpretation of utilitarianism (and nearly all the versions of it can be made susceptible to this treatment, except for some versions of rule-utilitarianism which are highly implausible on other grounds) the utilitarian is committed to prescribing an act which almost everybody will agree is wrong. Give your case as much verisimilitude as you can. Professional opponents of utilitarianism are not always as careful as they should be about this. Sometimes they use extremely jejune examples, thinking the game to be a push-over, so that they need not take too much trouble with them. But it is better if the case is something which your audience can be got to believe really could happen. Thus you will seem to have established a knock-down counterinstance to the utilitarian theory; it will have been shown to require us to say some act is right when we all know it to be wrong.

8.2 Now suppose by contrast that you are on the opposite side in the disputation. How will you answer the objection? First of all you must be quite clear what version of utilitarianism you are defending. Naturally I strongly recommend that you should choose the version defended in this book; for if you have understood what has been said in it so far, especially about the separation of levels, you will not find it hard to see the weaknesses in your opponent's position. Indeed, your first move should be to ask him what level of thinking he is talking about; for on this will depend what moves in the game are permissible, and in particular what examples can properly be adduced. In any case, if he has never heard of the difference between levels, mention of it will put him off his stroke.

Briefly, if he is talking about the critical level, he is allowed to bring up any examples he pleases however fantastic; but at that level no appeals to received intuitions are allowed, because the function of critical thinking is to judge the acceptability of intuitions, and therefore it cannot without circularity invoke intuitions as premises. If, on the other hand, he is talking about the intuitive level, he is allowed to appeal to any intuitions he thinks the audience will agree with, pending their examination by critical thinking, but must be very careful what examples he uses. For his audience's intuitions are the product of their moral upbringings (2.2), and, however good these may have been, they were designed to prepare them to deal with moral situations which are likely to be encountered (3.2); there is no guarantee at all that they will be appropriate to unusual cases. Even in the unusual cases, no doubt, the usual moral feelings will be in evidence; but they provide no argument.

The dispute is likely to resolve itself, therefore, into one about the admissibility and the treatment of examples. To illustrate this, suppose that your opponent's case is the following: there are in a hospital two patients, one needing for survival a new heart and the other new kidneys; a down-and-out who is known to nobody and who happens to have the same tissue-type as both the patients strays in out of the cold. Ought they not to kill him, give his heart and kidneys to the patients, and thus save two lives at the expense of one? The utilitarian is supposed to have to say that they ought; the audience is supposed to say that they ought not, because it would be murder. Let us suppose that your opponent manages to get the audience to treat murder as a descriptive, not a secondarily evaluative, word (1.5), and thus to call the statement that it would be murder a purely factual one, which can be established prior to any judgement that it would be wrong. I have simplified the case a little from the way it has sometimes been presented in the literature (H 1978c:164), because the complications will not affect the moves we shall be making.

On this example you have to mount a two-pronged attack. If we are to do intuitive thinking, the matter is fairly simple. It *is* murder, and *would* therefore be wrong. A utilitarian does not have to dissent from this verdict at the intuitive level. If he has been well brought up (and in particular if he has been brought up by a sound critical utilitarian thinker) he will have that intuition, and it is a very good thing, from the utilitarian point of view, that he will have it. For just think what would be the consequences of a moral education which contained no prohibition on murder!

Your opponent will now object that although on the utilitarian view it is a good thing for people to have these intuitions or feelings, it also follows from that view that they ought to overcome and act contrary to them in cases like this, in which, *ex hypothesi*, it is for the best to do so. Let us ask, then, whether the doctors in the hospital ought to do this if they are utilitarians. It will turn upon their estimate of the *probability* of hitting off the act which is for the best by so doing. The crucial words are, of course, '*ex hypothesi*'; for your opponent has constructed his example with the express purpose of making the murder the act which will have the best consequences. You must not allow him simply to *assume* that this is so; he has to convince the audience, not just that it really could be so in a real-life situation, but that it could be known to be so by the doctors with a high degree of probability. For utilitarianism, as a method of choosing the most rational action (the best bet for a utilitarian) in a moral dilemma of this sort, requires them to maximize the *expectation* of utility (i.e. preference-satisfaction); and since, if they get it wrong, the consequences will be pretty catastrophic, the doctors have to be very sure that they are not getting it wrong. There is perhaps no need to go into any technicalities of games-theory to establish this point, though a full account would need to contain a method of weighing combinations of probabilities with utilities against one another, by asking which combination one would prefer, after exposure to logic and the facts.

It is fairly obvious that this high degree of probability will not be forthcoming in many actual situations, if any at all. Have the doctors checked on the down-and-out's connexions or lack of them? (How? By consulting the police records, perhaps! But a colleague of my psychiatrist sister once wrote in his notes, about a dishevelled individual brought in off the streets very late at night by the police, 'Has delusion that he is a high-ranking civil servant', and it turned out that he was in fact a *very* high-ranking civil servant.) Have they absolute confidence in the discretion and support of all the nurses, porters, mortuarists, etc., who will know what has happened? Add to this the extreme unlikelihood of there being no other way of saving these patients, if they can be saved at all, and it will be evident that your opponent is not going to get much help out of this example, once it is insisted that it has to be fleshed out and given verisimilitude.

But perhaps that was not his intention. Perhaps, that is to say, he all along intended the example to be a dummy. Is he not allowed, after a brief introduction of the example to give its general shape, to skip the details and simply *posit* that it is a case where murder would be for the best? The audience, which is probably prejudiced against utilitarians anyway, will have no difficulty in imagining that the details could be filled in in a way that would suit his case and damage yours. But you must not let him get away with this. If we are talking about intuitive thinking in a real-life sort of situation, the example needs to be a real-life sort of example.

If, on the other hand, he claims the right to introduce any *logically possible* example, then he is exposed to the other prong of your attack. For then he has put himself beyond the range of intuition and cannot appeal to it. Critical thinking can certainly deal with such cases, and will give a utilitarian answer. If he tailors the case so that the utilitarian answer is that murder is the right solution, then that is the answer he will get. What you have to say to the audience is that this does not in the least matter, because such cases are not going to occur. This has two important consequences for the argument. The first is that allowing that in such a case murder would be justified commits us to no prescription to murder in the actual world, in which we have to live our moral lives. The second is a generalization of the first: the prima facie principles which the critical thinker will select for use in this world can also, and will, include a ban on murder, because for the selection of these principles this peculiar case, since it will not occur, is irrelevant.

Your opponent may say 'Are there not some cases occurring in real life, albeit rarely, in which murder is justified on utilitarian grounds?' To which you should reply that he has not produced any, but that if he really did find one, we should have to do some critical thinking on it because it would be clearly so unusual as to be beyond the range of our intuitions. If we then found that murder really was justified in that case, we still should not have shown that the rational moral agent would commit the murder; for he would be unlikely to have sufficient evidential grounds for saying that it was the right act. But, giving your opponent everything that he asks for, if he did actually have sufficient evidence (a very unlikely contingency), murder would *in that case* be justified; though even then the agent in question, if he had been well brought up, might not do it, because it would go so much against all his moral feelings, which in a good man are powerful. So, owing to being a good man, he might fail to do the right act. If he did bring himself to do it, it would haunt him for the rest of his life. But until your opponent produces actual cases, you should not let yourself be troubled overmuch with fictional ones. If the actual cases are produced, you will probably find that the critical discussion of them will leave you and the audience at one, provided that the discussion is serious.

8.3 We are now in a position to apply the same technique to some more genuine problems. Let us take first the objection commonly made to utilitarianism that it does not allow us to give any weight to the duties usually thought to exist towards particular persons, or to ties of affection and loyalty which bind us to them but not to mankind in general (Rescher, 1975; H 1979b:141). For example, it is usually held that we have special duties to our spouses and children, and ought to have greater affection and loyalty to them than to total strangers, and so seek their good more earnestly. Similar things are said about the relation between a doctor and his patient, or a teacher and his pupil. And similar things *used* to be universally, and are still quite widely, accepted about that between a citizen and his country. I have heard the same argued about the loyalty of a worker to his union.

These last two instances might make us pause before proceeding on the assumption that all commonly upheld loyalties can be used as a stick to beat utilitarians with. They show how palpable, and how dubious, is the appeal to intuition when people say that utilitarianism treats everybody's preferences as of equal weight (e.g. those of my children and other people's children), and therefore has to be rejected as giving no weight to these feelings of special affection which we all think it a good thing to encourage. We have first to be sure that, in a particular example, it *is* a good thing to encourage these feelings. Even family loyalties provide examples of extremely various intuitions. In some countries it is considered wrong if someone who has obtained a position of power does not use it to advance the interests of the members of his family; in others this is called nepotism and thought corrupt. And even in Britain there is dispute about whether it is right for a well endowed father to try to get the best possible education for his children by sending them to expensive schools which others cannot afford.

This should warn us that even where intuitions are all in agreement, they should not be taken for granted; it needs to be established by critical thought which of them ought, in our present circumstances, to be fostered. Anybody who asks himself whether, and in what sense, he ought to bring up his children to be patriotic will see the force of this question. So let us proceed as before and ask our anti-utilitarian objector what level of thinking he is talking about, intuitive or critical. In order to make it easy for him, let us allow him to choose an example in which nearly everybody will agree that the loyalty in question is a good thing. A mother, say, has a new-born child and her maternal feelings make her provide for this child, but they do not, or not to anything like the same degree, impel her to provide for other people's children. Ought a utilitarian to condemn this partiality?

At the intuitive level we all think that the mother is to be praised, in all normal circumstances (barring a few extreme radical advocates of communes, and Plato). Given our two-level structure, there is nothing in this that a utilitarian need object to. *If* the intuition is one that ought to be inculcated (and this cannot be determined without critical thinking), the most likely way of doing the right thing in normal circumstances will be to follow the intuition. If this were not so, then the intuition would not be the one which ought to be inculcated. If we ascend to the critical level and ask why it ought to be, the answer is fairly obvious. If mothers had the propensity to care equally for all the children in the world, it is unlikely that children would be as well provided for even as they are. The dilution of the responsibility would weaken it out of existence. Our traditional upbringing has taken account of this. And evidently Evolution (if we may personify her) has had the same idea; there are, we are told, a great many of these particular loyalties and affections which are genetically transmitted, and have no doubt favoured the survival of the genes which transmit them (Singer, 1981).

8.4 The general lines of the utilitarian answer to this objection should by now be clear. *In so far* as the intuitions are desirable ones, they can be defended on utilitarian grounds by critical thinking, as having a high acceptance-utility; if they can be so defended, the best bet, even for an act-utilitarian, will be to cultivate them and follow them in all normal cases; if he cultivates them seriously, or has had them cultivated for him by those who brought him up, all the associated moral feelings will be present, but will provide no argument whatever against utilitarianism. Unlike intuitionism, it is actually able to *justify* the intuitions, where they can be justified.

Faced with this argument the anti-utilitarian will produce examples in which we would all have the intuitions, but in which, he asks us to suppose, the utilitarian would have to prescribe that we acted contrary to them. This would be because in the particular cases sufficient information is assumed to be available to show that the intuitively right act would not be for the best. To take a pasteboard example with which I was once confronted by Professor Bernard Williams on television: you are in an air crash and the aircraft catches fire, but you have managed to get out; in the burning plane are, among others, your son and a distinguished surgeon who could, if rescued, save many injured passengers' lives, to say nothing of those whose lives he would save in his subsequent career. You have time to rescue only one person.[1]

It is hard to make Williams' example realistic. How do you know he is so distinguished a surgeon—perhaps he was only shooting a line when you struck up an acquaintance in the departure lounge? Has he got his tools with him, and can he do any more for the injured people than the first aid which the crew are trained to give (which probably prescribes keeping them warm and immobile and giving some common drugs which, we hope, they managed to extract from the aircraft)? How promising is your son's future (he can probably look forward to a greater span of it than the surgeon)? However, setting aside all these minor points, we find that you have a very strong feeling that you ought to rescue your son and let the surgeon burn. But what does this show?

It would take a very hardened intuitionist to think that it shows that to rescue your son is your undoubted duty. You almost certainly will rescue your son. But that is because you have (rightly from the critical utilitarian point of view) been brought up to attach dominant importance to these

---

[1] Godwin's example (1793:II, 2) of Fénelon's chambermaid's daughter, who has to choose between saving the Archbishop and saving her mother from a fire, has greater verisimilitude, because she may be presumed to have known Fénelon well. But if the archbishop really was such a paragon, perhaps it would be right to save him, as Godwin implies; the fact that it would go against the grain is hardly material. (In a later edition the female characters change their sexes to male.)

family loyalties. Of course no upbringing takes into account such rare cases as this (they are not what those who influenced you were preparing you for, nor would evolution be affected by them). To be in an air crash of any sort is, fortunately, a statistically very rare experience; to be in one in which one has the opportunity to rescue anybody is rarer still; to be in one in which one can rescue precisely one person and no more is hardly to be expected. So you come to this unhappy experience entirely unprepared for it. Your intuitions were simply not designed to cope with it. However, you do have the strong moral feelings and will probably act on them in the split second which is all you have in which to decide. And who is to blame you? Probably in a situation of complete uncertainty and panic it is the rational thing to do. The fraudulence of the example consists in suggesting that you can at one and the same time be in this emergency situation, and do the leisured critical thinking which would be necessary in order to justify you in going against your intuitions.

Undoubtedly critics of utilitarianism will go on trying to produce examples which are both fleshed out and reasonably likely to occur, and also support their argument. I am prepared to bet, however, that the nearer they get to realism and specificity, and the further from playing trains—a sport which has had such a fascination for them— the more likely the audience is, on reflection, to accept the utilitarian solution. I am thinking of their examples in which trolleys hurtling down the line out of control have to be shunted into various alternative groups of unfortunate people. I have myself, when helping to build a railway, seen trolleys run out of control, and therefore find the unrealism of the examples very obvious. The point is that one has no time to think what to do, and so relies on one's immediate intuitive reactions; but these give no guide to what critical thinking would prescribe if there were time for it. But, personal experience aside, I have done quite a lot of work on serious practical problems in medicine, war, politics, urban planning and the like, and have never come across any actual example in which this kind of anti-utilitarian argument was in the least convincing.

8.5 Before we leave the subject of loyalty it is worth while pointing out one unrelated mistake that is commonly made. Sometimes it is suggested, as an argument, not against utilitarianism, but against the universal prescriptivism on which I have sought to found it, that duties to particular individuals can exist which are not owed to any other individuals however similar in their universal properties. For example, it is said that I may have duties to my mother which I do not have to anybody else's mother however similar. To take an even clearer example which I have not seen in the literature, I have a duty to see to it that my own promises are fulfilled, but not anybody else's. These are said to be moral duties resting on principles which have to contain references to individuals, and this is held to impugn the universalizability of moral judgements.

This objection results from a logical confusion: that between individual constants and bound individual variables (H 1955). The principle that for all x, if x has made a promise, x ought to see that it is fulfilled, is as universal a principle as any; and so is the principle that for all x and y, if y is the mother of x, x ought to do certain sorts of things for y. No individual constant appears in them, and therefore moral judgements which rest on them are universalizable. It is surprising how seductive this confusion has been.

8.6 Another objection of the sort we are considering in this chapter is based on our common distinction between good and evil desires. We have, following Brandt, given some account of how *irrational* preferences might be adjusted in the light of logic and the facts (5.6). But we have done nothing to show that preferences commonly thought to be *immoral* could be similarly treated. A different move is needed to cope with this problem, which in another form troubled the classical utilitarians: John Stuart Mill's rather unhappy discussion of higher and lower pleasures is an instance (1861:ch. 2). But not all the examples adduced are of the same kind. Here, to start with, is an easy kind to demolish. According to the utilitarians, it is said, we should have to give as much weight to the pleasures or preferences of the Marquis de Sade as to those of Mother Teresa. The fact that the former likes to torture people, and the latter wants nothing so much as to supply the needs of the poor, should count for nought; a preference is a preference and weighs in the utilitarian calculation purely in proportion to its strength.

As before, if we are speaking of the intuitive level, we do have the intuitions which are being appealed to, and the utilitarian could give, at the critical level, good reasons why they should be encouraged. Obviously, the more people there are like Mother Teresa (within reason) and the fewer like the Marquis, the better. So if we have been brought up successfully by thoughtful utilitarians, these are the intuitions we shall have. If it is alleged that the intuitions and the moral feelings that go with them should be suppressed in particular cases where this would maximize preference-satisfaction, we have to ask what these cases would be, and how likely they would be to occur. Professor Amartya Sen (1979:473) has an example in which a morose and sadistic policeman gets so much pleasure (his only pleasure) out of torturing another character whom he calls the romantic dreamer that the latter's pain is more than compensated for in the utilitarian calculation. The dreamer, it appears, does not all that much mind being tortured (but if so, would it not be frustrating rather than pleasurable for the policeman to see him lying there happily on the rack?).

It is fairly obvious that no real case like this will occur. So, as before, nothing in the real world is going to be affected by having a method of *critical* moral thinking which allows one to say that *if* it occurred, the torturing should be done; at least, no harm would come of it unless the existence of this logical possibility were allowed to weaken our hold upon the prima facie principle which condemns cruelty. But if this did happen, it would be in contravention of the method, which forbids us, when

selecting prima facie principles, to attend to cases which
are not going to occur.

It may now be suggested that the case could be made
more difficult for the utilitarian by supposing that there
were not one but thousands of sadists, who could be, in
sum, given quite a lot of pleasure by torturing some
unfortunate victims quite badly. This example is not all
that fanciful; the Romans, though probably not many of
them were sadists in the narrow sexual sense, actually had
this kind of entertainment, and so did our own nearer
ancestors, except that the victims were bears not humans. I
say nothing of foxhunting and bullfighting and the like
which go on to this day. Ought the utilitarian not to
commend what happened in the Roman arenas?

The argument is plausible but fallacious. For what
ought to be done, on any theory including the utilitarian,
depends on the alternatives to doing it. It would be absurd
to suggest that there was no other way in which the Roman
populace could get its pleasures. The right thing to have
done from the utilitarian point of view would have been to
have chariot races or football games or other less atrocious
sports; modern experience shows that they can generate
just as much excitement. Mass sadism does occur, perhaps;
but it does not have to. It is in accordance with utilitarian
critical thinking to recommend the adoption of prima facie
principles which forbid its indulgence and encourage less
harmful pleasures. If we all had the right intuitions (the
ones which a wise critical thinker would seek to inculcate)
we would condemn such practices unhesitatingly. There
need therefore be no conflict between utilitarianism and
received opinion over this kind of example.

8.7   A somewhat more difficult kind of example is that
in which the pleasure or preference-satisfaction in question is not harmful to anybody, like that of the sadist, but
just repugnant to many of us. In the nineteenth century the
pleasures of deviant sex would have served as an example;
the fact that, if the pleasures cause no harm to anybody,
this is a less immediately convincing example nowadays is

in itself significant. We have seriously to ask ourselves what pleasures ought to be condemned; and critical thinking can supply the answers. A handier example for the anti-utilitarian is the so-called 'pleasure machine' (Smart, 1973:18 and refs.). This device is supposed, by electrical stimulation of the brain or other means, to give us unalloyed pleasure for so long as we keep pressing the button, without any adverse side- or after-effects. It is suggested that utilitarians would have to recommend the manufacture of large numbers of such machines, so that we could all have almost continuous pleasure operating them, taking just enough time off in turn to look after the machines, the electricity and food supply, and other necessities.

It is important here that our variety of utilitarianism is not formulated in terms of pleasure. The question really is whether, looking forward to a time when such devices become available, and putting ourselves into the shoes of those who could use them, we *prefer* a life for ourselves plugged into the machines to one devoted to pursuits now considered normal and enjoyable; and, whatever answer we give to this question, whether the answer is rational. I have, following the usual form of the argument, represented it as an all-or-nothing choice. Actually, I prefer that the machines should be available for occasional use (perhaps when I was feeling very depressed, or faced a very bleak future, as an alternative to suicide), but hope that I should be strong-minded enough to use them sparingly.

Is this a rational preference, or is it too much influenced by my existing attitudes, which ought to be discounted in such a decision (7.4)? Or is it simply that I lack knowledge of what it would be like to be on the machine, and so do not acquire the present preferences that such knowledge would bring with it? This does not much matter for the present argument. For if most people have the same existing preferences as I have, this readily explains why they find any suggestion that we should hook ourselves up to the machines for most of our waking hours repellent and counterintuitive. So it is open to a utilitarian to reply to the objection, that he understands very well why people say what they do, but that this does not provide a reliable answer to the question of what they would 'say if they were fully informed and rational.

Perhaps this hesitant answer is all that can be given at the present time. But I should be surprised if, when the machines became available, people did prefer a life hooked up to them; they would, I think, find it impossible to make the changes in their genetic make-up which would be necessary for adjusting to such a life. Perhaps we should have to do some genetic engineering as well, or at least massive indoctrination. As we saw (5.6), preferences can change; so the question is, Would it be rational to seek to change them? If I fully represented to myself what being on the machine would be like if my preferences changed appropriately, should I not rationally decide to set about changing them? Since I do not know enough about what it *would* be like, and since the example is in general so underdescribed, I am unable to answer this question; on certain assumptions I might rationally prefer to attempt the preference-change, on others not. But at any rate there is no difficulty in accounting for our present *intuitions*.

8.8   Science fiction aside, what are we to say about the pushpin-poetry question that troubled Mill (1861:ch. 2; cf. Bentham, 1825:III, ch. 1)? Are the preferences of those capable of only the grosser (but harmless) pleasures to have the same weight as those of their more refined contemporaries? Can we justify the reservation of funds for opera houses and programmes on television for the better-educated minority, which could have been diverted in order to increase the supply of mass entertainment? The question is a hot one politically, but perhaps a sane utilitarian solution can be found.

We are committed by the formality of our method to a Benthamite answer to the basic question: equal preferences count equally, whatever their content. This is because the only question the method allows us to ask is, What shall we rationally universally prescribe, or from an impartial standpoint prefer, if we are fully informed and make no logical mistakes? There is no place here for discrimination, at the critical level, between pleasures or preferences because of their content. We are not allowed to bring in intuitions that such and such pleasures are more worth while. But it can be argued even so that the 'higher pleasures' deserve some protection. To at least a great many people who are able to enjoy them, they afford *more* enjoyment than the modern equivalents of pushpin, so that the quantity of pleasure is *not* equal. So these people, at any rate, will prefer the higher pleasures. This step in Mill's argument is correct, and does not require him to disagree with Bentham.

Moreover, if the percentage of such people in the population were to be increased by better education, utility over the foreseeable future would also be increased, on the assumption, not only that the better educated people will get more pleasure, minded as they are, from Bach than from pop music, but that they will get more pleasure from Bach than they would have got if they had never known anything but pop music. I think this a not absurd assumption to make. Such a line of reasoning might lead us to the conclusion that, putting ourselves impartially in the places of all, now and in the future, who would be affected by such a decision, we would prefer to preserve what we have inherited of these civilized arts and try to get a bigger audience for them. This can be done at the cost of an amount of money which, if diverted to mass entertainment instead, would provide no noticeable addition to the present ample supply. Technological improvements (opera and ballet on television, video tapes, etc.) will reduce the cost and increase the market. So we can hope that if those responsible for these matters can hold the philistines off, preference-satisfaction will in the long run be increased overall.

The basic move in all these arguments is to show that, even if preferences are given weight in proportion to their strengths and regardless of their content, a sound critical thinker, in the actual state of the world, will come up with prima facie principles for general use which accord with most of our intuitions. Not all of them, perhaps. Maybe those who think that the desires of homosexuals are inherently evil and should be utterly discounted or given negative weight will have, if they do some careful critical thinking, to abandon this intuition. But in general critical thinking will result in prima facie principles which discriminate quite sharply between good and evil desires, and between higher and lower pleasures, even though at the critical level no discrimination is allowed on grounds of content. This is because, in the world as it is, the encouragement of good desires and higher pleasures will maximize preference-satisfaction as a whole in the long term, even when preference-satisfaction is assessed in an impartial and content-indifferent way.

9

RIGHTS AND JUSTICE

9.1 In the preceding chapter we dealt with some of the easier objections that have commonly been made against utilitarianism, and are likely to be made against my own theory, on the score of counterintuitiveness. We saw that the counterintuitiveness is indeed there, in the examples that are usually adduced; but that it is to be accounted for by the fact that our intuitions, if we have been well brought up, are schooled to deal with the sorts of cases we are likely to meet in real life, and may well give answers in unusual cases which conflict with what an archangel would decide. However, we would normally be acting rationally if we followed the intuitions, because of the dangers inherent in our human situation: our lack of information and our proneness to self-deception.

In this chapter we shall be dealing in the same way with two other objections of this sort which at first sight look more difficult, those concerned with justice and with rights. Besides the theoretical importance these questions have for the dispute between the utilitarians and their critics, they also clearly have a very powerful bearing on practical issues. Many of the vexed problems of national and international politics, including some of the most bitter and violent, would be nearer a solution if these matters were better understood. For the contending parties are often fighting for what they think are their just rights; and if we could find a way of arguing which would enable them to agree on what these were, an accommodation would be more easily reached. This could be the philosopher's contribution to world peace, though it would be optimistic to hope that it will be taken up very quickly.

9.2 Since the notion of justice is the more complex, we will deal with rights first. We have, initially, to get out of the way some complications which do not affect the argument, but will confuse us if we do not deal with them. First of all, there is thought to be some connexion between the notions of rights and of obligations, and between both and such other moral concepts as 'ought', 'right' (adjective), 'wrong' (adjective, noun, and verb), and in particular 'just'. If a person's rights are, as he thinks, infringed, he will be likely to complain that he has suffered an injustice, that he has been wronged, that a wrong has been done to him, that what has been done to him was wrong (not right), and ought not to have been done. And it is usually held that if somebody has a right (at any rate of the second and third sorts to be mentioned shortly) somebody else has a corresponding obligation.

It might at first sight be thought that all rights are based upon justice, and that the infringement of a right is always an injustice. This, if it were so, would simplify our argument; for I am going to deal in some detail with the concept of justice, and it would be convenient to be able to effect a simple translation of statements about rights into statements containing the word 'just', and thereafter treat the problem of rights as solved. But unfortunately it is not so, except in an extremely wide sense of 'just'. We shall see that there is such a sense. Those who think that all moral virtues can be subsumed under either charity or justice have to be using the word 'just' in such a wide way. But confusion would result if we used it so here, before distinguishing the senses of 'just'. Certainly in most ordinary senses of the words one may have a right infringed without suffering an injustice. I have a right to walk along the footpath through my neighbour's farm, which is a 'public right of way'; but if he comes out with a shotgun and orders me off, I shall not naturally complain that he has acted *unjustly*, but rather that he has failed to fulfil an *obligation* to allow me to pass without let or hindrance. To this notion, therefore, we must turn.

Philosophers sometimes make a distinction between its being the case that I ought to do something, and my having an obligation to do it. Others simply use the noun 'obligation' and the verbs 'obliged' and (in American usage) 'obligated' as syntactical variants of 'ought', so that, for example, 'I am obligated to' means just 'I ought to'. Examples like the following are adduced by the first party: if somebody is stranded by the roadside on a dirty night and asks me for a ride, it makes sense to say that I ought to give him one, but have no obligation to. It will be simplest, and will not affect our argument, if I hedge on this question and allow that there are wider and narrower senses of 'obligation' in current, or at least in philosophical, use, but use the narrower sense in what follows, unless otherwise indicated. The notion of a right is tied to that of an obligation in this narrower sense, not in the wider. It makes sense, similarly, to say that the stranded person has no right to a ride, though I ought to give him one.

The relation of rights to obligations is, however, confused by an ambiguity, well known since the work of Wesley Hohfeld (1923:36 ff.), in the notion of a right. It is not perhaps an oversimplification to say that there are three distinct senses of 'a right'. In the first of these I have a right to do something if I have no obligation not to do it. For example, I have a right to get myself elected to some body by the means which the rules for elections to that body allow. Equally, anybody else has the right to stop me, if he can, by advancing his own candidature, again in accordance with the rules. In this sense a right entails no obligation, but only the absence of one. In the second sense (which was that used in the 'right of way' case just mentioned), I have a right if others have obligations not to stop me. My right to get myself elected is not of this second sort. It is true that I have, in the second sense, a right to *try* to get myself elected (others have obligations not to stop me trying). But my right in the first sense is a right to get myself elected, not just to try. If I succeed and take my seat, I shall be in breach of no obligation; but nobody has an obligation not to stop me succeeding. In a third sense, I have a right if others (it is not always clear who) have obligations positively to see to it that I can do or have that to which I have the right. In this sense we speak of a right to equal educational opportunities, or to work, or to enough to eat. A possibility of confusion arises between this sense and the second, because where there is a right in the second sense, it is generally agreed that governments have an obligation to see to it that the right is preserved, by making appropriate laws and enforcing them. But the senses are distinct; it is not self-contradictory to say that I have an obligation not to interfere with a person's doing something, and that therefore he has a right to do it in the second sense, but that nobody has any obligation to stop me interfering, so that he has no right in the third sense.

9.3 But to get this matter clear we have now to distinguish between legal and moral rights, and between the corresponding obligations. Legal rights are the easier notion, because it is easier to say how we would establish that somebody had legal rights of these three sorts. Legislatures exist to make laws, and courts to interpret and apply them. There are complications here which jurists discuss. But in principle there is a decision-procedure for determining what the law is in a particular case. All societies which have laws have 'rules of recognition' (Hart, 1961:92) whereby they decide what the laws are. The status of these rules raises difficulties which bring the case of legal rights closer to that of moral rights (H 1967); but into these difficulties I shall not now enter.

The trouble with moral rights is that there seems to be no such decision-procedure. That is why disputes about rights are so intractable; all the difficult disputes, like that about 'women's rights', arise in cases where a moral right is being claimed, not a legal right in the strict sense. If people who campaign for women's rights were thinking of existing legal rights, they could go to court instead of demonstrating; the question, however, is one of what the law morally ought to be, not what it is. However, the problem of moral rights is not quite so difficult as it looks. If it is a feasible project, as I think it is, to produce a way of reasoning about moral questions in general, and if we could find a way of reducing questions about moral rights to moral questions of some tractable sort, we should have solved our particular problem in solving the general one.

A word should perhaps be said at this point about the concept of natural rights, which is apt to create perplexities in this area. This concept, like that of natural law, dates from a time when law and morality were not distinguished so carefully as for clarity they should be. Without detailed argument, for which there is no room here, I will say baldly that everything which people have wished to express in terms of natural law and natural rights (and many of these things are worth saying) can be much more clearly expressed in terms of morality, i.e. in terms of what the law morally ought to be. Appeals to natural rights and the natural law are really appeals to what legislators and courts ought to make the law and treat as law. The advantage of sticking to this terminology is that we shall then be able to use our method of moral reasoning in order to determine what, in particular, legislators and courts ought to do. Unless we clarify matters thus, we shall, instead of asking what the law ought to be, be led into the dead end of trying to decide what the natural law *really* is. The result of this is to throw us back on our own intuitions (in effect, on our moral intuitions), which are bound to vary from one party to another, without recourse to the critical thinking that would help us settle our differences. For it is obvious that those who appeal to the natural law and natural rights are relying entirely on the intuitions they contingently have as to what these are.

9.4 We have achieved, following Hohfeld, an account of rights in terms of obligations. We have also distinguished legal obligations and rights (which are what the legislature has determined and the courts will enforce) from moral obligations and rights (which can only be established by a quite different procedure). So if we could link up the notion of a moral obligation, in the narrow sense, with the moral concepts (especially 'ought' and

'must') which are somewhat better understood, the particular problem of moral rights would be on the way to
solution.

The gap here is between the general notions 'ought' and
'must' on the one hand and the seemingly narrower notion
of an obligation on the other. I am inclined to think that the
way to bridge this gap is to go back to what I said earlier
about the stricter and laxer uses of moral terms, especially
'ought' (1.6, 3.4). It is clear that the word 'ought' as used by
humans can be used to express overridable moral
prescriptions. Perhaps the word 'must', even in human
language, cannot; perhaps, that is, duties expressed by
'must' cannot be overridden. The word 'obligation' in its
narrower sense seems in this respect to lie between 'ought'
and 'must'. Obligations can be overridden, but not so
easily as duties expressed with 'ought'. If we look again at
the case of the person stranded by the roadside, it would
seem that we could have a moral opinion about this which
could be expressed without self-contradiction by saying 'I
ought (morally) to give him a ride; but it is not the case that
I must (morally) give him one; I have no (moral) obligation
to'. Here 'obligation' is like 'must'. But it is not self-
contradictory, either, to say, in some other case, 'I have an
obligation, but it would be going too far to say that I must'.
This reflects the overridability of obligation, even though
it is less easily overridable than 'ought'. Since rights are
linked, in the way we have described, to obligations, it is
not surprising that rights too can without self-contradiction be overridden, with what seems to be the same degree
of difficulty.

Another feature of obligations which links them to rights
is the fact that an obligation is normally *to* some particular
person, who has a corresponding right. Neither 'ought' nor
'must' is person-related in this way. Whether there are
other features which distinguish obligations and rights on
the one hand from the duties (if that is what they are to be
called) expressed by 'ought' and 'must' on the other, I
cannot say. But a picture is beginning to emerge of how we

might bridge our gap. It is understandable that within the general area of morality marked out by the use of 'ought' and 'must' (which is not the whole of morality, because the word 'good' and the virtues have been left out of this picture), there is a smaller field of obligations and rights, distinguished by being person-related and by being, unlike 'must', overridable, but not so easily as 'ought'.

It would also seem that obligations and rights are concepts belonging to intuitive thinking and governed by prima facie principles. That they are not concepts of critical thinking is shown by their overridability, which they must have since they often conflict; if what I said earlier is correct (1.6, 3.5), the 'ought' and 'must' of critical thinking are not overridable. This gives the key to the understanding of many problems about rights, as also about justice, as we shall see. If we can find a method of critical thinking which will enable us to select moral principles of all sorts, there is no reason why we should not use this same method for selecting principles which lay down rights and obligations in particular, as well as principles of justice (more or less in Professor Rawls' sense, 1971). And if we are able by critical thinking to decide which moral principle should override which in cases of conflict between principles, we ought similarly, by the same means, to be able to decide which right or obligation should override which. Just as the question of what intuitions we do have gives place to the question of what intuitions we ought to have, so the question of what rights we have (or on the basis of our intuitions can claim to have) gives place to the question of what rights we ought to have, i.e. what rights a system of principles selected by sound critical thinking would allow us. This thesis is similar to a parallel thesis about justice, which I shall shortly be putting forward, that the crucial question is not what acts are just, but what principles of justice sound critical thinking would select. The form of this transition between questions ought to commend itself to Rawls.

9.5 We have, then, as elsewhere, a two-level structure

of moral thinking, with claims about rights confined to the intuitive level. There is, however, one possible exception to this. There may be a right which everybody can be shown to have by logical considerations alone: what is called the right to equal concern and respect (Dworkin, 1977a:180, 272). The status of this right is similar to that of 'formal' justice, as it is called, which we shall be examining shortly. Both can be established by appeal to formal considerations alone; and for that very reason it is a mistake to think that these purely formal considerations can take the argument on farther and faster than they really can.

The 'right to equal concern and respect' that can be established by appeal to purely formal considerations is nothing but a restatement of the requirement that moral principles be universalizable. This requirement, as I hope to have shown, is potent in moral argument; but it must not be taken to prove, directly and by itself, conclusions about how in particular we should treat people. To treat people with equal concern and respect is to follow Bentham's principle already cited (1.1; *FR* 7.3), 'Everybody to count for one, nobody for more than one', which, in turn, is equivalent to the formal logical rule that individual references cannot occur in the principles which are the basis of our moral judgements. For if we put an individual's name into a moral principle, we should be giving him a privilege (or the opposite), and not treating with equal concern and respect him and others not so designated. There is a 'right to equal concern and respect' of this formal sort, which can be appealed to, unlike other rights which require substantial moral principles as their backing, in critical thinking.

It should be clear by now how lacking in substance is the common objection to utilitarianism, which might be advanced against my own theory of moral reasoning too, that it can give no place to rights, and can ride rough-shod over them in the interests of utility. We are very reasonably told (Dworkin, 1977a:184) that we should 'take rights seriously'. If we take them seriously enough to inquire what they are and what their status is, we shall discover that they are, indeed, an immensely important element in our moral thinking—important enough to justify, in many cases, the claim that they are 'trumps' (ib:xv)—but that this provides no argument at all against utilitarians. For utilitarianism is better able to secure them this status than are intuitionist theories.

Let us take any typical conflict between claims to rights. A racist organization seeks to reserve a public hall for a meeting, and it is obvious that, if the meeting is held, there will be incitement to racial hatred and a danger of violence (we need not ask who will start it). The public authority which controls the hall, urged perhaps by the police, refuses to make the hall available. The racist organization then protests that it is being denied its right to free speech. The public authority counters that it has an obligation to preserve the right of minorities not to have hatred preached against them, and that the public has a right to be protected against outbreaks of violence. Here we have a very typical case of conflict between rights, comparable in all respects to the conflicts of duties discussed earlier (2.1 ff.). Another instance is the well canvassed conflict between the right of a woman to dispose of her own body and the right of the foetus (or of the person whom the foetus would become, H 1975c) to life. In such conflicts both rights may be important *in general*; the problem is, which should be overridden in a particular case. Certainly, in the public meeting case, the right to freedom of speech is of great importance; but so are the other rights which conflict with it.

Faced with such situations, how is an intuitionist to decide which right is 'trumps'? Different people will have conflicting intuitions. What is needed is a method of critical thinking which will decide which of the rights, or the principles on which they are based, should override the other in this case. Intuitionists provide no method of critical thinking beyond the appeal (perhaps after 'reflection') to further intuitions, which have no more authority than the first lot. The most that such a method can achieve is consensus between those who happen to have been similarly educated.

The method I would advocate, by contrast, bases itself on logical considerations established by an understanding of the words used in the questions we are asking, and compelling on anybody who is using the words in the same senses, i.e. asking the same questions. If I am not mistaken in what I have said earlier about the logical character of the moral words, and here about the word 'rights', the method to be employed is one which will select moral principles for use at the intuitive level, including principles about rights, on the score of their acceptance-utility, i.e. on the ground that they are the set of principles whose general acceptance in the society in question will do the best, all told, for the interests of the people in the society considered impartially.

In the case we have described it is likely that a principle will be selected which guarantees freedom of speech but qualifies it by restrictions on what may be said. This is not the place to discuss precisely what those restrictions should be; for example, how to draw the line between incitement to violence and the expression of political dissent. What I hope to have made clear is that the method I have been advocating provides a way (and so far as I can see the only secure way) of reasoning about such questions. The use of this method at the critical level to select principles for general use does not in the least stop us entrenching those principles, once selected and inculcated, against too facile appeals to immediate utility; it is sound utilitarian wisdom to think that such appeals can tempt us into actions which are likely to turn out not at all for the best, given our human limitations. So perhaps the intuitionists can be praised for giving an adequate account of intuitive thinking about rights. Would that they had lifted their eyes a bit higher!

9.6 I shall now give a more summary treatment of the parallel problem of justice—more summary, because so many of the moves are the same, and because I have

discussed it elsewhere (H 1977d). As we saw, and as
Aristotle (1129ª26) already noticed, there are wider and
narrower senses of the word 'just', and also different kinds
of justice even in one of these senses. I spoke earlier of
'formal' justice. This, like the 'right to equal concern and
respect', is to be explained by a simple and direct reference
to the requirement of universalizability which, in turn, has
a logical basis. We are being formally unjust if we make
different moral judgements about identical cases, and act
on them. Note that there is no requirement not to make
similar moral judgements about different cases; the differences may or may not be morally relevant (3.9). Nor is it
necessarily morally wrong, or unjust, to *act* in a way which
treats identical cases differently. If I have to give a single
indivisible cream puff to one or other of my twins, who
both want it equally, it may be morally right to toss a coin,
rather than give it to neither, or cause it to disintegrate in
the attempt to divide it. What would be at fault (logically)
would be to make the moral judgement that I ought to give
it to one twin rather than the other, when there was nothing
to differentiate them. That is why we toss coins in such
cases, to introduce a difference.

As is widely recognized, formal justice will not take us
very far in our pursuit of prescriptions for substantial
justice. It will not, for example, tell us whether or not
people with big houses should get greater political power,
or whether or not they should pay more taxes; for the
principles that only people with big houses should have
votes, and that they should be exempted from taxation, are
both formally universal. In order to bring the requirement
of universalizability to bear on such substantial issues, we
have to go a longer way round, and add other premisses,
some of them empirical.

Besides formal justice, there are also very wide substantial uses of the word 'just', already mentioned. These were
perhaps commoner for the corresponding word in Greek,
'*dikaios*'. Plato used this very widely indeed; Aristotle is
referring to this wide use when he says that justice in this

sense is equivalent to complete virtue so far as it concerns
our relations with other people (1129ᵇ26). Probably
Aristotle's narrower 'particular' sense, which covers distributive and retributive justice and is perhaps best
translated 'fair', is the commonest meaning of the word as
applied to actions. But the Latin translation '*justus*' had or
acquired a much more general sense; Horace's 'just man
tenacious of his purpose' (*Odes* III, 3) was not especially
praised for his devotion to retributive or distributive
justice; nor were the '*justorum animae*', the souls of the
righteous who are in the hand of God (*Wisd.* iii, 1); they
were praised for their virtue in general.

It is easy to be confused by this variety of senses, and
philosophers probably have been. They belong to different
levels of moral thinking. Formal justice, as we have seen,
being essentially a logical principle or property, applies at
all levels. So, perhaps, does justice in the wide Platonic
sense; a superhuman critical thinker who never needed to
do any intuitive thinking could certainly be called just in
this sense, not only because he always observes formal
justice, i.e. impartiality between persons, in his critical
thinking, but because the results of the thinking are
prescriptions for a morally good life. But I shall be arguing,
analogously with my treatment of rights, that the principles of 'particular' substantial justice are prima facie and
not critical principles.

This is shown, as before, by the fact that they can on
occasion conflict. By this I mean not merely that people can
disagree about the just solution to a particular dilemma,
but that there may be no completely just solution. About
justice, those who like to agonize about situations in which
there is 'no right answer'[1] may well be right. But this is a
reason for insisting on the possibility of critical thinking.
This critical thinking will determine, not what is the
uniquely just act, but what, in these difficult
circumstances, we ought to do. There is probably no

---

[1] The expression, though not the view, is Prof. Dworkin's (1977b).

solution to the Palestinian problem which will be just to both the Israelis and the displaced Arabs; but that should not stop us looking for the *best* solution. It may even be that there are principles of justice, the best we can find by critical thinking (i.e. those with the highest acceptance-utility) which will give useful general guidance about such cases; but, because they are general, they will conflict in some particular instances, and this may be one of them. Note that to say that they conflict in particular instances is not to say that they are in themselves mutually inconsistent; it is logically possible that things should be different from how they are, and that the principles could therefore both be observed. The conflict is *per accidens* and not *per se* (2.2).

Our two-level structure of moral thinking thus helps to explain in what senses justice is overridable, and in what senses not; and also in what senses it is independent of contingent empirical facts about the situation, in what senses dependent on them. Formal justice is neither overridable, nor dependent on contingent facts; a sound critical thinking will always observe it. On the other hand, what prima facie intuitive principles of substantial justice are the best for a particular society to adopt will vary according to the circumstances of that society. These will include the propensities of its members; the fact that they are quite happy about social inequalities and would be made unhappy by the disturbance of them may make it best for them to have principles of justice which accord weight to them, until such time as social attitudes change. I say this not because I am an 'ethical relativist' (I am not), but because moral judgements about concrete situations have to be made in the light of facts about those situations (H 1977d *s.f.*), of which facts about attitudes and reactions are one very important kind. But of course it may well be right to seek to change social attitudes, if change would be for the best.

Our treatment of justice is thus a compromise between the view that justice is totally overriding and independent of contingent facts, and the view that it depends on circumstances and can be overridden. Formal justice is non-contingent and non-overridable; substantial justice has to be accommodated to varying societies and situations. It must be added that in so far as there still is a sense of 'just' so general that it encompasses all virtue, or a very large part of it, the person who acts on the deliverances of sound critical thinking will be virtuous, and therefore just in this wide sense. It will be seen that this treatment, like our treatment of rights, enables the utilitarian, and a supporter of my own theory, to give an account of justice which is in accordance with ordinary ideas. The intuitive principles of justice which sound critical thinking would select for a society ought to be given all the devotion that any intuitionist could demand, just like other prima facie principles. I am not seeking to diminish their sanctity, but only to say how to select them and how to adjudicate between them when they conflict. And within a society, if the critical thinking has been well done, we shall find ourselves as devoted as the intuitionists are to the *content* of the principles currently accepted; the difference will be that, when disputes arise, as they will, about the merits of rival principles, we shall have something to say and the intuitionists will not.

9.7   It is now time to distinguish between the different kinds of substantial justice. Aristotle (1131ª1) listed two main kinds, retributive and distributive justice, which have come to be thought of as the principal species of justice. This, however, is to oversimplify. If we look at all the matters on which lawcourts have the duty of giving just decisions, we see that only some of them are concerned with retribution in the strict sense (i.e. with rewards and penalties); for example, the decision that a trade union may not put pickets on the factory of a firm with which it is not in dispute seems to be answering a question neither about retribution nor about distribution. If the union goes on doing it in spite of the court's decision, it may be ordered to pay damages, or its officers may be imprisoned for contempt of court, either of which could in a loose sense be called retribution; but the original decision is not one to exact retribution. And what I have said about lawcourts applies also to other authorities which have the duty of dealing justly, and to parents; their duty is not confined to just distribution and just retribution in any narrow senses.

It seems therefore better to use a broader distinction between judicial or quasi-judicial justice on the one hand, and social and economic justice on the other, the former being justice in the decisions of courts and similar authorities, and the latter justice in the distribution of the various benefits and harms which arise from membership in a society and its economy, including small societies such as families and partnerships and groups of friends. One may even ask what would be the just division of some asset between *two* people. We may treat retributive justice as representative of the first kind of justice, and use the convenient term 'distributive justice' for the second.

We must next ask whether these two kinds of justice can be subsumed under a single genus, or one reduced to the other. I have maintained elsewhere (H 1977d) that retributive justice can be reduced to distributive. It might be objected to this that it is hard to see, in retribution, what is being distributed between whom. And it is indeed hard for anybody to see this who confines his thought to the intuitive level. For the prima facie principles which are usually accepted as governing retributive justice say nothing about distribution. It is only when we ask about the justification of these principles (which intuitionists do not need to do, because each of them thinks his own principles self-evident, however diverse from others' principles) that we need to bring in other parties, between whom we have to be fair.

Those who live in a polity governed by laws derive certain benefits, but also suffer certain disadvantages, from the existence and enforcement of those laws. The basis of political, economic, and social justice is the fair distribution of these benefits and disadvantages. 'Laws' here can be stretched to cover customs enforced by social pressures; but the principles involved can be sufficiently illustrated by laws in the narrow sense. There is, first, the question, faced by legislators, of what the laws are to be, including the question of what penalties are to be attached to breaches of them. The thinking which they should do in order to answer this question is a very close analogue of critical moral thinking, and was so used by Kant (1785:75). It also involves moral thinking itself, of all kinds; for the question of what the laws ought to be is in part a moral question.

Secondly, there is the question faced by judges, but not only by them, of how the laws should be administered. This too is in part a moral question. Prima facie moral principles are needed for the conduct of those who administer the law, and critical thinking has to select these principles. In selecting them it will have, as always, to observe formal justice, giving equal weight to the equal interests of all the parties affected, without favouring any individual as such. Thus the grounds of selection will be utilitarian; but the principles selected may not themselves look utilitarian at all. They are likely to be, rather, of the sort dear to deontologists and intuitionists; they will insist on things like not punishing the innocent, not condemning people unheard, observing procedures in court which are calculated to elicit the truth from witnesses and cause the jury to attend to it, and so on. These prima facie principles of substantial, including procedural, justice in the administration of the law will be selected by critical thinking because their general acceptance is likely to further the interests of those affected, all in all, considered impartially, i.e. with formal justice. So, though the principles may accord with those defended by intuitionists, their justification is utilitarian.

Let us suppose that a judge is asked to justify his sentencing a convicted prisoner (Kant, 1785:68n.; *FR* 7.2, 4). He can answer first at the intuitive level, pointing out that the prima facie principles of justice have been observed: there is a law against the crime of which the prisoner has been found guilty by due process, and the penalties fixed for it lie within a certain range which has not been transgressed. In choosing the particular sentence within this range, he has been guided by well-tried and accepted principles. If the laws themselves are questioned, the judge can refer the questioner to the legislature, together with the sound prima facie principle that judges should not depart from what is laid down by statute (though, if he came to think that the legislators were radically immoral, he ought to do some critical thinking, and perhaps give up his job as judge and join the revolution).

If he is then asked 'Why *these* principles?', he will have to appeal to critical thinking. Given that the legislators could justify their choice of the laws themselves by such an appeal, it should not be difficult for the judge similarly to justify the principles he has been using in administering them. But there is nothing to prevent the principles being amended if it turns out that they are not in the best interest of all, considered impartially. The well-worn 'problem of the justification of punishment' is thus easily solved. The retributivists are right at the intuitive level, and the utilitarians at the critical level. It is proper and necessary for judges to sentence in accordance with the law, and sentence only those who have been duly convicted. But the reason why this is proper and necessary is that a legal system in which judges have not been brought up to treat this principle as in practice unbreakable is likely to be a bad system for nearly everybody subject to it. And if a justification is demanded for the laws themselves, or for a particular law, with the penalties attached, it too will be utilitarian: these are the laws which it is best, in the general interest, to have.

I hope that nobody will now be tempted to bring up unusual cases in which a breach of the prima facie principles would, exceptionally, be for the best. No such cases are likely to arise in practice, and it is for the world as it is that prima facie principles have to be selected and firmly inculcated. The good judge will not consider the possibility of the case before him being of such a sort. If he could consider it, he would certainly be a worse judge—one who would not act for the best in *other* cases. Only in extreme situations in which the system of law was disintegrating could such considerations come in, and probably not even then. Perhaps, *pace* Kant, the murderer should be let off by the society which was about to disperse to the ends of the earth; but even this is doubtful from a utilitarian point of view, and we are unlikely to be faced with such a situation. Perhaps the sheriff should hang the innocent man in order to prevent the riot in which there will be many deaths, if he knows that the man's innocence will never be discovered and that the bad indirect effects will not outweigh the good direct effects; but in practice he never will know this (3.2).

9.8 I have dealt at length elsewhere (H 1977d, 1979c) with two applications of the accounts of rights and justice that I have just been giving, and can therefore merely summarize them. The first concerns the relation between justice and equality in distribution. For reasons of space I shall have to leave out of account the distinction between different things that have to be distributed: wealth, power, status and so on. These require separate treatment; but the method which I shall be suggesting for determining the just distribution of wealth can be used, with necessary changes in empirical premisses, for determining the just distribution of power and of status.

Reasons can be given why the principles of economic justice which would be chosen by an impartially benevolent critical thinker would be moderately egalitarian. Two of them are well known. The first is the diminishing marginal utility, over the ranges that matter, of money and of most goods. This has the effect that the possession of his latest increment of money by a poor man gives him more utility than the same increment does to a rich man. In terms of preferences, the impartial critical thinker who put himself in the shoes of both these people would prefer that he should, in those cases, be given the increment if he were the poor man than if he were the rich man, supposing that he could not have it in both roles.

I deliberately put it in this somewhat cumbrous way in terms of increments, because it is not the case that to *take away* a hundred pounds from a rich man will always cause him less disutility than the utility conferred on a poor man by giving him the same amount; for people tend to resent having money taken away from them more than they enjoy having it given to them. But all the same this principle does favour gently managed egalitarian redistributions, for example by progressive taxation. For the reason just given, it does not except in extreme cases favour violent revolutions or abrupt confiscations; for the evils caused by these are likely to outweigh the good from the redistribution itself. Another factor which favours gradualism in redistribution is that a steady increase in wealth is likely to give cumulatively more satisfaction than a sudden steep one; those whose wealth increases year by year are likely to savour the increments more than those who win fortunes in sweepstakes. The *prospect* of huge windfall gains has, indeed, an attraction for gamblers which induces them to accept less favourable odds than the probability of winning would justify. But I am speaking not of the prospect, but of the utility of the actual access of wealth; this is seldom so great as was expected. And similarly a gradual decrease in wealth, with time to adjust, is likely to cause less pain than a sudden plunge to the same level. None of this, however, can be used to argue against the immediate relief of extreme poverty where it exists.

The second potent egalitarian argument is based on the human propensity to envy. Envy has been accounted a sin; but its existence is a fact relevant to moral thinking. If there were good arguments in favour of inequalities, there would be equally good arguments in favour of suppressing envy. But if there are already arguments against the inequalities, it is likely to be better to remove the envy by removing the inequalities than by preaching against it as a sin.

There are perhaps good arguments for some inequalities (e.g., the need for differentials to provide incentives, which are inseparable from a certain amount of envy; the need for a spread of capital accumulation to all those willing to save, and of patronage of the arts and education, both of them in order to avoid too much concentration of the power of investment and patronage in the hands of officials, as tends to happen in too radically 'egalitarian' societies). On these matters a philosopher cannot as such be an expert. Both of the arguments in favour of moderate equality, and all of those against extreme egalitarianism, rest on contingent empirical facts or conjectures.

That is really the main point. We should mistrust anybody, be he philosopher, economist, sociologist, or politician, who bases arguments for egalitarianism, or for that matter against it, on intuitions. It is not *a priori* true or self-evident, either that the kind of liberty to which, for example, Professor Nozick (1974) appeals in favour of allowing inequalities, is an overriding principle, or that to have shown statistically that Britain remains a somewhat unequal society is to have proved without further premisses that new egalitarian measures are called for. Neither political liberty nor economic equality are of necessity good things in themselves; it all depends on how much people want them and therefore on what sacrifices of their own or other people's other interests are worth making in order to attain them. A critical thinker who does his job will need to find out a lot about people's actual preferences in a given society (and they may be different in different societies) before he commits himself even to prima facie principles requiring the subordination of other important goods to equality, or to liberty, in any of their many senses.

If I were compelled to guess at a solution, for a typical Western industrial society, to the dispute between the egalitarians and their opponents, I should come down in favour of a moderate egalitarianism; but I should do this on the basis, not merely of the philosophical understanding which I hope I have achieved of the nature of the argument, but of empirical conjectures about what people are like in that kind of society, and what they prefer.[2] I should not mind being shown to be wrong about these conjectures, provided that the experts in these matters then gave us more reliable estimates, with an understanding of how they would have to be fitted as premises into the argument, whose form I have, as a philosopher, been trying to clarify.

9.9 Exactly the same has to be said about the other chief question remaining, that of personal and political liberty; so I will say it briefly. It might have been contingently the case that societies could prosper under tyranny and slavery. Perhaps it even has been the case in some cultures and periods. By 'prosper', I mean that the members of the societies as a whole could prosper, not that a favoured section of them could. I firmly believe that as a matter of fact no likely society is going to be better off with a system allowing slavery (H 1979c); and I also firmly believe that all societies which are capable of operating a democratic system (an important qualification) would be well advised in their own interests to adopt one. But my reasons for these judgements are beliefs about contingent matters of fact. If these were shown to be false, then the same philosophical views about the nature of the moral argument involved might make me advocate slavery and tyranny.

It has been thought to be a defect in utilitarianism that it is in this way at the mercy of the facts. But in truth this is a strength and not a weakness. Likewise, it shows the lack of contact with reality of a system based on moral intuitions without critical thought, that it can go on churning out the same defences of liberty and democracy *whatever* assumptions are made about the state of the world or the preferences of its inhabitants. This should be remembered

---

[2] For other relevant empirical considerations see Gellner (1979).

whenever some critic of utilitarianism, or of my own views, produces some bizarre example in which the doctrine he is attacking could condone slavery or condemn democracy. What we should be trying to find are moral principles which are acceptable for general use in the world as it actually is.

POINT

. . . who showed by his life and his logic that man
Grows good and grows blessed the self-same way.
ARISTOTLE, *Epigram on Plato*

10

FANATICISM AND AMORALISM

10.1 In Part I, by distinguishing the levels of moral thinking, we cleared away one of the main sources of confusion which have prevented people understanding the method of moral thinking which the logic of the moral concepts imposes. In Part II we outlined the method itself, and applied it in some fields which have been thought to present difficulties. In Part III we shall be discussing, from various angles, why anybody should want to use this method—what the point of it is. This divides into two questions. The first is, Why should we engage in moral rather than in some other kind of practical thinking (e.g. prudential)? This will be the subject of the next two chapters. The second is, What makes one method of moral thinking better than another? We have been assuming that what we are after is rationality in moral thinking. Others have demanded that moral thinking be shown to lead to the discovery of objective moral facts. These two notions, rationality and objectivity, will be the subject of the final chapter.

The most obvious way to start the discussion of the first question will be to examine the position of somebody (I shall call him the amoralist) who is unwilling to think morally, either in general or on a particular occasion (*FR* 6.6; 6.3). In this chapter I shall be formulating the position and showing that only one version of it, out of those considered, is really tenable. In the next I shall try to show why, nevertheless, there are good reasons for adopting the moral concepts and thinking in accordance with their logic. But before we come to the amoralist it will be instructive, for purposes of comparison, to give an account of another way of thinking, which has been thought to create trouble for my theory and on which I spent quite a lot of space in *FR*: that of the person whom I there called the fanatic. After what has been said in the first two parts, we are equipped to anatomize him.

The anatomy I shall give is not different in essentials from that given in *FR*; but I have seen some distinctions more clearly, and the moves made in chh. 2 and 5 of this book help to clear up the problem. It may be of use if I briefly explain, to start with, why the possible existence of fanatics was thought by me to present a difficulty for my theory. Already in *FR* I had been flirting with a theory of a broadly utilitarian sort; and it seemed that there could be a person who could dissent from the conclusions of such a theory because he was firmly wedded to certain ideals, and in accordance with them made moral judgements, compliance with which would be far from maximizing utility or preference-satisfactions. I instanced a racist Nazi or South African who, in pursuit of ideals of racial supremacy or purity, thought it right to oppress or exterminate members of certain races, even though he might admit that the harms to them exceeded the good to members of his own race. It would expose a gap in the defences of utilitarianism if such a person could listen to, and understand, all the arguments, and admit all the facts, adduced by the utilitarian, and still sustain his opinion.

Already in *FR* 9.8 I made one necessary distinction, that between (as I shall call them) 'impure' and 'pure' fanatics. The first are those who hold moral opinions divergent from those of utilitarians only because they are unable or unwilling to engage in what I now call critical thinking. This may be because of refusal or inability to face facts or to think clearly, or for other reasons. This kind of 'fanatic' (who can be so called only in a less than pure-blooded sense) presents no theoretical difficulty for us, though his undoubted existence in large numbers in the world creates enormous practical problems (H 1972d:71; 1979g). It cannot be held against the method of critical thinking that its arguments have no effect on someone who cannot understand them or will not admit the facts on which they rely.

Only the 'pure fanatic' would present a difficulty. This would be someone who was able and willing to think critically, but somehow survived the ordeal still holding moral opinions different from those of the utilitarian. But now we have to distinguish between two ways in which this might happen. The first, which would indeed present a difficulty, would be if a case could be found in which the pure fanatic went on holding his opinions, and could not be budged from them by critical arguments, and in which these opinions proved to be indeed different from those which a utilitarian would reach. The second, which would not present a difficulty of the same (or perhaps in the end of any) kind, would be if the pure fanatic went on holding his opinions, but it turned out that these were not, after all, inconsistent with utilitarianism. It is this latter case whose possibility I had not envisaged when I wrote *FR*. The tactic of the present chapter will be, after first discussing the impure fanatic (to which class all real-life human fanatics, as I think, belong), to show that the second kind of pure fanatic logically can exist, though we shall not in practice meet him, and that this possibility raises no difficulty for our theory; but that the first kind of pure fanatic cannot exist, if the argument of ch. 5 is correct. The impression that he might exist is created only by failing to distinguish him from, on the one hand, the impure fanatic, who certainly exists in quantity, and, on the other, the second kind of pure fanatic, who does not exist but logically could.

That the second kind logically could exist will seem counterintuitive to intuitionists, and they will certainly use this as an argument against me. It is to be rebutted, as always, by appeal to the separation of levels advocated in ch. 2. Because his existence is only a logical, not a practical possibility, critical thinking, although it can handle his case, will pay no attention to it when selecting prima facie principles for use in intuitive thinking in the real world. Therefore the intuitions of the well brought up man will not be adapted to deal with such a case, and even its existence will seem counterintuitive. This, so far from being an objection to our theory, is exactly what it leads us to expect.

10.2   The roots of fanaticism lie in intuitionism and in the refusal or inability to think critically. We have seen (2.2) that a necessary part of moral education lies in the acquisition of moral attitudes—i.e. dispositions to have moral intuitions with a certain content and the associated moral feelings, and to act in accordance with them. It is a good thing that we should have these attitudes firmly implanted; a wise utilitarian educator would wish his pupils to be so equipped to face the stresses of the moral life. But there are several things that can go wrong with this process of moral education. First of all, the content of the attitudes, i.e. òf the prima facie principles which they embody, may not be such as a wise critical thinker would have chosen; for not all those who influence the attitudes picked up by the young are wise. We have already mentioned as an example the deeply implanted attitudes of racial, religious or political intolerance which have characterized those growing up in certain cultures. Although it is a good thing to grow up with intuitions, there are some intuitions with which it is bad to grow up. This would not stop intuitionist philosophers in any culture, however strange from our point of view, defending as sacrosanct the shibboleths characteristic of that culture. They would do this even after consideration of 'all relevant philosophical arguments' (Rawls, 1971:49); for they would not allow themselves to count as relevant any argument which threatened the security of their intuitions.

However, this is not the only possible, nor even the

commonest, source of fanaticism. For there are some intuitions which it is good to have, but unthinking subservience to which in extreme forms may be an evil. An example is provided by some pacifists. It is certainly a good thing to implant in ourselves and in our children a moral antipathy to killing and other forms of violence. A sound critical thinker would select prima facie principles with some such content, and a wise utilitarian educator would seek to inculcate them. Since simple principles are the easiest to inculcate, there will be a tendency to oversimplify the principles, at any rate in the initial stages of education. Probably most children are at first taught simply not to tell lies, not to steal, not to use violence on other people, and so on. They will later learn what count as exceptions to these principles (either what does not count as lying, or what lies are permissible; either what is not properly called violence, or what forms of violence are morally justified—*LM* 4.3). But it is easy here too for things to go wrong, especially if the original simple principles have been very firmly implanted and critical thinking has been neglected.

It has been suggested that many extreme radicals in the sixties and seventies of this century came from homes where an advanced liberal attitude to such political questions as race and war was accepted. The extreme and rebellious and often very illiberal radicalism of the young was a shock to their parents; but, we are told, these ought to have blamed themselves. For what the young were doing was to take the principles of their parents and live them out in a more thorough and consistent way without the evasions which the parents had devised to soften their impact. The young were being 'logical' in a sense of 'logic' in which it consists in taking some intuitive principle and following out its implications regardless of any other principles which might be equally important, and regardless of the critical thinking which could cope with conflicts between them and determine which should override which in a particular case.

If the parents were to blame, however, it was not, as has

sometimes been suggested, for being too liberal in the first
place, nor for not following their own liberal principles to
the bitter end, but for failing to introduce their children to
critical thinking at an early enough age. By this failure they
produced a generation which contained more than its fair
share of fanatics incapable of critical thought. And some
other, illiberal, parents contributed their own contingent
to the radical army by trying to force on their children
principles so rigid, and in some cases so absurd, that in the
prevailing climate the children, not having been taught
how to think critically, rebelled and adopted opposite but
equally uncritical principles. It is my hope that this book
may help towards an understanding of these unhappy
events.

A pacifist is usually somebody who has got hold of an
intuitive principle forbidding violence and clings to it
regardless of what other equally important principles this
compels him to disobey. He solves the conflict of
principles, not by critical thought, but by elevating one
principle, quite irrationally, over all the others. The
dispute between pacifists and non-pacifists is not to be
resolved at the intuitive level; both sides have perfectly
good intuitions to appeal to and will simply go on affirming
them. The solution lies in asking which of these principles
should override which in a particular case. Only critical
thought can answer this question. And it can do more. If
cases are given weight in accordance with the probability of
their occurrence, critical thinking will come out with a set
of prima facie principles which are appropriate for a given
society and period. These may well be different from those
appropriate to *other* circumstances; for both new weapons
and newly available ways of settling disputes without
violence get devised, and alter the conditions in which the
principles have to be applied. If my own critical thinking is
any guide, the principles appropriate to the present time in
the United States and Europe are not pacifist ones, though
they are more pacific than those appropriate in other
centuries, or in this century in countries like Israel, at times

when they are under constant threat from their
neighbours.

One may be fanatical about moral opinions even when
they are sound ones. There are a great many prima facie
principles which we do right to hold, but which can make
us fanatics if we stick to them in cases to which other
principles also apply, and in which these other principles
would be the ones we should act on if we did our critical
thinking thoroughly. For example, it is an excellent
principle for doctors to save lives when they can; but if any
doctor says 'My job is saving lives, therefore I must keep
people alive to the last possible moment whatever the cost
to them in suffering', he is showing himself a fanatic in
elevating this good principle above another which would,
after critical thinking, override it in particular cases,
namely the principle requiring him to prevent suffering. It
is not the content of a person's intuitive principles that
makes him a fanatic, but his attitude to them.

10.3   The fact that even good intuitions can be fanati-
cally adhered to has generated an argument against my views
which some have found attractive. They have complained
that in *FR* 9.1 I chose as an example of fanaticism the Nazi,
thus, they thought, prejudicing the issue against my
opponents. For, they said, there are a great many perfectly
respectable and even lovable people who hold views which
cannot be defended by an appeal to utilitarian critical
thinking of the sort that I am advocating. Am I not just
smearing these nice intuitionists by comparing them with
the Nazis? I foresaw this objection, noted, and briefly
answered it in *FR* 9.5; but I will amplify the answer.

It is not fanatical to have moral intuitions. There is,
however, a difficulty in distinguishing the fanatic from the
ordinary good man who, as I have said he should, sticks to
his intuitions in the face of stressful situations and does not
readily go over to critical thinking, which might lead him
astray (3.1 f.). But the difficulty disappears once we look at
such decisions in their context. It is not fanatical, *in a
particular situation of stress and relative ignorance*, to keep

off critical thinking for fear of getting it wrong. Nor is it fanatical, though it is regrettable, if those who suffer from a general lack of confidence in their own powers of critical thought renounce it entirely, not because they cannot do it, but for fear of doing it badly. What distinguishes the ordinary less than pure-blooded fanatic is his determination in principle to think with his blood: that is to say, to put his ingrained convictions beyond the reach of critical thought even when he is in a position (has the facts and the leisure) to examine and appraise them. And it is not only the Nazis and other such detestable people who do this.

10.4 Both the pure and the impure fanatic cling to their intuitions in the face of critical thinking, but for different reasons. The pure fanatic, by contrast with the impure, is able and willing to do the critical thinking, and does it. The question is, what then happens in our argument with him. The difficulty which the fanatic represents for my theory is supposed to be this: it is said that a sufficiently determined fanatic could admit all the facts adduced by a critical thinker, and all the logical inferences which he used, and still, without offence to logic, reject his utilitarian conclusions. It is obviously going to be irrelevant to this argument if there can be a less than pure-blooded fanatic who rejects the conclusions only because he has not absorbed the facts, or because his own logic is faulty, whether through enthusiasm for his ideals or intuitions, or from some psychological cause. It is only the fully-informed and logically impeccable fanatic that would present a difficulty for our theory if he were able to reject our utilitarian prescriptions. I shall now proceed to show that he cannot.

It is clear that he cannot, if the argument of chh. 5 and 6 is correct. For the steps in that argument from universal prescriptivism to utilitarianism were all based on the logic of the concepts involved. The fanatic is not rejecting this logic; he is not the amoralist with whom we shall be dealing later in this chapter. So if the steps really are all conceptual, he cannot refuse them. The objection based on the alleged possibility of his existence is in effect a denial that the argument of chh. 5 and 6 can be correct. It will therefore be useful to go over it again with the case of the fanatic in mind. In order further to assuage the objectors of 10.3, let us take an example in which the opinions of the fanatic are not in the least extreme. Our doctor in 10.2 will serve very well; he exists, perhaps, in many hospitals the world over and is probably a most amiable person.

The argument could appropriately take the form of a dialogue between the fanatical doctor and our archangel of 3.1, who can reason with perfect logic, and knows all the facts. If there are any facts which the less than angelic doctor does not know, or any logical moves he is not clear-headed enough to make, the archangel can put him right. Let us assume that the relevant facts are these: the patient will die at once if not put under intensive care: if he is put under intensive care, he will suffer a great deal and die in any case within a month or so; but the doctor has a very strong moral aversion to omitting any step which could prolong life. In a real case there would be questions about probabilities; for it could never be certain just when the patient would die or how much he would suffer; but if I put the argument in a simpler form which treats as certain what is only highly probable, the reader will be able, if he wishes, to complicate it by bringing in probabilities with, I am sure, the same outcome to the dispute. This is not a 'dummy' example such as I satirized earlier; it is like what happens all the time in hospitals. The archangel, of course, does not need to make judgements of probability, because he *knows* what the consequences of alternative actions would be.

If the doctor knows that the patient will suffer to that extent if he lives, he will himself have acquired a preference that, were he the patient, he should not, *ceteris paribus*, suffer in that way. If he has not acquired that preference, equal to that of the patient when he is suffering, then the archangel has not managed to convey to him the full extent of the patient's suffering. But let us suppose that the doctor is thus fully informed, as critical moral thinking demands. He will then have to set this preference for what should be done to him in the hypothetical case in which he is the patient, against his own present preference, based on moral conviction, for not letting the patient die. If the first of these preferences outweighs the second, the doctor will accept the universal prescription that in such cases the patient should be allowed to die, rather than that which prescribes that the patient be kept alive at all costs. For the second of these prescriptions goes against the balance of the doctor's own preferences.

10.5   If the doctor wishes to avoid this consequence, given the facts which we have supposed, he can do it only by somehow boosting his own preference for keeping the patient alive. It will be suggested at this point that he can do this by claiming that, after all, his is not just a mere *preference* like that of the patient not to suffer; it is a *moral conviction*. Do not moral convictions take precedence over mere preferences? Are not moral principles supposed to be overriding (3.5)?

A full understanding of our method will dispel this objection. First of all, moral convictions at the intuitive level are *not* overriding (3.6); they cannot be, because they frequently conflict with one another. Secondly, what are in conflict here are not a moral principle and a mere personal preference not to suffer, but two moral principles. The doctor is faced with a choice between two *universal* prescriptions, one of which says that in such cases suffering should be prevented, and the other of which says that the patient should be kept alive. So no appeal to overridingness will help the fanatic.

It is important to be clear that what is at issue here is not whether our theory is the correct one; we have already argued that question. It is, rather, whether, assuming that it is correct, we can use it to defeat the fanatic in argument. So let us assume that it is correct, and see what it will do. First of all, our method is based on the falsity of descriptivism. If some form of descriptivism were true, the doctor might be able to say 'I just *know* that I ought not to let the patient die; what are his preferences against that?' But on the view here assumed to be correct, this is nothing more than an appeal to his own intuitions, which cannot be made without circularity, since they themselves are in dispute. It is critical thinking that we are supposed to be doing.

Our method, because it is purely formal, relies on nothing but the choice between alternative prescriptions, some universal and some singular, given that the parties start with the prescriptions they do start with. These prescriptions are all the expressions of preferences. None has greater authority or dignity than another, so far as the reasoning goes. The only advantage given to moral prescriptions over others is that the prescription finally chosen has to be universal or universalizable; this is the requirement rejected by the amoralist whom we shall be discussing shortly. But the fanatic is not an amoralist. If the doctor says 'My initial preference is based on moral conviction, so it has to prevail', he is taking the argument in the wrong order; it is an argument whose purpose is to *arrive at* a moral conviction by critical thought. To insist on the *prior* authority of the moral intuitions that one starts with is simply to refuse to think critically.

So then the doctor cannot boost his own preferences by claiming that they are moral ones. If he wants to make them prevail, he has to show that they are stronger than those of the suffering patient. In real life (which is what we are concerned with) it is highly unlikely that this will be so in all cases. No doubt there will be cases in which the patient does not very much mind being kept alive in a mildly distressing condition in order not to offend the doctor's moral susceptibilities. But that is not the sort of case we are considering; we are assuming that the patient will suffer a great deal.

10.6   However, let us change the case to tilt the balance the other way. Let us suppose for the sake of argument that the doctor is, because of his moral attitudes, so averse to letting the patient die (his preferences are so strong) that his own suffering if he does it will exceed that of the patient if he is kept alive. In that case even critical thinking will say that the suffering of the two taken together will be minimized by putting the patient under intensive care. The case is now beginning to look a bit far-fetched. But perhaps by bringing in the moral repugance of the nurses and a few medical colleagues who are involved, and making the patient's suffering not too extreme, we can tilt the balance enough to make it right, according to critical thinking, to do what the doctor wants. However, we must now make a move which has a decisive impact on the argument: that of asking whether these moral attitudes are alterable, in a way in which the patient's sufferings and consequent preferences are not.

Preferences are certainly often alterable, and this fact has very wide implications for utilitarian theory. We have already mentioned this in our brief discussions of prudence (5.6) and of evil desires (8.6). It is in accordance with our method to assign equal weight, strength for strength, to all preferences alike, provided that they survive exposure to logic and the facts, and to account for any counterintuitive consequences by appeal to the separation of levels and the inadmissibility of fantastic examples. The present case will serve as an illustration. If it is alleged that the doctor's preference for keeping the patient alive can be boosted by adding to it all the preferences of those who think it his sacred duty to do this, then we have to ask whether both these kinds of preference are not in fact fairly easily alterable, and whether they ought not to be altered. Might not our critical thinking, in that case, come out with the result that the best universal prescription to adopt for this case would be that the doctor and all the others should overcome their aversion? The critical thinking itself might help them to do this.

We have already considered the move of appealing to what I said earlier about the utility of sticking to our intuitions in situations of stress. This move is now inadmissible, because we are here embarked on critical thinking, and the question is what its results would be. But it might be claimed here, not that the doctor and his colleagues *ought* not to put their preferences in question, but that they might not be *able* to. Perhaps their moral convictions are so deeply ingrained that they will in sum suffer more than the patient would, however hard they try to get over them. The case is now getting pretty fantastic; but even on this supposition, it may be that by going against his conviction in this case, albeit at the cost of great suffering, he may make it easier for himself and others to overcome it in future cases, so that in the end the attitude will get generally abandoned, and replaced by one which requires doctors to keep patients alive only when it is likely to be what the patients themselves would prudently prefer (which will still be so in the overwhelming majority of cases). If so, then the results of this change in attitude may be so beneficial as to outweigh the initial jar to the doctor's and other people's moral susceptibilities.

The fanatic is therefore in a dilemma. Either he has to admit that his own preferences, including those based on his moral convictions, are not enough to outweigh the preferences of the others who will be harmed by implementing them. In that case, if he fully represents to himself the stronger preferences of the others, he will come to have preferences of his own that, were he they, he should not suffer as he is proposing to make or let them suffer. But then he will abandon his fanatical line of action and the universal prescription which requires it. So, on this horn of the dilemma, the fanatic will cease to be a fanatic. Or else he has to claim that his own preferences (together with those of people who think like him) are so strong and unalterable that they will continue to prevail over those of the others whom his actions will cause or allow to suffer. If this claim be granted, then critical thinking will endorse the universal prescription that in such cases the fanatic's preferences should be implemented. In this case, the fanatic does not *need* to be a fanatic—only a person with quite fantastically strong preferences. In neither case is critical thinking controverted; nor is utilitarianism. In both, the right solution is the utilitarian one. But in the second, the opponents of utilitarianism will try to claim that the result of critical thinking is counterintuitive.

The answer to this move should by this time be obvious; it is the same as we have given many times before. If these fantastic cases really have to be considered, critical thinking will give those answers. But since they are not going to occur, the counterintuitiveness of the answers provides no argument against the method. For our intuitions were not made for use in such cases; they are, perhaps, good intuitions, and critical thinking would endorse them for use in the world as it is, as having the highest acceptance-utility; but if we address our critical thinking to queer cases, we shall get queer answers. This does not in the least matter; if the answers are counterintuitive, that just shows that our intuitions were, rightly, not chosen to cater for such unreal cases.

One last difficulty must be mentioned. It might be thought that our failure to take a firm position on the inclusion or exclusion of external preferences (5.6) leaves us vulnerable to attack here. It does not. For if external preferences are to be taken into consideration, then both those of the fanatic and those of others will have weight; but if not, then neither will. In both cases the argument will be as I have outlined it; no new factor is introduced by the inclusion of external preferences. It might be thought that the fanatical doctor's case becomes stronger if he is allowed to appeal to his own and his fellow-fanatics' external preferences; but these will in practice be counterbalanced by the external preferences of those who hold contrary opinions. Although it is easy to devise logically possible cases in which this is not so, they provide no better ammunition for our intuitionist opponents than the logically possible but in practice unreal cases already discussed.

10.7 The problem presented by the amoralist is quite

different from that presented by the fanatic. The former
refrains from making moral judgements at all (in the sense
characterized in ch. 3), or makes only judgements of moral
indifference; and he does this either always, or in connexion with particular cases (*FR* 6.6). The latter makes
moral judgements, but clings to them in a peculiarly
obdurate way, which resists critical thinking in one of the
ways described. The position of the amoralist is best
explained, as it was in *FR*, by considering a possible
escape-route from the form of moral argument which I
have been advocating.[1] It can be set out schematically as
follows, in a way already outlined (6.3). Suppose that *A* is
proposing to do something to *B* which *B* prefers should not
be done, but which *A* prefers to a lesser degree should be
done. By the method we have been pursuing, it is possible
to bring *A* to reject the moral judgement that he ought to
do it, because, having thought what it would be like to be in
B's position, he will not accept the universal prescription
that this be done in such circumstances. But having
rejected this universal prescription, he is not compelled to
accept a universal prohibition on such acts, which is what
we want him to do. He can, instead, refuse to accept any
universal prescription, affirmative or negative, for such
situations, and this leaves it open to him to say that it is
neither the case that he ought to do it, nor the case that he
ought not. To say this is consistent with also accepting the
singular prescription that it not be done to him were he in
B's position; so he does not have to stop wanting it not to be
done to him on that hypothesis. He only has to stop
thinking that it ought not to be done to him (for that would
commit him to saying that he too ought not to do it in the
actual case).

In this way he can escape the argument by simply

[1] Substantially the same escape-route was later noticed by Prof. Gauthier
(1968), who repeats the point already made on p. 100 of *FR*, but does not discuss
the answer to the objection given on the next page. He later rightly says that
permissions are of various kinds, but makes the mistake of treating 'Let *C* put me
into prison' as the expression of a permission, which it can hardly be. For other
discussions see Gensler (1976) and Torrance (1977, 1981).

refraining from accepting any universal prescription, or any moral judgement except judgements of indifference; and he may take up this amoralist position either universally, or only about cases like this in particular. I cannot deny, and did not deny in *FR*, that the former, universal amoralist, position is possible. We shall ask later what costs it imposes on one who takes it up. But it cannot be claimed that he has to give up using moral language. He may be perfectly well acquainted with this and able to use it, but only use the moral words in sentences beginning 'It is not the case that'. He is like a person who knows how to use the word 'witch', but does not believe that there are any witches; he knows what a duty would be but (like Mr. Mackie on one perhaps uncharitable interpretation) does not admit that there are any. This will be his position if he takes the same line in every case in which a moral question is asked. It is of course possible for him, alternatively, to take it only in some cases and not in others.

Another way of characterizing the two positions is this: when we ask moral questions about proposed actions, we often assume that the answer must be either 'I ought' or 'I ought not'; that is to say, we have already ruled out the possibility that the action is morally indifferent. He, however, has not ruled it out. We can perhaps ask him therefore whether he has any policy about when he is going to say actions are morally indifferent and when he is going to admit the 'ought'/ought not' dichotomy. This is one version or aspect of a question which it is legitimate to ask of anybody who wishes to discuss moral questions (even in an amoralist spirit), namely what his morality as a whole is—i.e. what set of moral principles, if any, he has and how they are related to one another. For it is legitimate to ask that a man's moral principles, if any, at the critical level, should be consistent with one another, and this can be determined only if he says what they are. In practice this is difficult or impossible; but the archangel can do it, and that is all that is relevant for the present argument in which we are concerned with perfect critical thinking.

Is the amoralist a total moral abstainer? He might answer that his policy is to say 'The action is morally indifferent: no universal prescription is applicable here' just when it suits him. That is to say, he might claim such moral indifference for actions whenever that claim would obviate his making a moral judgement about them which it would not be in his interest to make or act on. His real principle in that case would be 'Acts are morally indifferent if to say that they ought *or* that they ought not to be done is against my own interest'. But this is a moral judgement, albeit one of indifference. It is hard to see how he could universalize it so as to get rid of the reference to his individual self. If he substitutes for 'my own interest' some universal terms which, as things are, single him out, he is open to the same objection that we have used on other occasions, viz. that he will not be prepared to extend this principle to hypothetical cases in which he has ceased to answer to that description (*FR* 6.8; 6.4). So it looks as if this line is closed to him.

10.8   The matter becomes clearer if we remember that all prescriptions, including moral ones, are expressions of preferences or of desires in a wide sense (6.1; *FR* 9.4; H 1968). To say that an act would be morally indifferent, therefore, is to refrain explicitly from expressing any desire that acts of just this sort should be done in *all* circumstances of just this sort, or any desire that they should not. This, as we have seen, is consistent with desiring that in *some* circumstances of just this sort such acts should be done, and in *some* not. This can be said sincerely, however, only if the speaker really has no such universal desires. It is not difficult to imagine the state of mind of someone who has no universal, and therefore no moral, desires at all. But I find it hard to imagine that of someone who has universal desires concerning cases in which his own interests are not affected, but has none for cases where they are, both actual and hypothetical. Whence could come the difference, if not from a differentiation of cases where *his* interests were concerned? Since he is not claiming to have universal desires about those cases, this does him no harm in the argument. But the same move which separates off those cases by an individual reference to himself, also separates off the other lot of cases about which he claims to be making moral judgements. If these latter are distinguished by an individual reference (as they must be, if the former, their complementary class, are) then the judgements cannot really be moral ones after all.

I do not see, therefore, how such a person can avoid becoming an amoralist *universally*, i.e. refraining from making moral judgements altogether. Nor can I see anything logically inconsistent in his position, if that is what he does. We shall be asking in the next chapter whether there are any non-logical reasons for not being an amoralist.

The logical possibility of consistent whole-hogging amoralism, unlike the picking and choosing kind that we have just been excluding, may seem a defect in our theory. But it carries with it one advantage; for it establishes my *bona fides* as a non-descriptivist. Many readers will by this time have become inclined to accuse me of going back on Hume's Law ('No "ought" from an "is"'); for the tenor of my argument has been consistently rationalist, and people find it hard to distinguish rationalism, which I favour, from descriptivism, which I reject. This distinction will be gone into in ch. 12. I have even, because of my zeal for stopping loopholes in the rationalist argument, been accused of reverting to some form of naturalism. 'Are you not saying', the objection goes, 'that, given sufficient facts about your own and other people's preferences, and about the other circumstances, a moral conclusion can be deduced by strict logic, "the logic of the moral concepts", as you call it? And does this not make you into a naturalist after all?'

The amoralist, for all his awkwardness for my theory, at least saves it from this imputation. For he is a man who, on my theory, can admit all the above facts and still refuse the moral conclusion, because he will not make any moral judgements at all. So, although I have elsewhere (*LM* 3.2; H 1977b:468), made clear that Hume's Law requires qualifications, its main substance, that to which one is committed by being a prescriptivist, remains untouched by the arguments in this book. Hume would not have liked what Kant said, but if he had read and understood it he would not have had to deny at least those parts of it that I have borrowed.

In other words, the 'net' of morality (H 1968), although much ampler than is provided by those who put *material* restrictions on what can count as a moral judgement, is not wide enough to catch those who will make no affirmative judgements having a universal prescriptive *form*. Mr. Warnock (1967:52 ff.; 3.8) is compelled to admit that he is not having any moral dispute with, for example, Homer and Aristotle, because they are not making moral judgements in his sense. I, by contrast, can dispute, and indeed reason, with them and with Nietzsche, if they are prepared to offer some affirmative universal prescriptions (as no doubt they would be). But my net, though larger, is not infinitely large; there is a way of escape, and all I can do is to point out its hazards, as I shall be doing in the next chapter.

11

PRUDENCE, MORALITY AND SUPEREROGATION

11.1   In this chapter we shall first deal with some inter-related problems, all of which could be expressed in the form of the misleading question 'Why should I be moral?' They are all to be resolved by coming to understand the relation between morality, at its different levels, and prudence. Then we shall briefly discuss a further problem which has similar features: the problem of what are called 'works of supererogation'. This has been thought to be an awkward problem for utilitarians, because on some accounts their theory could leave no room for such a class of acts. The problem yields, as might be expected, to the distinction between levels of moral thinking.

It might be thought an objection to our method that it does not enable us to deal with a determined and consistent amoralist such as I described in the last chapter. Looking at the matter more broadly, we can see that this difficulty might take several different forms. First of all, it might be objected that by claiming that the moral words have certain logical properties, and then founding a theory of moral reasoning on them, we have put out of the range of our artillery the person who says 'I agree that what you call "the moral words" have these properties, and that, if they have, a system of "moral reasoning" can be founded on them which will lead to certain conclusions; but for that very reason I am not going to use those words, or not in those senses, because I do not intend to be forced to those conclusions'. Have we not plugged gaps *within* our system of reasoning only at the cost of leaving an enormous hiatus *outside* it (*FR* 10.1 ff.)?

But the matter, as we saw, may be even worse than that; for it is possible for somebody even to use the moral words in the senses, and with the logical properties, that we have claimed they have, and *still* not make, using them, any moral judgements except ones of indifference. Provided that he is consistent in doing this, we have no logical power to make him do otherwise.

Thirdly, it might be claimed that even if someone does make moral judgements which are not judgements of indifference, he may still not act on them; so we have, by providing a system of reasoning, done little to improve people's morals. And if, as prescriptivists are entitled to do, we reply that on our view there can be no gap between a prescriptive moral judgement and the disposition to act on it (for if a person were not disposed to act on his moral judgements, he would not be treating them as prescriptive), still it may be objected that there has to be a gap somewhere. Logic cannot take us all the way from beliefs in non-moral facts to dispositions to action; we have a choice, therefore, whether to put the gap between the factual beliefs and the moral judgements, as prescriptivists do, or, as descriptivists prefer, between the moral judgements and the dispositions to action, leaving a tight connexion between the factual beliefs and the moral judgements. In either case there will be a gap, and the 'is'-'ought' debate is thus revealed as trivial (Singer, 1973), since nobody can claim to remove the gap altogether, and it therefore does not much matter where it is put.

This particular objection, however, has been circumvented by our method. For, leaving the prescriptivity of moral judgements intact, and therefore the tight connexion between them and dispositions to action, it also shows how, given certain claims about the logical properties of the moral and other concepts, and given certain factual premisses about people's preferences, we shall reach certain conclusions if we do our moral thinking correctly, and have ruled out 'It doesn't matter' as an answer to our questions. But, as we are not descriptivists, we cannot claim that there is a tight connexion between factual beliefs and moral judgements; and this results, as we saw, in leaving an escape-route for the consistent amoralist: he can admit all our facts, and still either make no moral judgements at all, or make only ones of indifference. So the first two forms of the objection have to be dealt with. I do not think it is possible to close this escape-route; amoralism is an option left open by our system of moral reasoning. All we can do is to give reasons of a non-moral sort why it should not be chosen.

11.2   Although the question 'Why should I be moral?' was coined by Bradley (1876), the modern discussion of it begins effectively with a famous article by Prichard (1912), who was consciously reviving a question asked in the *Republic* of Plato, whom he specifically attacks. Prichard thought it misguided of Plato and others to try to show that to live morally is in our interest, i.e. in accord with prudence. He maintained that it is not universally the case that morality and prudence coincide, and that the question 'Ought I to do my duty?' is one to which the answer is, trivially, 'Yes' if 'ought' is understood morally, but admits of no answer in general if 'ought' is understood prudentially; and that it is mistaken to ask for a prudential justification for living morally. By contrast, some have insisted that rational justifications for living morally have to be in the end prudential. This seems to have been Plato's view in his *Republic*; and he has recently been supported by Mrs. Foot (1958a).

It is possible to take the word 'rational' in such a sense that this must be true. The word is sometimes used as more or less synonymous with 'prudent' (i.e. with 'doing what is, to the best of one's belief, in one's own interest'); and Professor Rawls (1971:142) follows this use when he calls his 'people in the original position' rational. One of the keys to clarity in this particular area is to avoid the use of the word 'rational'; if it is used in the way I have just mentioned, it begs the main issue, and if it used in such a sense that it can be rational to act morally even against one's own interest (and no doubt there is such a sense), then it begs it in the opposite direction. I shall therefore not use the word in this chapter, but shall postpone discussion of it to the next. It will be best to use the word 'prudent' instead for the former sense. As we have seen (5.6), this word itself presents difficulties. However, for the purposes of this chapter the rough account given earlier will suffice, along with a corresponding account of 'in someone's interest'. This we shall take as meaning 'such as he would choose if he fulfilled the "requirement of prudence"' (ib.).

11.3   It must be admitted from the start that it is not the case, and it is hard to see why anybody should ever have thought that it was the case, that to do what we morally ought to do is always in our prudential interest. At least, it is hard to see how anybody could ever have thought this in default of divine rewards and punishments in this world and the next. To that extent Prichard was right. But we can abandon this extreme view and still achieve something more modest, which nevertheless is adequate for the defence of morality. The clearest way of seeing this is to consider what our position would be if we were bringing up some child, and had *only* the child's interests at heart. It would be his preference-satisfactions alone, over his life as a whole, that we were seeking to maximize. That is to say, we would be concerned neither with our own interest, nor with that of other members of society, in the child's subsequent behaviour, but simply with the interests of the child himself. How would we bring the child up? It might be thought that what we would do would be to inculcate in the child a purely egoistic principle, namely the principle to do on every occasion what his own interest most demanded.

We must notice the analogy between this view and the view, *within* morality, of an extreme and crude act-utilitarian of a sort whose views we have rejected (2.4), but who constantly figures as Aunt Sally in the writings of anti-utilitarians. This is a one-level act-utilitarian who thinks that, when confronted with actual moral problems in daily life, the correct thing to do is to work out on every occasion what will maximize utility and then do it. What such an act-utilitarian does in order to determine his moral duty, our crude egoist, if educated in the manner I have suggested, will do in order to determine what is in his interest. It will be equally misguided in the two cases. In the moral case, if we tried to do a felicific calculation on each occasion, we should not have time and should miss the bus on most occasions, and should very often deceive ourselves into thinking that some act was in the general interest when really it was only in our own obvious and immediate self-interest. For this reason we would be wise to be guided, not by a felicific calculation on each occasion, but by a set of well chosen prima facie principles, if we want to achieve those acts which even act-utilitarianism (in the person of the archangel) would in full knowledge pronounce to be right.

When discussing this transition from crude act-utilitarianism to a more sophisticated sort which was also a sort of rule-utilitarianism, I used examples from prudential questions—e.g. the question of whether to make it a principle to wear seat belts when driving (3.2). Exactly the same considerations apply when we come to discuss how to be a successful egoist. It would be just impracticable, and misguided even if practicable, to follow a policy of doing an egoistic or self-interested cost-benefit analysis on all occasions of prudential decision. There would not be time; and we should often cook up our answers in order to pretend, not, as in the previous case, that what was really only in our own interest was morally required or allowed, but that what was only the demand of the immediate desires of the present moment was prudentially required. We should nearly always put off going to the dentist.

In order to counteract this tendency, we need prima facie prudential principles just as much as moral, and need to develop a lot of the same attitudes to them. Many of the so-called 'moral' virtues, including some of those listed by Aristotle (1107^a28 ff.)—namely those which I shall call the *instrumental* moral virtues—are required as much for success in egoism as in morality. Such virtues are courage, self-control, perseverance and the like. They are necessary instruments, if we are going to make a success of practising the more intrinsic virtues such as beneficence or justice. Whether we are seeking to do what is morally right or what is in our own interest merely, we are unlikely to be very successful unless we cultivate these instrumental virtues. This is one fortunate point at which the demands of morality and prudence coincide. One is unlikely to be even a successful criminal without courage and perseverance.

It follows that some, but only some, of the prima facie moral principles which we are likely to adopt will be replicated by precisely similar prima facie pruden-tial principles. Such a principle is the principle of 'temperance', as the Greek word '$s\bar{o}phrosyn\bar{e}$' is conven-tionally translated: the principle that, unlike the 'profligate', who thinks it right always to pursue the pleasure of the moment (Aristotle, 1146^b22), we should cultivate a settled disposition not even to *want* to do that, but to seek more long-term good ends. It was this coincidence, in the instrumental sphere, between the requirements of morality and prudence, which, among other causes, led to confusion between the two spheres in Plato and Aristotle. They often, indeed, speak as if the moral virtues *as a whole* were no more than means to the good life, i.e. instrumental to it; and though this is not in the end a fair interpretation of Aristotle, because he means at least half the time that the practice of the virtues is *constitutive of*, not merely *conducive to*, the good life (e.g. 1177^a1, 1144^a5), it is easy to be confused on this point.

11.4 Our original problem about the relation between morality and prudence can now be restated thus: To what extent will the *prudential* principles, which we shall inculcate in the child whom we are educating in his own best interest, coincide with the *moral* prima facie principles which we should, instead, inculcate if we were seeking to secure, not just his interest, but the interests of all those affected by his actions—i.e. if we were utilitarian educators of the sort considered earlier (2.2, 3.2), and not a vica-

riously self-interested educator such as we are now thinking of ? We have made a modest, though by itself not large,
step forward by establishing that the principles corresponding to the instrumental virtues will be the same in
both cases.

But this is not much so far. It will be at once objected that
that is not the main point. Granted, we have to be
courageous and self-controlled and all that, in order to live
successfully either the life of morality or the life of crime;
but it is the *intrinsic* moral virtues that we ought to be
talking about, and the principles corresponding to these
will diverge from those which egoistic critical thinking
would select. The key question is, How much would they
diverge, in the world as it is? The last phrase is, as always,
crucial, because it is sufficient for our purposes to reconcile
morality with prudence in the world as we have it; it should
not trouble us if they were at odds in logically possible
worlds which are not going to be actual.

Plato seems to have thought it relevant to the argument
that if, by putting on our finger a 'ring of Gyges', we could
render ourselves invisible, this would enable us to escape
detection for crimes which we could not, as things are, get
away with; he thought that the moral act had to be shown to
be prudent even in those circumstances (*Rep.* 359 c). But
one supremely relevant empirical fact is that there are no
rings of Gyges. And there are many other such empirical
facts which are relevant, not all of them so indisputable. On
such matters I can only give my opinion; they are not the
province of the philosopher, though they have an important bearing on his discussions. But if I were bringing up
the child we have been speaking of, I would bring him up
on moral prima facie principles of just the same sort as the
act-utilitarian archangel would select, so far as I could
determine what these were. I should do this, not because it
would suit my own book to have the child well behaved
(though that is a motive for most human educators), and
not because it would be in the interests of society in general
(though that is what an act-utilitarian educator would be

after); for we have supposed that we are not to be guided by either of these motives. I should do it because that would be best in the child's own interest.

There are several reasons for this, of which I shall mention first the most obvious. It is impossible for us to predict the future course of the child's life in any detail. After we have lost control over him (e.g. by dying, which we shall do sooner or later), he will be in all sorts of situations which perhaps we cannot even imagine. We have, therefore, to guess at the best principles for him to have in his own interest. Should we try, for example, inculcating in him the principle that he should always look around carefully and, if he thinks he can get away with it, do immoral things when it is in his interest? I am quite sure that it would not be in the child's interest to teach him this principle.

Why am I so sure? I ask in return, What would living by this principle involve? To be a successful immoral egoist of this sort requires capacities far beyond the reach of all but the most gifted human beings. There is a curious mirror-image effect here which is worth noticing, because it may be illuminating when we come to discuss the life of extreme virtue and acts of supererogation. Just as, to adopt principles requiring extreme saintliness and get away with it, one would have to be godlike, so, to adopt principles of extreme criminality and get away with it, one would have to be a quite exceptionally talented devil. And fortunately people lack this anti-virtue. By 'extreme criminality' I do not mean 'doing atrocious things every minute'. I mean 'Always doing without scruple what is to one's own advantage, and always getting away with it'. Our devil might be superficially very respectable.

But there is another empirical reason, besides human incapacity, why the principle I have mentioned would not be in the child's interest to adopt. It is a physical and not a social fact that there are no rings of Gyges. But the more important empirical facts here are social ones. It is no accident that the world and society are such that crime does not in general pay. People have made it like that because they did not want crime to pay; it is more in the general interest if criminals are brought to book. We must not think here merely of the legal system and courts and policemen; they are, in fact, not the most load-bearing part of the apparatus for 'the enforcement of morals',[1] and would be ineffective unless backed up by much more powerful social pressures. Mankind has found it possible to make life a great deal more tolerable by bringing it about that on the whole morality pays. It is better for nearly all of us if social rewards and penalties are attached to socially beneficial and harmful acts; and so it has come about that on the whole they are.

However, this too takes us only a little way. For it will now be asked, Why not bring up the child to conform to the accepted mores for the most part, but to transgress them cynically when he can escape detection or at least retribution? Part of the answer is that by far the easiest way of seeming to be upright is to be upright.[2] We have seen already that successful crime is for nearly everyone an impossibly difficult game and not worth the candle. If it is alleged against this that in the past people have amassed large fortunes in business careers which were far from unspotted, I reply that the money did not on the whole bring them happiness, and that with their talents they could have done better for themselves by making less money in a more socially beneficial career. If there are exceptions, they are rare enough to be unpredictable by an educator.

11.5   If we ask the reason for this, we shall see that there is another move to be made which reinforces the last. If we set about bringing up our child to have the principles which are most likely on the whole to conduce to his own well-being (and I have argued that some of these will coincide with moral principles) we shall have to bring him

---

[1] The title of Lord Devlin's lecture (1959) which aroused so much controversy.

[2] If we are to believe Xenophon (*Mem.*I, 7), this was Socrates' view. Contrast Plato, *Rep.* 361b, 362a.

up to have not merely a *policy or practice* of obeying these principles, but *firm dispositions of character* which accord with them. Some of these dispositions (perhaps the most important of them) will be positive: the dispositions which make possible mutual cooperation and affection, without which all our endeavours would miscarry, and all the joy and warmth in life would disappear. Those who do not love their fellow men are less successful in living happily among them. Others are negative, but none the less necessary if imperfect human beings are to be got to live in accordance with principles of any sort: dispositions which will make them feel bad if they transgress the principles.

I am not saying that this will be the *same* feeling as a morally well brought up person will have when he transgresses moral principles. I might have said this in relation to the instrumental virtues. Can we really distinguish the self-condemnation of a soldier in a righteous cause when he has displayed want of courage from that of a burglar who has done the same thing and thus gone without his loot? The feeling might be the same in both cases, though not the enterprise. This, however, is not true of the intrinsic virtues; if a man fails, when in pursuit of his own interest, to display single-minded devotion to it, and so out of weak humanity does a kindness to somebody to his own financial loss, he may subsequently kick himself, but he does not suffer remorse, as does the moral man who has, say, in a fit of vindictiveness, done an act of cruelty. But all the same, *some* aversive feeling is required in order to secure consistent obedience to the principles. And perhaps the most effective way of bringing up our child to obey the principles would be to inculcate *moral* feelings. Given that the principles are the same in either case, the moral feelings will be more effective because they receive a great deal more reinforcement from his fellows.

Let us suppose, then, that, in the cause of his doing what is in his own interest on the whole, we have inculcated into this child some moral prima facie principles and the feelings that go with them. The further move I mentioned

at the beginning of this section consists in pointing out that
he has thus acquired an *extra* prudential reason for obeying
his principles. For he will have come to feel repugnance
and shame when he breaks them, and that is an added
disutility to him. In the extreme case, if he has been
successfully brought up, he will suffer great self-loathing if
he has gone back in a serious way on his moral principles,
and that is not in his interest.

But now it will be said, Why not temper the moral
education in such a way as to leave him with the disposition
to follow the principles to the extent that will keep him in
good standing with society, but omit the inculcation of this
disposition to self-loathing? Here again we trespass on the
empirical; but has not the difficulty of bringing this off
been underrated? It is a question of what dispositions are
co-viable. My guess is that the safest and best way of
bringing up our child is to implant in him, if one can, a
good set of moral principles plus the feelings that go with
them, the feelings being strong enough to secure observance of the principles in all ordinary cases, but not, of
course, neurotically strong, or stronger than is needed for
their purpose. We do not want our child to have feelings of
remorse whenever he has failed to wash for a couple of
hours.

11.6   It therefore becomes crucial what the principles
are to which these feelings are attached, and in particular
how stringent they are. This gives us the cue to take up the
other question I mentioned at the beginning of the chapter,
that of works of supererogation. Ought we, to borrow the
title of Professor Urmson's well known paper (1958), to
bring up our children to be saints and heroes? It is
commonly objected to utilitarianism that it would compel
us to make no distinction between ordinary duties and acts
of supererogation which are praiseworthy but not
obligatory. The topic is familiar, and our separation of
levels sheds a good deal of light on it. Utilitarianism is
thought to have this consequence by those who consider
only one level of moral thought (it is seldom clear which)

and therefore think that at this one level we must, if utilitarianism is correct, always have a duty to do what will maximize the furtherance of the interests or the satisfaction of the prudent preferences of our fellow men and ourselves considered impartially, counting everybody for one and nobody for more than one. And if this is translated into practical terms it seems to mean that I have a *duty* (not merely that it would be praiseworthy) to give away all my worldly goods until I have just enough to keep me on a level with the most poverty-stricken Bangladeshi, whom the distribution of my goods will have made by an infinitesimal amount less impoverished. It is claimed by objectors to utilitarianism that this is counterintuitive—a claim whose force as an objection is by this time getting rather small.

This is surely a case in which our intuitions would need defence, even if they were confident and unanimous, which they are not. It is a serious question whether we ought to give away our goods to feed the poor throughout the world—one which demands critical thought, not just an appeal to intuition. Our intuitions are suspect; they date from a time when it was not possible to do very much about poverty in remote parts of the world, and they may owe something to a natural desire to insulate our morality from these problems. When we do examine and seek to justify or else reject them, critical thinking asks what intuitions in this area it is good for people to have; and the answer is not as obvious as might at first be thought (Singer, 1972; 1979: 158 ff.).

It may be that archangels give away all their goods; and obviously some saints do. But the question each person has to ask himself is what prima facie principles are appropriate for *him*; and this may depend on his capacities. It also depends partly on his situation, because there is a limit to which one person's prima facie principles can diverge from other people's without causing serious and damaging misunderstandings. So, to oversimplify a bit, it looks as if the best system of prima facie principles will have more than one sub-level, all within the intuitive level of thinking.

First there will be those principles which nearly everyone has to accept if they are to be workable and fulfil their purpose: principles requiring honesty and truthfulness, for example (for if there are too many dishonest and untruthful people mutual confidence, which is the chief advantage of having those principles, will evaporate); and principles forbidding cruelty and aggression (for a few predators at large will destroy confidence in a different but just as harmful way). Then at another sub-level there will be principles which each person takes as binding on himself and on those like him, but which he does not expect to find obeyed by everybody. And there may be many variations in these. It would be wrong to think that there is no level intermediate between the prima facie principles which have to be common to nearly everybody, and the highly specific principles of critical thinking, each tailored to a particular detailed situation. I may well think it right to have personal but fairly general principles which I do not expect to be the same for everybody, but which are suited to my own capacities and condition.

For example, if I were very saintly like Albert Schweitzer or Mother Teresa, I might have much more exacting principles than in fact I have; and the same would apply in the case of conduct in the face of danger if I were more courageous than I am. This last case illustrates very well the point that principles have to be suited to those who are to follow them (Aristotle, 1106ª36); it is common to find people who try to be more courageous than they have it in them to be, getting themselves and others into serious trouble by, for example, attempting feats of mountaineering or seamanship which are beyond their powers. We say then that they have demanded too much of themselves; that they have set their standards for their conduct too high, and that they have no *vocation* for that kind of exploit.

This last is a useful notion here. The prima facie principles I would do well to set myself to observe will of course include those minimal requirements which are the foundations of life in society. But they will include, too, principles which are desirable in those who occupy certain roles, or vocations in the professional sense, like that of doctor or lawyer or jobbing builder. And they will also include principles proper to my vocation in a much more personal sense, akin to that which it has in theology. And for some these will be pretty stringent; but others would be foolish to aspire to these, because they will never bring it off.

Although it would probably be disastrous if moral education were devoted to the sole purpose of producing saints,[3] it would be detrimental to nearly everybody if those who are able to be saints failed to become such, according to their capacity. Each of us, therefore, has to ask himself what is the level of saintliness of which he is likely to be capable, and strive for that. It is quite hard enough. And of course there are many more ways than one of being a saint, or even a moderately good man (Strawson, 1961; FR 8.6; contrast Aristotle, 1106ᵇ35).

11.7 Returning for a moment to the question about feeding the hungry, it has to be realized that this is not simply a question of what duties individuals have to help other individuals, though this is an important aspect of it. Just as important is the question of what economic, political and social arrangements will result in the long run in people being less hungry, consistently with the avoidance of other evils to which political arrangements are prone. It is difficult in the world as it is to conceive of any system for organizing these matters which does not depend on assigning specified territories to specified groups of people (called nations) and giving responsibility for looking after those territories and nations to governments either freely chosen or somehow thrown up by the nations themselves. Any other system is likely to be condemned as interference or even as imperialism; and it is unlikely that it could be successful from a utilitarian point of view under present conditions.

---

[3] 'Saints' in Urmson's sense and not in that of *Eph.* i, 1.

If we are to have a system of sovereign states, there is a limit to what individuals from outside, even operating through well organized voluntary agencies, can achieve. Oxfam does wonders, but it cannot put to rights the economy of Bangladesh, nor regulate the population of India. It is a commonplace that aid, whether given by governments or individuals, has to be very carefully directed if it is not to be dissipated in projects which do not help with the main problem and may divert effort from enterprises which could help much more. The developing countries which have developed quickest have in general been the smallest recipients of aid; and, although this may not be a causal correlation, it at least shows that massive aid is not *necessary* for development in all cases.

It is much more likely that the most beneficial targets for aid are areas which have suffered natural or man-made disasters and which require temporary relief, and, on the other hand, places where aid can stimulate self-help. This perhaps puts a top limit on the scope of voluntary aid—a limit which, though it leaves most of us doing far less than we should, would allow us to retain the greater part of our resources to use for other good purposes nearer home. Among these is prudent investment, in default of which the resources will dry up. This is an instance of the paradox mentioned earlier (8.3) that particular loyalties at the intuitive level are compatible with complete impartiality at the critical. The reason is that prima facie principles requiring partiality have in some cases a high acceptance-utility even when judged from an impartial critical standpoint. Even a certain degree of self-love in the Butlerian sense is justified from this point of view; for sometimes, when I do things for myself, I know that I benefit, but when I do or try to do things for other people, they may not be the right things, or, even if they are, may be ineffective without their cooperation. I have myself during the course of my life been much more successful in doing good for myself than in trying, with the same or greater expenditure of effort, to do good for other people, because often they do not have the same notion of their good as I have.

11.8 These considerations support the picture we gave earlier, involving at least three sub-levels of prima facie principles, the ones common to all, those common to particular roles, and those personal to individuals. In terms of this picture it is not hard to give an account of works of supererogation. The run-of-the-mill prima facie principles, common to all, and the principles proper to particular roles, give rise to what are called, on the conventional account, duties, or obligations in the widest sense. But 'so likewise ye, when ye shall have done all those things which are commanded you, say, We are unprofitable servants: we have done that which was our duty to do' (Luke, xvii, 10). The saint or hero will do more and will be praised for it. This is easily reconcilable with the rather sophisticated utilitarian method that I have been advocating: the run-of-the-mill principles are the ones with the highest acceptance-utility, if we consider society as a whole; and it is in accordance with utility to condemn breaches of them. They are the least that even a saint has to do. But it is also in accordance with utility to praise those who are able and willing to do more, but not to condemn those who fail. The morality with the highest acceptance-utility must be a practically workable one. And it is hard enough for most of us to live up consistently even to the run-of-the-mill principles, especially when we are tired or frightened or very angry.

I have argued that, if we were bringing up a child purely in his own interest, we should try to inculcate into him some prima facie moral principles, with the attendant moral feelings. Will these include only the run-of-the-mill principles, or should some more exacting principles be also absorbed, if it is within his capacity to live by them? I would answer 'Yes'; for it does look as if people who set themselves higher moral standards which are within their capacity, or not too far outside it, are in general happier than those who do not set their sights so high. But this is an empirical judgement for which I am not able to offer hard evidence; I can only ask the reader whether, from his own experience of life, he does not agree with it.

But there are hazards. Both in the case of prudential principles and of moral, especially the more exacting, even if we grant that the best bet is to adopt them and make them second nature—even if, that is to say, we shall in general and on the whole do best for ourselves if we do this— instances may nevertheless arise in which to have done it will lead us into great troubles. Although it is the best bet to wear seat belts always, it may be that a very few people have been burnt alive through wearing them when they might have survived without them (2.9).

In the same way, it may be that to absorb a certain moral principle (say one requiring self-sacrifice) will be in general in a person's interest (for in general people who are self-sacrificing lead happy lives, to the surprise and discomfiture of those of us who are more selfish). But occasions will arise in which their principles will require them to make very great sacrifices, if they are not to go back on all they have learnt to hold sacred; and this latter they will not be able to bring themselves to do. In that case, if the cause is a good one, we shall admire them, and perhaps, significantly, even wish that we were more like them; but we are not required to say, *contra* Prichard, that they were acting *on that occasion* in their own interest (perhaps they were getting themselves killed when they could have had long and happy lives if they had been less courageous). It may be that the best sort of person to try to become is one who on such rare occasions will act contrary to his own interest in real truth and not, as he often will, merely seem on the surface to be doing that.

In general, when we are educating our children, we know that, in teaching them to admire and practise virtue, we may be bringing it about that in some unlikely contingencies they will have to pay a very high price for their upbringing. But we do not know that that will happen. Even allowing for that possibility, may it be that, all in all, to bring them up to be virtuous—even to practise a higher virtue than the run-of-the-mill principles require—will be in their interests if they are the right sort of people? I think it may be; for it is usually the case that people who are so brought up are happy.

This all depends on empirical assumptions about the way the world goes. I am not making any assumptions about what happens in an after life; but, confining ourselves to this world, we have, if morality is to be a viable enterprise, to believe that if we adopt moral purposes and principles we stand a reasonable chance of carrying them out and not perishing uselessly in the process (H 1973b). And I myself would bring up any children that I had charge of accordingly. This is the secular equivalent (or not perhaps so secular) of seeing that they are, as the Marriage Service puts it, 'christianly and virtuously brought up'. And if we ought so to bring up our children, even in their own interests, it would seem that the same could be said of what we ought to do to ourselves, so far as we are able.

It can safely be predicted that, saints aside, any even moderately good man will react to the above defence of morality in terms of prudence with as little enthusiasm as I do. That is because our intuitions are not even utilitarian, let alone egoistic. And I have given good reasons for thinking that it is desirable from a utilitarian standpoint that they should be like that; and less solid, but perhaps adequate, reasons for saying the same thing from the point of view of an egoist.

12

OBJECTIVITY AND RATIONALITY

12.1 Moral philosophers of the present time, with a few honourable exceptions, all seem to think that they have to take sides on the question of whether 'objectivism' or 'subjectivism' is the correct account of the status of moral judgements. Most of them have the ambition to establish their objectivity, that being the more respectable side to be on; but quite a number are attracted by subjectivism (sometimes, without any clear distinction of meaning, called 'relativism'), as being more go-ahead and free-thinking. Hardly any of them give any clear idea of how they are using the terms 'objective' and 'subjective'; and almost none realizes that, in the most natural senses of the words, moral judgements are neither objective nor subjective, and that the belief that they have to be one or the other is the result of a fundamental error (viz. descriptivism) which both objectivists and subjectivists, in one of the senses of those words, commit (H 1976b:195). It will be the first task of this chapter to clear up these confusions in a rather summary way; I shall then go on to the more serious question of whether moral thought can be rational and in what sense. It is this latter question to which those engaged in the spurious battle between objectivism and subjectivism should have been addressing themselves, because it has an answer, and one which ends the anxieties which generated the objectivist–subjectivist dispute, in a way which no solution of the dispute ever could—for it has none.

We must first distinguish between various senses of the words 'objective' and 'subjective'. Consider the three utterances:

(1) She is over 5 ft. tall;

(2) I love her;
(3) Please come before four o'clock.

The first two state facts of different sorts, but both state facts. It is possible to use the word 'objective' in such a way that both can be said to make objective claims, whereas (3) cannot. In the case of both (1) and (2), if we know their meanings we know their truth-conditions. To put the matter in other words (and less ambiguously than can be achieved by using the word 'objective') both (1) and (2) are (purely) descriptive statements.

But there is another sense in which (1) makes an objective claim but (2) does not. In this sense, statements about people's states of mind are said to be not objective but subjective. To claim objectivity in this sense, a statement has to say something about objects which are in principle publicly observable; and, unless we are behaviourists, my love for her does not fall into this category. If we are behaviourists, the distinction is in danger of breaking down; but it can perhaps be preserved by admitting a class of (behaviourally identified) states of mind, descriptions of which count as subjective, and all other factual statements as objective. So someone who thinks that approval, for example, is a pattern of behaviour and no more, may still call himself a 'subjectivist' if he thinks that to say that an act is right is to say that one approves of it.

But the important point is that the sense of 'objective' which makes (1) objective and (2) subjective is a different sense from that which makes both (1) and (2) objective, and (3) not. The distinction between (1) and (2) on the one hand, and (3) on the other, is much better marked by some other pair of terms; I shall be using 'descriptive' for the property shared by (1) and (2) and 'non-descriptive' for the lack of it. An utterance can be non-descriptive and yet have a descriptive element as *part* of its meaning, as I have explained very fully elsewhere (*FR* 2.8; *LM* 7.2, 7.3; 1.5). The chief relevance of all this to moral philosophy is that the term 'subjectivist' is sometimes used, narrowly, to cover those who think that moral judgements state subjective facts in the sense in which (2) does but (1) does not; but sometimes it is used more widely to cover anybody who denies that moral judgements have the property possessed by (1) but not by (2). In this wide sense, both a subjectivist in the narrow sense, who thinks that moral judgements state facts about people's states of mind, and a non-descriptivist, who thinks that an essential part of their role in their central uses is something different from the stating of facts, have to be called subjectivists.

This would not matter so much if it were not that the issue between objectivists, in the sense of those who believe that moral judgements are like (1), and subjectivists, in the sense of those who believe that they are like (2), is a totally different issue from that which divides both these people (who might be called objectivists in a wide sense but are better called descriptivists) from the non-descriptivist who thinks that moral judgements are typically not pure statements of facts but in part, for example, expressions of attitudes, prescriptions, or something else non-descriptive. The arguments on these two issues have to be different, and it is a great source of confusion if the issues are not distinguished. In particular, non-descriptivists are immune to arguments which serve to demolish subjectivists in the narrow sense (4.5).

I am myself a non-descriptivist—though I am far from thinking that moral judgements are just like (3) (*LM* 11.5; H 1976b:196); however, I still often meet philosophers who think that it is an argument against my views to show that what is right or wrong cannot depend on what somebody prescribes. I find it extraordinary that anybody should attribute to me the view that it so depends.[1] For if it

---

[1] Prof. Basil Mitchell says (1980:32) 'To be an objectivist is to hold that whether something is or is not morally right is independent of the attitudes or inclinations of any particular speaker or set of speakers. It is to deny what Professor R. M. Hare explicitly asserts. . . . ' But of course I *am* an objectivist in that sense. A quotation, out of context, from *FR* follows, which (a) is not

did so depend, then we should be able to derive the statement 'It is wrong' from a factual statement about the utterances or perhaps the thoughts of some prescriber; and I have repeatedly made clear that I do not think that such a statement can be derived from *any* statement of fact. What has happened is that people who are unable to distinguish between the wider and the narrower senses of 'subjectivist' think that because subjectivists in the narrow sense make moral judgements depend on statements of fact about people's thoughts or attitudes or even utterances, non-descriptivists must do the same (in spite of the fact that their non-descriptivism makes this impossible).

This is particularly clear in the case of the variety of non-descriptivism which I have advocated, namely universal prescriptivism. We have to distinguish between

(4) Never do a thing like that,
and
(5) Jones said 'Never do a thing like that';

and thus to understand that it is possible consistently to say that a central element in the meaning of moral judgements has the form of (4), without committing oneself to the absurd view that moral judgements are, or are derivable from, or are dependent for their truth on the truth of, statements like (5). But evidently many are not able to grasp this point.[2]

There is another sense which might be given to 'objectivist' and which is relevant here—though I doubt whether the word has been much used in this sense. This is the sense in which to say something objective is to say something about observable objects. Note the expression 'say something about', which might be thought to mean the same as '*state* something about', but in fact has a much

---

inconsistent with objectivism in this sense, and (b) comes from a passage in which I was talking about something quite different (see 12.7 fn., below).

[2] In H 1976b I falsely accused Prof. Alan Gewirth, through misreading him, of committing this confusion, and have already eaten my words (H 1977b).

wider extension. (3) above, 'Please come before four o'clock', *says* something about an observable object, though it does not *state* anything about it, because it is not a statement. It says something about the presence of your body (an observable object) in the place in question before a certain time; if the body is not there, the request will not have been complied with. As a non-descriptivist, I certainly think that moral judgements can say something about observable objects in this sense, though they may not (for example, 'You did wrong to feel like that' does not).

12.2   In yet another sense moral judgements might be called objective (though I do not think they often have been), if they not merely say something *about* observable objects and their properties, but are made, and can properly be made, *because* those objects have those properties. Thus, I may say that he did wrong because he hit her; what was wrong about what he did is that his hand forcibly struck her body; if he had merely pushed her away it would not have been wrong. Needless to say, my own prescriptivist view makes moral judgements objective in this sense.

For the sake of completeness some other possible senses of 'objective' must be mentioned.[3] It may mean 'unbiassed', and as so used it and its opposite 'subjective' can be used of statements of fact of any sort. For example, if I am a proud father, I may think and say that my daughter was singing in tune when in fact she ended up one key lower than she started; and then I shall be accused of a lack of objectivity. This sense must be carefully distinguished from that in which the results of championships in speed skating are determined objectively by who gets first to the tape, whereas those in figure skating are determined subjectively by a panel of judges; the judges, we hope, are not biassed, but they cannot check their subjective opinions against any physical measurement.

It must also be distinguished from a sense used by

---

[3] I am indebted here to an unpublished paper by Mr. Mackie.

lawyers, who say that the test of whether an act was due to provocation is subjective if it asks merely whether the agent was in fact, being a man of an irascible disposition, moved to do it by what the other man did; but objective, if it asks whether a reasonable man would have been provoked by what he did. This distinction is not especially relevant here; but it may warn us not to confuse the application of a more or less consistent intersubjective norm (which can be done with moral judgements or with any other kind of prescriptions if we wish) with objectivity in the sense of factuality or descriptivity, which prescriptions cannot have.

Perhaps the most crucial sense of 'objective' for ethics, if it exists, is one that has nothing essentially to do with factuality, and can apply equally to prescriptions, but is at least closely allied to the sense 'unbiassed'. It is sometimes claimed that moral judgements have to be made from an impersonal standpoint.[4] This might mean merely that they have to be impartial, i.e. that who is in which role in the situation being judged is not treated as relevant. Objectivity in this sense is preserved by any system of reasoning which, like my own, insists on the universalizability of moral judgements. Whether 'impersonal' means any more than this I am in some doubt. The negative form of the adjective might suggest that the judgement has to be made not by a person but, perhaps, by an 'imperson'; but it is hard to attach sense to this. We have in this book made use of the notion of a very perfect moral judge, the archangel, who is able to make moral judgements without personal bias or partiality; but even his judgements would not be objective in the sense, if there is one, that they issued from no person. Theists believe that God is such a perfect judge; but they also believe that he is one or more persons. Without going deeply into this suggestion, which does not look promising on the face of it, I shall affirm baldly that there can be objective prescriptions in the sense of

---

[4] I hesitate to attribute this view to Prof. Thomas Nagel; but this paragraph was prompted by reflection on his Tanner Lectures at Oxford (1980:77 ff.).

impartial prescriptions, but that I cannot extract more from the notion of impersonality than this.

It is hard to know just how sophisticated a discussion of these matters is appropriate. My impression is that the points on which most people, including some very sophisticated people, trip up are quite simple and indeed elementary ones; and that, if they were to get these clear, they could return to their more ambitious discussions with greater hope of getting somewhere. For this reason I have not scrupled to use the word 'factual'—a very elusive notion. It needs discussion whether there is any determinate class of factual statements from which moral judgements have to be excluded. I feel much safer with the expression 'descriptive', whose definition I have discussed at length in *FR* 2.1 ff. Everything of importance in the above account of objectivity could be put in terms of this word, which, applied to statements, means that their meaning completely determines their truth-conditions. If this were done, we should not need the word 'factual'.

12.3 But before we leave the notion of objectivity for the more promising one of rationality, it may be helpful to mention a problem which troubles many people, and whose solution is to be found by erecting a bridge between the two notions. Many readers will complain that I have not dealt with the main reason why people want moral principles and values to be objective. What they feel the need of is a decision-procedure—an algorithm even—for moral dilemmas. This demand can sometimes take the crudest forms. For example, it may be asked of the moral philosopher that he should produce some yardstick which has only to be applied to actions or to people in order to determine whether they are right or good. To ask this is to ask for a way of escaping from the labour of moral thought.

But the demand is not always so unreasonable. Seen in the light of our distinction between levels of moral thinking, it may be perfectly just. If one has been brought up with certain moral intuitions, and doubt has been cast on their reliability, what more natural than to look for a

way of thinking which can resolve the doubt in a determinate way? We wonder whether our intuitions are
giving us the right answer, so we ask for a way of deciding
'objectively' what *is* the right answer; and this could be an
entirely laudable demand to be shown the proper method
of critical thinking. This demand I hope to have met, and
indeed from time to time I have actually used the word
'right' and near synonyms to signify what the results of
such thinking would be if it were done in accordance with
the rules which the logical properties of the moral concepts
generate (2.8).

However, this entirely reasonable demand might be
confused with another which is based only on a misunderstanding of the word 'right'. The crucial point to get
hold of is that statements containing 'right', like those
containing 'true', get their logical character and status
from the 'that'-clauses inside them which specify what is
being said to be true or right. Thus, if 'She is over 5 ft. tall'
states a fact, then so does 'It is true that she is over 5 ft. tall'
state a fact; and likewise 'It is right to say that she is over 5
ft. tall'. But by contrast, if anybody maintains that 'He did
wrong' does not state a fact, it will be no argument against
him to point out that we can say 'It was right to say that he
did wrong'; for this is to assume what needs proof. If 'He
did wrong' did not state a fact, then neither would 'It was
right to say that he did wrong'.

I have discussed at tedious length elsewhere (H 1976b:
201) how much or how little can be shown by pointing out
that we can use the words 'right' and, in certain limited
contexts, 'true' of moral judgements. Since the conclusion
was that the fact has very little bearing on the question of
objectivity, I shall merely point out here that anybody who
requires us to show how it can be established that it was
right to say that he did wrong is only asking over again the
question to which almost the whole of this book has been
addressed, namely, how it can be established that he did
wrong. It has been our aim to find a system of moral
reasoning which we can use when faced with moral

questions. If such a system can be found which is rational, then the question of the objectivity of its results can be left to look after itself. We may therefore pass on without further delay from the notion of objectivity to that of rationality, which we should have been discussing all along.

12.4 Rationality is in its primary sense a property of thought, and of actions in so far as they are the product of thought. More precisely, it is a property of thought directed to the answering of questions, among which may be the question of what to do next. In much of the literature the word has been used too narrowly, because the questions which we might seek to answer by our thought are more various than writers have sometimes realized. We have already illustrated this (5.6) by considering three different questions which might be asked in a choice-situation, namely 'What would my present preferences be, if I exposed them to logic and the facts?', 'What would maximize the satisfaction of my now-for-now and then-for-then preferences?' and 'What shall I now do?' We saw that a rational answer to the third question depends on the answer to the first, but that the second is a different question. We have now to add to these a fourth question, 'What (morally) ought I now to do?' Since these are different questions, it may be that they demand different properties in thought directed to answering them, if it is to be rational.

To say this is not to claim that no single definition of 'rational' can be given. Professor Brandt (1979:10) has offered a promising one, of which we have already made use: 'I shall preempt the term "rational"', he says, 'to refer to actions, desires or moral systems which survive maximal criticism by facts and logic.' He subsequently elaborates and explains this definition in such an exemplary way that I feel excused from trying to improve on his account. In particular, he explains how to be rational under conditions of incomplete information. It is clear that the definition could also be used for the special case where the question we are trying to answer is a purely factual one like 'Is the professor reading my papers before he grades them?' A paranoid student might answer 'No' on insufficient grounds; and then we should say that his thought-processes had been irrational because, if more criticized and corrected by facts and logic, they would have become different.

However, there is one point which, though I am sure Brandt is aware of it, is not sufficiently stressed by him. 'Criticism and correction by logic' presumably require some cognizance of the logical character, determined by the meaning, of the question being asked. May it not be that if one is asking what one *ought* to do, the thought-processes one has to go through if one is going to be rational, and the sorts of criticism to which these thought-processes are open, are different from what they would be if one were asking 'What shall I now do?', i.e. wondering what *to* do?

It has been the purpose of this book to set out the requirements for rational thinking about moral questions; and I have claimed that logic can determine what these requirements are. But this logic is the logic of certain concepts, namely those which are expressed by means of such words as 'ought', as used in moral contexts. The requirements may well be less stringent, or at least different, if we are asking, not these questions, but others such as 'What shall I do?' In order to answer rationally the question 'What shall I do?' we have, according to Brandt, to submit our own desires (preferences) to logic and the facts. But facts about other people's preferences and their satisfaction are not made relevant by the question itself, in the way that they are by the question 'What ought I to do?' This is because in answering the latter question I am prescribing universally; I must, in order to answer it rationally, rationally prefer that the answer should be acted on whatever role I play in the resulting sequence of events. Brandt himself does not accept that one of the cardinal features which distinguishes moral questions is the universalizability of answers to them. I have already given my reasons for dissenting from this rejection of universalizability, which is based on too facile an appeal to what people say who have not thought enough about what they are saying (4.7).

12.5 Nevertheless, it is possible to accept Brandt's account of the rational answering of the question 'What shall I do?', and extend it into an account of moral rationality, by bringing in the requirement of universalizability as we have done. We simply require that the answering prescription be a universal one. But to complete the picture it is necessary to say a little more about the concept of rationality itself, in order to guard against certain misconceptions.

The commonest of these is to think, following Hume (1739: II, 3, iii; III, 1, i), that rationality can only be displayed in thinking about factual or about logical questions. If this were so, then any question that could be rationally answered would be a factual or logical one. This is what ethical descriptivists commonly think. If moral questions cannot be rationally answered unless they are factual or logical, a would-be rationalist cannot avoid the conclusion that any moral judgements which are not analytically or logically true are about matters of moral fact. In order to understand why this is wrong, we have to explain how 'criticism by facts' enters into our appraisal of moral thought-processes.

It should at once be clear that it does enter. It is common ground that anybody who makes his moral judgements in disregard of the facts about the action he is judging is thinking irrationally (5.1). Moral judgements are about properties which actions have (e.g. the property of resulting in someone's death). The properties of the actions are the reasons for the judgement; that is another way of stating the requirement of universalizability, which is generated by the logical properties of the moral concepts. But the properties which are the reasons for the judgement are not themselves moral properties, and therefore the facts which we have to discover before we can make it rationally are not moral facts, but ordinary facts whose factuality nobody need deny, like the fact that he killed her.

It is not necessary, in order to show the rationality of moral thinking, to bring into existence any specifically moral facts additional to these ordinary facts (H 1979a). If somebody in his moral thinking has taken cognizance of such ordinary facts as are available and relevant (3.9), he has done all the fact-finding that rationality requires. What it requires in addition are thought-processes governed by logical rules, and I have tried to explain what these are.

If one thinks that this is not enough, one may look around for moral facts to fill the gap, and be misled into thinking one has found them. To repeat what I said earlier (4.3), there are two kinds of facts (which are not moral facts at all, but can easily be mistaken for them), with which descriptivists can seek to plug this supposed gap. The first are facts about our feelings and dispositions. We are indeed disposed to condemn certain actions, and that is a fact, but not a moral fact. The vice of intuitionism lies in the surreptitious transition from these psychological facts to alleged moral properties which actions are supposed to have, but which are really nothing but the tendency to evoke these feelings. Intuitionism is only a cloak for subjectivism of the sort which regards moral judgements as statements that we have feelings of approval, disapproval, etc. There is no more of substance to the intuitionist account than to the subjectivist; both are infected with the same error (4.5).

The other kind of fact which can be used in the hope of plugging the gap consists of facts which are the reasons for the moral judgement. It is a common mistake, whose name is 'naturalism', to think that a fact cannot be a reason for a moral judgement unless the moral judgement is deducible from the fact with or without some other factual premises. This is not so. A fact can be a reason for a moral judgement for anybody who accepts a substantial *moral* principle from which, in conjunction with the fact and other non-moral premisses, the moral judgement is deducible. Thus we say 'He did wrong because it resulted in her death', thereby giving as a reason for the wrongness of his action the fact that it resulted in her death; and this reasoning may be quite all right, if we have as premiss the substantial moral principle that one ought not (with whatever qualifications are appropriate to the case) to do what will result in people's deaths. But there is no deducibility of the moral judgement from the factual premiss without the inclusion in the premisses of this substantial moral principle. Since the whole of this book has been about how to establish such principles, I shall not be accused, I hope, of introducing irrationality by saying this.

The rationality of moral thought rests, indeed, on there being a system of reasoning for deciding which of such principles to adopt. This system I have called 'critical thinking'. It does not, and does not need to, ascertain any moral facts, though it does need to ascertain facts of a more genuine sort. We are rational in our critical thinking if we make use of the available facts, and reason in accordance with the logical requirements generated by the concepts used in the questions we are asking.

12.6   Before I end, I must answer a question which will certainly be asked. I have repeatedly throughout my career as a moral philosopher condemned naturalism and all other forms of descriptivism, and have just been doing it again. But, it might be asked, have I not now screwed up my system of moral reasoning so tight that I have myself become a descriptivist? For if to be a descriptivist is to think that moral judgements are descriptive, and if for a statement to be descriptive is for its meaning to determine its truth-conditions, surely I am a descriptivist? Have I not, by appealing to the meanings of the moral words, and thus to the logic of the moral concepts, set up a system of moral reasoning which compels us to adopt certain moral principles and reject others? Could it not be said, therefore, that the truth or rightness of these principles follows from the meanings of the words? And is not this a form of naturalism and thus of descriptivism?

Consider any moral principle adopted at the critical level. It may be highly specific, stating what ought to be done in all cases of some minutely specified kind. I have been maintaining that critical thinking, if done in accordance with the logic, i.e. with the meaning-rules, of the moral concepts, and given determinate assumptions about the facts of the case, will lead to our acceptance or rejection of the principle (in cases where the interests and preferences of ourselves and others are affected). But what is the difference, it may be asked, between saying this, and saying that the meaning of the words used in stating the principle determines its truth-conditions? If there is no difference, then moral principles are after all purely descriptive.

In order to assess this imputation of descriptivism, we must briefly remind ourselves of the route by which the result was reached. The order of this recapitulation will not be the same as that of the original exposition, because, now that we have traversed the entire route, we can pick out the most crucial steps more clearly in a different order. First we stipulate, in accordance with the logic of the moral concepts, that in accepting a moral principle we are accepting a universal prescription or prohibition (*FR* 2.7, 6.2). Next, in rejecting amoralism (but not for logical reasons, since it is a consistent position) we stipulate that some universal prescription or prohibition shall be adopted for the case under consideration. The admission that amoralism can be a consistent position marks a departure from descriptivism, as we saw (10.7); for if logic cannot compel us to abjure amoralism, provided that it is consistently followed, that leaves it open to us, when any universal prescription or prohibition is proposed, either to accept it, if it is consistent with the other prescriptions that our preferences commit us to, or, if we are an amoralist, to reject it. We argued against consistent amoralism, but on prudential grounds not logical (11.3 ff.).

12.7   That, then, is one feature of our system which makes it non-descriptivist; but not the only one, as we shall shortly see. Faced with the choice between accepting and rejecting some universal prescription or prohibition, we have to reconcile it, if we are to accept it, with the sum-total of our preferences; that is, we have to prefer, all in all, that it should be (universally) observed than that it should not be (universally) observed. But these preferences will include, if we are fully informed, preferences about what should happen were we in the positions of those affected by the observance or non-observance of the principle, preferences which correspond exactly to the preferences which the people in those positions have (5.3). Leaving on one side the amoralist escape-route, the imputation of descriptivism arises because *facts* about other people's preferences seem, according to this system of reasoning, to constrain us to form *preferences* ourselves as to what should happen were we in their positions. This looks at first sight like an inference from a statement of fact to a prescription; for preferences have, as we saw, prescriptions as their expressions. Are we then saying that, the facts about other people's preferences (the prescriptions they accept) being what they are, we cannot rationally (i.e. if fully informed about those preferences and consistent in our thinking) escape having similar preferences ourselves for the hypothetical situations in which we would occupy their roles, and therefore cannot escape accepting the prescriptions which are the expressions of those preferences? And is not that an inference from facts to prescriptions?[5]

It must be noticed that this point has nothing in particular to do with universalizability. The prescription to which we seem to have to assent is a singular one (e.g. 'Let that not happen to *me* if I am in that situation'); and no

---

[5] This is the kind of 'dependence' on people's 'inclinations' that Prof. Mitchell (12.1 fn., above) mistook for a lack of 'objectivity'. But if the admission of it makes someone a subjectivist, anyone will be a subjectivist who thinks, e.g., that to do *that* would hurt her very deeply, and would therefore be wrong. It is her not liking it being done to her that makes it wrong, which is one kind of preference or inclination.

requirement to assent to universal prescriptions has to be made *en route* from the fact about the other person's singular prescriptions or preferences to our own singular prescription or preference. The only point at which universalizability enters the argument so far is in the requirement, for the sake of rationality, to ascertain the facts, including facts about others' preferences; for as we saw (5.1), our final moral judgement will be irrational unless we have done that first. But even there universalizability was not indispensable; for, as we saw, it can be claimed that cognizance of the facts is a necessity for rationality even in singular prescriptions.

We must also at this point notice that what we said about personal identity has a bearing on our present problem (5.4). If it be accepted that 'I' has a prescriptive element in its meaning, then, when I entertain the thought that the person who is actually now suffering might, in a hypothetical case, be myself, I acquire some hypothetical prescriptions by doing this. In general, when I say that somebody who would be in a certain situation would be *myself*, in so saying I express a concern for that person in that hypothetical situation which is normally greater than I feel for *other people* in the same situation. To recognize that that person would be myself is already to be prescribing that, other things being equal, the preferences and prescriptions of that person should be satisfied. This is what is involved in 'identifying' with that person.

It is, as we have seen, possible to identify to a greater or lesser degree with other people also. Aristotle found in this the essence of love, and the language he uses bears out the strength of the conceptual connexion between personal identity and non-contingent sharing of prescriptions and preferences. He defines the *philos* or loved one as 'another oneself' (1166ª32, 1169ᵇ7). This is the origin of the expression '*alter ego*' which has passed into our language. It might be claimed that, even if we *can* form such a relation with other people, we must, if we are to have continuing identity, maintain it with ourselves. Self-sacrifice is certainly possible, but without this there would be no self to sacrifice. I may sacrifice the preferences of that future person to ends which I value more; but to think of that person as myself, I must at least give the same weight to his preferences as he does.

Stripped of inessentials, the reason why the method expounded in chh. 5 and 6 has put me in danger of being called a descriptivist is the following. I claimed that it is a conceptual truth that if I know that I would be prescribing something were I in exactly someone else's position with his preferences, I must now be prescribing the same thing with the same intensity. This looks as if it made possible an inference on conceptual grounds alone from a *fact* about what I should be prescribing were I that person to a present *prescription*. And it would be impossible for a consistent pure-blooded prescriptivist to admit such an inference. But now it turns out, if the view about personal identity which I have been suggesting is correct, that the alleged fact itself contained a prescriptive element. For in identifying the person in the hypothetical situation as *myself*, I should, if that view be accepted, already be committed to prescribing that his prescriptions be satisfied. So the suggested view about personal identity would have the two merits from my point of view of preserving me from any form of descriptivism and of making the thesis maintained in ch. 5, on which our whole method depends, even more clearly a conceptual one. In the baldest terms, it is the thesis that to the extent that I know what it is like for a certain person to be prescribing or preferring something in his situation, and identify hypothetically with him (i.e. think that I might be he, which involves prescribing that if I were, his prescriptions, which would in that hypothetical case have become mine, should be satisfied), I shall prescribe that those prescriptions should in that hypothetical case be satisfied. And this is obviously a tautology.

But it is a far from trivial one. For it is the key to understanding what happens when we advance to morality from prudence. To be prudent is to think of the future states of a certain person (normally the person whose body one's present body will be) as *oneself*, and thus to acquire a concern for the satisfaction of the future preferences of that person. To become moral is, first of all, to contemplate the hypothetical situation in which what are actually going to be states of another person would be states of oneself, and thus to acquire a hypothetical concern for the satisfaction of the preferences of oneself in that hypothetical situation; and then, because of universalizability, to find oneself constrained (unless one takes the amoralist escape-route) to turn this merely hypothetical concern into an actual concern for the satisfaction of the preferences of the actual other person.

In plainer terms, morality requires us to argue: Since, if *I* were going forthwith to have the preferences which *he* actually has, I must now prescribe that they *should* be satisfied, and since morality admits no relevant difference between "I" and "he", I am bound, unless I become an amoralist, to prescribe that they *be* satisfied. This prescription will have to compete with others (6.2), but it is enough to have secured it a place in the competition. And what establishes the truth of the first 'since'-clause is the implicit prescriptivity of the word 'I'.

12.8 If this claim about personal identity were sustained, it would provide a further reason for not classifying me as a descriptivist. It must be noted however that I am not, and have never been, a completely unqualified non-descriptivist either. I am referring, not to the fact that I have always allowed as much importance to the descriptive meaning of moral judgements as to the prescriptive, but to the fact that at the very beginning, when in *LM* 2.5 I suggested the rule that no imperatives can be deduced from indicatives alone, I said that it might require qualifications, and I at once made some (in relation to so-called hypothetical imperatives and some other compound imperatives which *can* be deduced from indicatives). I have later allowed (H 1977b:469), in response to examples produced by Professor Sen and others, that other qualifications are needed, in particular that which is demanded by the thesis of universalizability itself, the admission of the inference from '*A* did exactly as *B* did' to 'If *B* did wrong, then *A* did wrong'. This latter is an inference to a moral judgement, and inferences of this sort cannot be made to plain imperatives, because they are not universalizable. Nevertheless, if moral judgements are a kind of prescriptions, this inference and others like it represent exceptions to the rule that there are no valid inferences from facts to prescriptions.

I did not, however, until very recently, contemplate the possibility of the exception (if, in spite of what I have said in the preceding section, it is an exception) which would be constituted by inferences from facts about other people's prescriptions to prescriptions of my own as to what should be done to me were I in their positions. In order to clarify matters further, let us make, for the sake of argument, the assumptions (which I think are actually false) that I could close the amoralist escape-route by some conceptual manoeuvre, and that what I have said about the prescriptivity of 'I' could be shown to be mistaken. Could I then defend myself against the imputation of being a descriptivist?

There is one defence which might be suggested, but of which I shall not avail myself. This would consist in saying that I do not require any inference from a fact to a prescription, but only from a fact about a prescription to a fact about another prescription. All I am saying, it might be claimed, is that if I know or believe that another has a certain preference, I must myself form a similar preference as to what should happen, were I in his position with his preferences. But this, it might be said, only requires an inference from the fact that Hare knows or believes to *the fact that* Hare prefers. No actual prescription is being deduced. However, this is not a strong defence; for if I cannot consistently claim to know or believe but withhold the prescription or preference, then, whether or not we call this a deduction of the preference from the knowledge or belief, i.e. of the prescription 'Let it be done if I were in the other person's position' from the statement 'The other person prescribes that it be done', it is as good as a deduction.

If we grant that there are some facts about prescriptions whose admission entails the acceptance of prescriptions, how big a dent does this make in my non-descriptivism? I am inclined to say 'Not a very big dent', for reasons which I shall now give. We must remember that what will determine our final moral judgement is our total system of preferences. Of these, the preference whose prescriptive expression is derived from the fact about another's preference is only one. We are therefore compelled only to assent *ceteris paribus* to the prescription that, should we be in the other person's position, that preference should be satisfied. We may, however, have many other preferences which will make *cetera* not *paria*, and may override this one. So to admit this inference, though it would influence our final judgement, would not determine it. Our other preferences may outweigh this one; what we prefer all in all is determined by the balance of them without external constraint, and in this sense we remain free to prefer what we prefer. This is not in the sense (perhaps favoured by some existentialists) that we can simply abolish or create preferences at will, but only in the sense that our resultant preference all in all is a function of our separate and perhaps conflicting preferences and their respective intensities and of nothing else.

But before we can be satisfied with this freedom we shall have to proceed further and see what happens when universalizability is introduced into the argument; for that might make the dent bigger. Universalizability requires us to choose our final moral judgement or principle *as if* it were going to be applied in all the hypothetical cases in which we occupied the roles now occupied by the others. This is what the requirement to treat hypothetical identical cases on a par with the actual case, and universalize over them, really amounts to. This exercise of reason does

substantially reduce our freedom; for now all the preferences for what should happen to us in hypothetical
situations in which we were in the others' roles have
acquired the same weight as they would have if we were
actually going to be in those roles and were perfectly
prudent. This, indeed, is what makes utilitarians of us
(6.2). Is this move consistent with non-descriptivism?

The answer may depend on what we said about the
fanatic (10.5). We said that it was in theory open to him to
have a preference for the realization of his ideal strong
enough to outweigh all the preferences of all the others who
would suffer through its realization; and that in that case
even we as utilitarians would have to allow him to have it
satisfied. We also said that practically speaking such a
contingency would never occur. However, the logical
possibility of its occurrence, though perfectly consistent
with our theory, illustrates a point which is relevant here:
our preferences can change; and so also can other people's.
We have to remember that preferences are not fixed but
fluid.

This means that we, and others too, retain the freedom to
prefer whatever we prefer. Some preferences, even in the
prudential sphere, may be more rational than others, as
Professor Brandt rightly maintains (1979: 110); but there
remains an irreducible and large minimum of sheer
autonomous preferences which rational thinking can only
accept for what they are, or will be. To that extent Hume
was right (1739: II, 3, iii). The effect of universalizability is
to compel us to find principles which impartially maximize
the satisfaction of these preferences; it does not constrain
the preferences themselves. The move in ch. 5 does
constrain them, but only to the limited degree already
admitted—i.e. the move which requires us to form hypothetical preferences for cases in which we are in others'
roles.

12.9 The upshot of all this is very interesting. We
retain, all of us, the freedom to prefer whatever we prefer,
subject to the constraint that we have, *ceteris paribus*, to

prefer that, were we in others' exact positions, that should happen which *they* prefer should happen. The requirement of universalizability then demands that we adjust these preferences to accommodate the hypothetical preferences generated by this constraint, as if they were not hypothetical but for actual cases; and thus, each of us, arrive at a universal prescription which represents our total impartial preference (i.e. it is that principle which we prefer, all in all, should be applied in situations like this regardless of what position we occupy). What has happened is that the logical constraints have, between them, compelled us, if we are to arrive at a moral judgement about the case, to coordinate our individual preferences into a total preference which is impartial between us. The claim is that this impartial preference will be the same for all, and will be utilitarian. This process of reasoning is very similar to what economists call the transition from individual welfare (or utility) functions to a social welfare (or utility) function. It is my hope that the argument of this book has shed some light on the means of achieving this transition.

But is it a kind of descriptivism or of non-descriptivism that we are advocating? A kindly philosophical friend might take us aside and say 'Why go to so much effort to keep the tattered flag of non-descriptivism flying? Does it matter what you call your view? You have, following your wise policy of swallowing the truths propounded by your opponents while castigating their errors, admitted that much of what descriptivists were trying to achieve can be achieved, though, you hope, by clearer and more rigorous arguments than they could command. Why not leave it to other people to say whether you are a descriptivist or a non-descriptivist or a mixture of the two?'

There is much good sense in this advice. On the other side, it could be argued that to admit the possibility of my calling myself a descriptivist might lead people to suppose that I no longer think the many errors of the usual kinds of descriptivists to be errors, which I still do. And there are particular points at which my theory is inconsistent with at

any rate a pure-blooded descriptivism. We have documen-
ted the amoralist escape-route, which is one such point.
Another is the liberty we all have to prefer what we prefer;
this liberty has the consequence that the facts from which a
descriptivist might seek to deduce moral judgements are
shifting facts about people's prescriptions, which can
change. So it is not so much a matter of us all confronting
ineluctable objective facts to which our moral judgements
have to conform. Rather, in preferring what we prefer,
morality compels us to accommodate ourselves to the
preferences of others, and this has the effect that when we
are thinking morally and doing it rationally we shall all
prefer the same moral prescriptions about matters which
affect other people (though in matters which do not, we
remain free). Moral thinking is thus revealed as something
that we have to do in concert, though each individual has to
play his own part. What I am advocating, then, is less a
form of descriptivism than, as I have called it, of rational
universal prescriptivism. Reason leaves us with our
freedom, but constrains us to respect the freedom of
others, and to combine with them in exercising it.

REFERENCES AND BIBLIOGRAPHY

1. *Writings of R. M. Hare*

For completeness, all works published since 1971 are listed. References are also given to works cited in this book and published before 1971. A complete bibliography up to 1971 is printed in H 1971b. References in the text of the form 'H 1963a:75' are to this part of the bibliography, the last figure being the page. References to *The Language of Morals* (1952) and *Freedom and Reason* (1963) take the form of the letters '*LM*' or '*FR*' followed by the chapter and section numbers. Internal references to this book are to chapters and sections, and either stand by themselves or are preceded by a semicolon.

1952   *The Language of Morals* (Oxford U. P.). Revised 1961. Translations: Italian, *Il linguaggio della morale* (Astrolabio-Ubaldini, 1968); German, *Die Sprache der Moral* (Suhrkamp, 1972); Spanish, *El Lenguaje de la Moral* (Mexico U. P., 1975).

1955   'Universalisability', *Aristotelian Society* 55. Repr. in H 1972b. Spanish translation in *Problemas de Etica*, ed. F. Salmeron and E. Rabossi (Mexico U. P.).

1960   'Philosophical Discoveries', *Mind* 69. Repr. in *Plato's Meno*, ed. A. Sesonske and N. Fleming (Wadsworth, 1965), *The Linguistic Turn*, ed. R. Rorty (U. of Chicago P., 1967), *Philosophy and Linguistics*, ed. C. Lyas (Macmillan, London and St. Martin's P., 1971), and H 1971c. German translation in *Linguistik und Philosophie*, ed. G. Grewendorf and G. Meggle (Suhrkamp, 1974).

1962   Review of M. Singer, *Generalization in Ethics*, *Ph. Q.* 12.

1963a   *Freedom and Reason* (Oxford U. P.). Translations: Italian, *Libertà e ragione* (Il Saggiatore, 1971); German, *Freiheit und Vernunft* (Patmos, 1973).

1963b   'Descriptivism', *British Academy* 49. Repr. in 1972b.

1964   'Pain and Evil', *Aristotelian Society* supp. 38. Repr. in *Moral Concepts*, ed. J. Feinberg (Oxford U. P., 1969) and H 1972b.

1967   'The Lawful Government', in *Philosophy, Politics and Society* 3, ed. P. Laslett and W. G. Runciman (Blackwell). Repr. in 1972d.

1968   Review of G. J. Warnock, *Contemporary Moral Philosophy*, *Mind* 77.

1971a   Review of L. van der Post, *The Prisoner and the Bomb*, *New York Review of Books* 17 (20 May).

1971b   *Practical Inferences* (Macmillan, London and U. of California P.).

1971c   *Essays on Philosophical Method* (Macmillan, London and U. of California P.). Italian translation, *Studi sul metodo filosofico* (Armando, 1977).

1971d   'Drugs and the Role of the Doctor' and other contributions to *Personality and Science*, ed. I. T. Ramsey and R. Porter (CIBA Foundation Report, Churchill Livingstone).

1971e   'Wanting: Some Pitfalls', in *Agent, Action and Reason*, ed. R. Binkley *et al.* (Toronto U. P. and Blackwell). Also in 1971b.

1972a   'Principles', *Aristotelian Society* 72.

1972b   *Essays on the Moral Concepts* (Macmillan, London and U. of California P.)

1972c   'Rules of War and Moral Reasoning', *Ph. and Pub. Aff.* 1. Repr. in *War and Moral Responsibility*, ed. M. Cohen *et al.* (Princeton U. P.).

1972d   *Applications of Moral Philosophy* (Macmillan, London and U. of California P.). Japanese translation forthcoming.

1972e   Review of G. J. Warnock, *The Object of Morality*, *Ratio* 14 (English and German edns.).

1973a   Critical Study: 'Rawls' Theory of Justice—I and II', *Ph.Q.* 23. Repr. in *Reading Rawls*, ed. N. Daniels (Blackwell, 1975).

1973b   'The Simple Believer', in *Religion and Morality*, ed. G. Outka and J. P. Reeder (Anchor P.).

1973c   'Language and Moral Education', in *New Essays in the Philosophy of Education*, ed. G. Langford and D. J. O'Connor (Routledge). Repr. in H 1979e.

1973d   'Sad Moralny' ('Moral Judgement'), *Etyka* (Warsaw) 11 (in Polish with English and Russian summaries).

1974a   Comment on R. Edgley, 'Reason and Violence', in *Practical Reason*, ed. S. Körner (Blackwell and Yale U. P.).

1974b   'The Abnormal Child: Moral Dilemmas of Doctors and Parents', *Documentation in Medical Ethics* 3. Repr. as 'Survival of the Weakest' in *Moral Problems in Medicine*, ed. S. Gorovitz (Prentice-Hall, 1976).

1974c   'Platonism in Moral Education: Two Varieties', *Monist* 58.

1974d   'What Use is Moral Philosophy?', television discussion with A. J. P. Kenny, in *Philosophy in the Open* (Open U.).

1975a   'Contrasting Methods of Environmental Planning', in *Nature and Conduct*, ed. R. S. Peters (R. Inst. of Ph. Lectures, 1974, Macmillan. London and St. Martin's P.). Repr. in *Ethics and Problems of the 21st Century*, ed. K. Goodpaster and K. Sayre (U. of Notre Dame P., 1979).

1975b   'Autonomy as an Educational Ideal', in *Philosophers Discuss Education*, ed. S. C. Brown (Proc. of R. Inst. of Ph. Conference, Macmillan, London, 1973).

1975c   'Abortion and the Golden Rule', *Ph. and Pub. Aff.* 4. Repr. in *Philosophy and Sex*, ed. R. Baker and F. Elliston (Prometheus, 1975).

1975d   'Euthanasia: A Christian View', *Ph. Exchange* 2 (Proc. of Center for Philosophic Exchange, Brockport, N. Y.).

1976a   'Ethical Theory and Utilitarianism', in *Contemporary British Philosophy* 4, ed. H. D. Lewis (Allen and Unwin).

1976b   'Some Confusions about Subjectivity', in *Freedom and Morality*, ed. J. Bricke (Lindley Lectures, U. of Kansas).

1976c   'Political Obligation', in *Social Ends and Political Means*, ed. T. Honderich (Routledge).

1976d   'Value Education in a Pluralist Society: a Philosophical Glance at the Humanities Curriculum Project', in *Proc. of Ph. of Ed. Soc. of G. B.* 10, ed. R. S. Peters.

1976e   Review of H.-N. Castañeda, *The Structure of Morality*, *J. Phil.* 73.

1977a   'Medical Ethics: Can the Moral Philosopher Help?' in *Philosophy and Medicine* 3: *Philosophical Medical Ethics, its Nature and Significance* (Reidel).

1977b   'Geach on Murder and Sodomy' (on 'is'–'ought' inferences), *Philosophy* 52.

1977c   'Opportunity for What?: Some Remarks on Current Disputes About Equality in Education', *Oxford Rev. of Ed.* 3.

1977d   'Justice and Equality', *Etyka* (Warsaw) 15 (in Polish with English and Russian summaries). English Version (revised) in *Justice and Economic Distribution*, ed. J. Arthur and W. Shaw (Prentice-Hall, 1978). Discussion in *Dialectics and Humanism* (Warsaw) 6 (1979).

1978a   'Prediction and Moral Appraisal', *Mid-West Studies* 3.

1978b   'Relevance', in *Values and Morals*, ed. A. I. Goldman and J. Kim (Reidel).

1978c   'Moral Philosophy', interview with B. Magee in his *Men of Ideas* (B. B. C. Pubs.).

1979a   'What Makes Choices Rational?', *Rev. Met.* 32.

1979b   'Utilitarianism and the Vicarious Affects', in *The Philosophy of Nicholas Rescher*, ed. E. Sosa (Reidel).

1979c   'What is Wrong with Slavery', *Ph. and Pub. Aff.* 8.

1979d   'Non-descriptivist Ethics' and 'Utilitarianism', in *Encyclopedia of Bioethics*, ed. W. Reich (Free Press).

1979e   Repr. of H 1973c with criticism by G. J. Warnock and reply, in *The Domain of Moral Education*, ed. D. B. Cochrane *et al.* (Paulist P. and Ontario Inst. for St. in Ed.).

1979f   'Universal and Past-tense Prescriptions: a Reply to Mr. Ibberson', *Analysis* 39.

1979g   'On Terrorism', *J. of Val. Inq.* 13.

1980   'Moral Conflicts', in *Tanner Lectures on Human Values*, ed. S. McMurrin (U. of Utah P. and Cambridge U. P.).

1982   *Plato* in Past Masters series (Oxford U. P., forthcoming).

2. *Other Writings*

ARISTOTLE, *Nicomachean Ethics* (refs. to Bekker's pages and columns given in margins of most edns. and translations).

ARROW, K. J. (1963), *Social Choice and Individual Values*, second edn. (Wiley).

—— (1977), 'Extended Sympathy and the Possibility of Social Choice', *Am. Econ. Ass.*

AUSTIN, J. L. (1956), 'A Plea for Excuses', *Aristotelian Society* 57. Repr. in next item.

—— (1961), *Philosophical Papers* (Oxford U. P.).

—— (1962), *How to Do Things with Words* (Oxford U. P.).

BAKER, J. (1977), *A Select Bibliography of Moral Philosophy* (Oxford University Sub-faculty of Philosophy).

BENTHAM, J. (1825), *The Rationale of Reward*.

BERGSTRÖM, L. (1971), 'Utilitarianism and Alternative Actions', *Noûs* 5.

BERLINER, H. (1980), 'Computer Backgammon', *Scientific American* 242 (June).

BRADLEY, F. H. (1876), 'Why Should I be Moral?', in his *Ethical Studies* (Oxford U. P.).

BRANDT, R. B. (1979), *A Theory of the Good and the Right* (Oxford U. P.).

CAMUS, A. (1942), *L'Étranger* (Gallimard).

DEVLIN, Lord (1959), *The Enforcement of Morals*, British Academy 45.

DWORKIN, R. M. (1977a), *Taking Rights Seriously* (Harvard U. P.).

—— (1977b), 'No Right Answer', in *Law, Morality, and Society: Essays in Honour of H. L. A. Hart* (Oxford U. P.).

FISHER, E. M. W. (1962), 'A System of Deontic-Alethic Modal Logic', *Mind* 71.

FOOT, P. R. (1958a), 'Moral Beliefs', *Aristotelian Society* 59. Repr. in her *Theories of Ethics* (Oxford U. P., 1967).

—— (1958b), 'Moral Arguments', Mind 67. Repr. in *Contemporary Ethical Theory*, ed. J. Margolis (Random House, 1966). This and preceding item repr. in her *Virtues and Vices* (Blackwell and U. of Chicago P., 1978).

GAUTHIER, D. P. (1968), 'Hare's Debtors', *Mind* 77.

GELLNER, E. (1979), 'The Social Roots of Egalitarianism', *Dialectics and Humanism* (Warsaw) 6.

GENSLER, H. (1976), 'The Prescriptivism Incompleteness Theorem', *Mind* 85.

GODWIN, W. (1793), *An Enquiry Concerning Political Justice*.

GRICE, H. P. and STRAWSON, P. F. (1956), 'In Defense of a Dogma', *Ph. Rev.* 65.

HAMPSHIRE, Sir Stuart (1972), 'Morality and Pessimism', Leslie Stephen Lecture, Cambridge. Repr. in his *Public and Private Morality* (Cambridge U. P., 1978).

HARSANYI, J. C. (1953), 'Cardinal Utility in Welfare Economics and in the Theory of Risk-Taking', *J. Pol. Econ.* 61.

—— (1955), 'Cardinal Welfare, Individualistic Ethics and Interpersonal Comparisons of Utility', *J. Pol. Econ.* 63. This and preceding item repr. in his *Essays in Ethics* (Reidel, 1976).

—— (1977), *Rational Behaviour* (Cambridge U. P.).

HART, H. L. A. (1961), *The Concept of Law* (Oxford U. P.).

HASLETT, D. W. (1974), *Moral Rightness* (Nijhoff).

HOHFELD, W. (1923), *Fundamental Legal Conceptions* (Yale U. P. and Oxford U. P.).

HUDSON, W. D., ed. (1969), *The Is–Ought Question* (Macmillan, London).

HUME, D. (1739), *A Treatise of Human Nature.*

KANT, I. (1785), *Grundlegung zur Metaphysik der Sitten* (*Groundwork to the Metaphysic of Morals*), translated as *The Moral Law* by H. J. Paton (Hutchinson and Barnes and Noble, 1948; refs. to pages of second edn. in margin).

KOHLBERG, L. (1970), 'Education for Justice', in *Moral Education*, ed. T. Sizer, (Harvard U. P.).

LEWIS, C. I. (1946), *An Analysis of Knowledge and Valuation* (Open Court).

LOCKE, J. (1690), *An Essay Concerning Human Understanding.*

LYONS, D. (1965), *Forms and Limits of Utilitarianism* (Oxford U. P.).

MACKIE, J. L. (1946), 'A Refutation of Morals', *Austr. J. of Ph.* 24.

—— (1977), *Ethics: Inventing Right and Wrong* (Penguin).

MILL, J. S. (1861), *Utilitarianism.*

MITCHELL, B. G. (1980), *Morality, Religious and Secular* (Oxford U. P.).

MOORE, G. E. (1903), *Principia Ethica* (Cambridge U. P.).

—— (1912), *Ethics* (Williams and Norgate and Holt).

MONSARRAT, N. (1951), *The Cruel Sea* (Cassell).

NAGEL, T. (1980), 'The Limits of Objectivity', in *Tanner Lectures on Human Values*, ed. S. McMurrin (U. of Utah P. and Cambridge U. P.).

NOZICK, R. (1968), 'Moral Complications and Moral Structures', *Natural Law Forum* 13.

—— (1974), *Anarchy, State and Utopia* (Basic Books).

PARFIT, D. (1971), 'Personal Identity', *Ph. Rev.* 80.

PLATO, *Euthyphro, Protagoras, Meno, Republic.* Refs. to Stephanus' pages.

POPPER, Sir Karl (1947a), 'Logic without Assumptions', *Aristotelian Society* 47.

—— (1947b), 'New Foundations for Logic', *Mind* 56.

PRICHARD, H. A. (1912), 'Does Moral Philosophy Rest on a Mistake?', *Mind* 21. Repr. in his *Moral Obligation* (Oxford U. P., 1949).

PRIOR, A. N. (1960), 'The Runabout Inference Ticket', *Analysis* 21. Repr. in his *Papers in Logic and Ethics* (Duckworth, 1976).

QUINE, W. V. (1951), 'Two Dogmas of Empiricism', *Ph. Rev.* 60. Repr. in his *From a Logical Point of View* (Harvard U. P., 1953).

RAWLS, J. (1955), 'Two Concepts of Rules', *Ph. Rev.* 64.

—— (1971), *A Theory of Justice* (Harvard U. P. and Oxford U. P.).

RESCHER, N. (1975), *Unselfishness* (U. of Pittsburgh P.).

RICHARDS, D. A. J. (1971) *A Theory of Reasons for Action* (Oxford U. P.).

ROBINSON, R. (1948), 'The Emotive Theory of Ethics', *Aristotelian Society* supp. 22.

ROSS, Sir David (1930), *The Right and the Good* (Oxford U. P.).

ROYCE, J. (1908), *The Philosophy of Loyalty* (Macmillan, New York).

RYLE, G. (1949), *The Concept of Mind* (Hutchinson).

SELLARS, W. (1980), 'On Reasoning about Values', *Am. Ph. Q.* 17.

SEN, A. K. (1970), *Collective Choice and Social Welfare* (Holden Day and Oliver and Boyd).

—— (1979), 'Utilitarianism and Welfarism', *J. Phil.* 76.

SIDGWICK, H. (1907), *The Methods of Ethics* (seventh edn., Macmillan, London, 1907; first published 1874).

SINGER, P. (1972), 'Famine, Affluence and Morality', *Ph. and Pub. Aff.* 1.

—— (1973), 'The Triviality of the Debate over "Is–Ought" and the Definition of "Moral"', *Am. Ph. Q.* 10.

—— (1979), *Practical Ethics* (Cambridge U. P.).

—— (1981), *The Expanding Circle: Ethics and Sociobiology* (Farrar, Straus and Giroux, and Oxford U. P.).

SMART, J. J. C. (1973), in J. J. C. Smart and B. A. O. Williams,

Utilitarianism: For and Against (Cambridge U. P.).

SPINOZA, B. de (1677), *Ethics.*

STEVENSON, C. L. (1942), 'Moore's Arguments against Certain Forms of Ethical Naturalism', in *The Philosophy of G. E. Moore,* ed. P. Schilpp (Northwestern U. P. and Cambridge U. P.).

STRAWSON, Sir Peter (1961), 'Social Morality and Individual Ideal', *Philosophy* 36. See also GRICE.

STROUP, T. (1981), 'In Defense of Westermarck', *J. of Hist. of Ph.* 19.

TAYLOR, C. C. W. (1965), Review of R. M. Hare, *Freedom and Reason, Mind* 74.

TORRANCE, S. B. (1977), 'Non-Descriptivism: a Logico-Ethical Study', doctoral thesis deposited in Bodleian Library, Oxford (MS. D. Phil. d 6345).

—— (1981), 'Prescriptivism and Incompleteness', *Mind* (forthcoming).

URMSON, J. O. (1958), 'Saints and Heroes', in *Essays in Moral Philosophy,* ed. A. I. Melden (Washington U. P.).

—— (1975), 'A Defence of Intuitionism', *Aristotelian Society* 75.

VENDLER, Z. (1976), 'A Note to the Paralogisms', in *Contemporary Aspects of Philosophy,* ed. G. Ryle (Oriel P.).

WARNOCK, G. J. (1967), *Contemporary Moral Philosophy* (Macmillan, London and St. Martin's P.).

—— (1971), *The Object of Morality* (Methuen).

WIGGINS, D. (1976), *Truth, Invention, and the Meaning of Life, British Academy* 62.

WILLIAMS, B. A. O. (1970), 'The Self and the Future', *Ph. Rev.* 79. Repr. in his *Problems of the Self* (Cambridge U. P., 1973).

—— (1973), in J. J. C. Smart and B. A. O. Williams, *Utilitarianism: For and Against* (Cambridge U. P.).

—— (1976), 'Utilitarianism and Self-Indulgence', in *Contemporary British Philosophy* 4, ed. H. D. Lewis (Allen and Unwin).

WITTGENSTEIN, L. (1953), *Philosophical Investigations* (Blackwell).

XENOPHON, *Memorabilia Socratis.*

INDEX